DAILY LIFE DURING

African American Migrations

Recent Titles in
The Greenwood Press Daily Life Through History Series

DAILY LIFE DURING

African American Migrations

KIMBERLEY L. PHILLIPS

The Greenwood Press Daily Life Through History Series

Daily Life in the United States
Randall M. Miller, Series Editor

 GREENWOOD

AN IMPRINT OF ABC-CLIO, LLC
Santa Barbara, California • Denver, Colorado • Oxford, England

Library of Congress Cataloging-in-Publication Data

Phillips, Kimberley L. (Kimberley Louise), 1960–
    Daily life during African American migrations / Kimberley L. Phillips.
        p. cm. — (The Greenwood Press daily life through history series)
    Includes bibliographical references and index.
    ISBN 978-0-313-34373-5 (acid-free paper) — ISBN 978-0-313-34374-2 (ebook)
1. African Americans—Migrations—History.   2. African Americans—Social life
and customs.   3. African Americans—Social conditions.   4. African diaspora—
History.   5. Migration, Internal—United States—History.   6. Migration,
Internal—Social aspects—United States—History.   7. United States—
Emigration and immigration—History.   8. United States—Race relations—
History.   I. Title.
    E185.P44   2012
    304.80896'073—dc23   2011051652

ISBN: 978-0-313-34373-5
EISBN: 978-0-313-34374-2

16   15   14   13   12   1   2   3   4   5

This book is also available on the World Wide Web as an eBook.
Visit www.abc-clio.com for details.

Greenwood
An Imprint of ABC-CLIO, LLC

ABC-CLIO, LLC
130 Cremona Drive, P.O. Box 1911
Santa Barbara, California 93116-1911

This book is printed on acid-free paper ∞

Manufactured in the United States of America

Contents

Series Foreword

The books in the Daily Life in the United States series form a subset of Greenwood Press's acclaimed, ongoing Daily Life Through History series. They fit its basic framework and follow its format. This series focuses on the United States from the colonial period through the present day, with each book in the series devoted to a particular time period, place, or people. Collectively, the books promise the fullest description and analysis of "American" daily life in print. They do so, and will do so, by tracking closely the contours, character, and content of people's daily life, always with an eye to the sources of people's interests, identities, and institutions. The books in the series assume the perspective and use the approaches of the "new social history" by looking at people "from the bottom up" as well as the top-down. Indian peoples and European colonists, blacks and whites, immigrants and the native-born, farmers and shopkeepers, factory owners and factory hands, movers and shakers and those moved and shaken—all get their due. The books emphasize the habits, rhythms, and dynamics of daily life, from work, to family matters, to religious practices, to socializing, to civic engagement, and more. The books show that the seemingly mundane—such as the ways any people hunt, gather, or grow food and then prepare and eat it—as much as the more profound reflections on life reveal how and why people ordered their world and gave meaning to their lives. The books treat the external factors shaping people's lives—war, migration, disease, drought, flood, pest infestations, fires, earthquakes, hurricanes and tornados, and other natural and man-made disasters that disrupted and even shattered daily lives—but they understand that the everyday concerns and routines of life also powerfully defined any people. The books therefore go inside homes, workplaces, schools, churches, meeting halls, stores, and other gathering places to find people on their own terms.

Capturing the daily life of Americans poses unique problems. Americans have been, and are, a people in motion, constantly changing as they move across the land, build new communities, invent new products and processes, and experiment with everything from making new recipes to making new governments. A people always in the process of becoming does not stand still for examination of their most private lives. Then, too, discovering the daily life of the diverse American peoples requires expertise in many disciplines, for few people have left full-bodied written accounts of their prosaic but necessary daily activities and habits and many people have left no written record at all. Thus, the scholars writing the books in the series necessarily borrow from such fields and resources as archaeology, anthropology, art, folklore, language, music, and material culture. Getting hold of the daily life in the United States demands no less.

Each book at once provides a narrative history and analysis of daily life, set in the context of broad historical patterns. Each book includes illustrations, documents, a chronology, and a bibliography. Thereby, each book invites many uses as a resource, a touchstone for discussion, a reference, and an encouragement to further reading and research. The titles in the series also promise a long shelf life because the authors draw on the latest and best scholarship and because the books are included in Greenwood's Daily Life Online, which allows for enhanced searching, updated content, more illustrative material, teacher lesson plans, and other Web features. In sum, the Daily Life in the United States series seeks to bring the American people to life.

Randall M. Miller

Preface

In their individual search for freedom and equality, the 9 million African Americans who collectively left the South between 1865 and 1965 irrevocably altered the political, social, and cultural history of the United States. How they established communities elsewhere, often under constrained economic and spatial circumstances, adds an equally compelling drama to this long history of migration. And there is more. In the decades after 1965, African Americans have continued to leave the South, but more have returned than left. Overall, the total number participating in this multidirectional migration remains significant. More than 1.3 million Africans and nearly 500,000 migrants from the Caribbean have arrived into the United States over the past 40 years. Compare this recent voluntary immigration with the involuntary arrival of about 400,000 Africans into British North America during the two centuries of the trans-Atlantic slave trade. In the 21st century, migration remains integral to black life in the United States.

Daily Life during African American Migrations is not only part of scholars' ongoing attention to black migration, but it also has been informed by scholarship in the growing field of African Diaspora studies. Black migration studies focuses on the internal movement of people in the United States. African Diaspora studies considers peoples of African descent who have voluntarily or through duress settled far from their native homes, and it gives attention to how these immigrants and their children have created new communities while they maintained or remade cultural connections with Africa. This study draws from these two fields. While this book focuses on the everyday experiences of migrants who participated in the large-scale internal movement out of the South and then helped establish communities in other regions, it also uses the concept of the African Diaspora as an analytical category to assess the experiences of these migrants alongside those of black immigrants who arrived between 1865 and the present. Each groups' experience across the century differed, but black migrants and immigrants have shared the impetus to seek greater social, political, and cultural freedom through movement. In my attention to the daily lives of migrants in the United States as part of the larger African Diaspora, I address blacks' labor and urban experiences, social and political activism, and cultural and communal identities in new ways.

This study has benefited immeasurably from the input of numerous scholars. Gregory Wilson, Zachary Williams, and other faculty in the Department of History at the University of Akron invited me to work with middle-school and high-school teachers in the 2008 and 2009 Akron Teaching American History. The teachers' questions and suggestions helped sharpen the focus of my approach. Patricia Sullivan, Waldo Martin, and the scholars in the 2006 and 2009 Civil Rights Institutes held at the Du Bois Institute at Harvard University offered helpful comments and suggestions that were especially useful for the final chapters. I especially want to thank Randall Miller, editor of the Daily Life in the United States series, for the invitation to contribute this volume. Randall read the manuscript with great care and his helpful comments and suggestions corrected many of my mistakes. I take responsibility for whatever errors remain. Mariah Gumpert, who is the in-house editorial contact for the Daily Life in the United States series at Greenwood Press, has been most attentive and patient. I have appreciated her guidance in prodding and shepherding this volume through the production process. Maya Johnson provided excellent research assistance. Mark, Peter, and Nina Shmorhun showed remarkable forbearance when I disappeared into my office to write this book. Even though this expression of my gratitude is hardly sufficient, I thank them for their daily love.

Introduction:
Black Migration and
the African Diaspora

During the mid-1910s, Sarah Rice watched African Americans leave central Alabama after the boll weevil infested the cotton crops:

In the train station it was just like an exodus of black people traveling, going north to better their lives, because the boll weevil had eaten up all the cotton and ruined their farms. It was pathetic, these people escaping for their lives with the bundles and stuff like that, because they didn't have suitcases. They just had sacks to put their clothes in, headrags on and everything, going north.[1]

About the same time Sarah Rice watched trains crowded with migrants leave Alabama, teenager Langston Hughes followed his mother and stepfather from Kansas to Cleveland to Chicago as the family moved on a quixotic quest for financial stability. Nearly a decade later, Hughes published a poem that captured black migrants' urgency, expressing how the "cold-faced North" would enable the oppressed to "escape the spell of the South."[2]

Other, equally vivid, descriptions of migrants fleeing the Mississippi Delta filled the black press. Some contemporary observers variously described the mass departure as a flood, a "great dark tide," or a deluge. Northern black newspapers described it as an

Exodus, language used by 19th-century migrants who saw their departures from the South as a biblical reenactment of the Israelites' escape from Egypt. The *Chicago Defender,* the nation's most popular black weekly newspaper, described the new and vast movement of African Americans as a Great Migration, a description that referenced other significant population movements in the United States, including the mass movement into California during the previous century. As *Exodus* and *Great Migration* became the defining terms, participants and observers alike placed this new and significant migration within the global movements of people spurred by personal and communal desires for more personal, cultural, and political freedoms.

African Americans' mass departure from the South for the urban Midwest and Northeast cities during World War I was voluminous, but the mass movement had antecedents in the decades after the Civil War. This new migration began within the South after 1890 as changes in the region's agricultural economy, racial violence, and the availability of work in new industries in rural areas or nearby cities precipitated blacks to leave farms. African Americans' quickened departures out of the South around 1915 coincided with the cessation of foreign immigration stemmed by the war in Europe, but the decades of movement within the South meant that a significant population of these southerners had experience with leaving rural homes and farms.

White southerners left the South as well and in numbers that surpassed blacks' departures, but proportionately, blacks' mass and permanent departure from the region signaled something different from their earlier periods of migration and from other groups on the move. The number of black men, women, and children leaving the South soared to over half a million between 1910 and 1920, and then by another million by 1930, eclipsing and replacing European immigrants to cities outside the South. African Americans' migration waned after 1930 as the financial downturn of the Great Depression became protracted, but over the next half century larger numbers left the South and became permanent residents in every other region of the United States. Overall, more than nine million African Americans left the South permanently between 1900 and 2005.

As African Americans left the South in droves in this long period, more than four million blacks left the former Caribbean colonies of Great Britain, France, and Spain and resettled in cities in the United States. In Harlem, Philadelphia, and Baltimore, black migrants from the South encountered black immigrants from the Caribbean, Latin America, and Africa. The protracted upheavals in agriculture, the diminished ability to participate in political and civic life, and the myriad individual needs and desires motivated a century of blacks' migration out of the segregated South, while similar and other events, particularly the limited access to land and steady work, shaped the mass migrations from elsewhere in the hemisphere. By the 1930s, many cities in the northern United States had nearly equal numbers of migrants from the Caribbean as from the southern United States. The cross-currents of this migration and immigration are better understood as the 20th-century African Diaspora.

This book focuses on the century-long migration of African Americans who first moved within the South and then left to make permanent homes in other regions. This study emphasizes the specifics of migrants' movements out of the South and their settlement in other regions within the broader historical, political, and cultural context of the African Diaspora. At the same time, it considers the specificity of blacks' migration as part of their long struggle for freedom and equality. The majority of these migrants who moved in the decades after the Civil War were newly emancipated people and their movements demonstrated their aspirations for equal and full citizenship. As white supremacy established legal and casual segregation in the last two decades of the 19th century— a process that continued into the 20th century—African Americans' need for safety from violence and their desire for better economic, cultural, political, and educational opportunities sustained their movement and settlement outside the South. As the internal events within the South encouraged black migration, external events, such as world wars, economic opportunities and depressions, and social and cultural aspirations, shaped and directed these departures.

A variety of data, including federal census reports and county and state population surveys, demonstrated that African Americans' century-long migration and settlement had four distinct periods, each lasting roughly 20 years. While discontinuous in their departures and diverse in their destinations, black migrants' experiences share important characteristics across time and space. Black migration was a process, but black migrants as a group tended to be working age (16 to 54 years old) and connected to family and friends. Migrants rarely "disappeared." While many young men set out on their own, most traveled to specific destinations and settled among and with familiar people; young women tended to depart with family, or traveled to specific cities where family already resided. Family and friends provided powerful incentives for migrants' departures and these connections extended important resources as migrants settled in new places. In each period of their migration, African Americans understood their departure from the South as part of a global movement of people seeking work, community, and freedom. And as migrants searched for better work, living, and social conditions, they aspired toward and demanded full citizenship and equality.

POST-CIVIL WAR MIGRATION, 1865–1900

Blacks' voluntary and mass migration began in the decade before the Civil War as thousands of free and enslaved people escaped the Deep and central South for cities in the border states of Missouri, Kentucky, and Maryland. Others departed for the upper Midwest states of Ohio and Illinois, or to New England and the upper mid-Atlantic states; thousands more fled to Canada. On the eve of the Civil War, the black populations of Louisville, St. Louis, and Baltimore increased by thousands. Many antislavery activists housed and protected the fugitives who settled in these towns and cities. The new residents established vibrant communities in Philadelphia, New York City, New Bedford, and other northern cities. Once four million enslaved African Americans acquired and claimed emancipation after the Civil War, many defined their new freedom as an ability to leave plantations and former owners and seek their own communities and labor arrangements. In the 50 years after the war, many sought refuge away from white-owned farms and plantations with oppressive labor practices that too closely resembled slavery. Others considered towns and cities safer as violence targeted at black political activists dramatically increased in the rural areas. By the 1880s, the black populations of every major city in the South, including those in Georgia and Alabama, had significantly increased. As the rural agricultural economies stagnated in the 1890s, new industries and the mechanization of older industries, including tobacco, made cities appealing to black Americans seeking steady work, better wages, and greater safety.

Along with claiming control over their own movements, African Americans considered landownership a marker of their new freedom, but former slaveholders organized to restrict them to plantations in conditions much like slavery. Almost immediately, these efforts inhibited blacks' movement and their ability to purchase land. While blacks formed the majority population in the rural areas of the Deep South states of Mississippi, Louisiana, Alabama, Georgia, and South Carolina, they had neither economic nor political autonomy. Between 1865 and 1892, white landowners used violence and coercion to assert their political authority. They consolidated their social and economic power by preventing blacks' participation in politics and they relegated them to single-crop sharecropping or farm tenancy that insured their indebtedness and immobility. Along with political and economic coercion, these landowners used the ideology of white supremacy and blacks' racial inferiority to justify blacks' removal from participating in American life. In the late 19th century, landowners further consolidated their power by forming alliances with owners of the new industries of coal, railroad, textiles, and lumber. These landowners and industrialists used the courts and state governments to limit blacks' mobility; control their participation in nonagricultural and nondomestic wage labor; and thwart their access to education.

African Americans responded to the violence and the restrictions in their access to work, education, and the ballot by making short-term moves within the South. Moving somewhere else, even for short periods of time, provided some choice. This short-term migration in the South during the late 19th century revealed two important and overlapping characteristics that informed blacks' movements in the next century. In the first, throughout the year, young men and women moved back and forth between work in rural areas and work in towns and cities. As the rural economies of cotton in the Deep South and tobacco in the Upper South declined, many young black adults moved to labor intermittently on railroads, in households, and on docks. By the turn of the century, black men traveled greater distances and for longer durations of time to work in lumber, turpentine, steel, and coal industries. Some traveled to help dig the Panama Canal. Black women left rural areas to pick crabs in Baltimore, work as domestics in towns and cities, or labor in tobacco factories in Richmond and Durham. As these departures became more frequent and lasted longer, families and friends frequently followed and settled in camps, towns, and cities. Steadier wages and extended households provided new opportunities to create communities in small towns and in cities. These new arrivals established significant businesses, churches, and community organizations in Durham, North Carolina; Richmond, Virginia; and Atlanta, Georgia.

1900–1930: "THE WHOLE BLACK WORLD IS ON THE MOVE"

This intraregional migration dramatically shifted in the first decade of the 20th century as the cessation of immigration from Europe into cities outside the South opened unskilled industrial and service work to African Americans. Since 1860, millions of immigrants from Europe had provided the labor for these jobs, but with the widening political unrest across Europe and then the Great War, employers considered new groups of workers. The American South proved fertile for labor recruitment as many northern industries, particularly railroads and steel manufacturers, had plants and shops in the South. Certainly employers' appeals and the promise of higher wages encouraged African Americans to leave the South, but hurricanes, floods, and the boll weevil infestation made agricultural work more precarious. While the lure of wages and the press of natural disasters set some African Americans in motion, other, equally important, reasons made the North a collective and permanent destination for many more.

More than their desire for steady work and higher wages, African Americans' longing to escape segregation sustained their mass departure. African Americans faced the daily humiliation, intimidation and assault under the system known as *Jim Crow*. Beginning in the 1870s and becoming pervasive in the 1890s, state-mandated and socially enforced racial segregation became the "southern way" to define racial relations and confine blacks to the bottom of the economic and social order. By the first two decades of the 20th century, the public and private separation along racial lines through laws and extralegal practices expanded rapidly. While all of the states in the South had established similar laws that barred blacks from political life, public accommodations, jobs, recreation, and transportation, the everyday *practice* of these laws was arbitrary and violent. Terror, including lynching, mutilations, and rape became accepted responses to African Americans who breached the elaborate and capricious racial codes. While lynching appeared to decline in the 1920s, the daily violence and humiliation of Jim Crow continued and expanded as African Americans traveled and worked in a wider geography in the South. For many migrants, leaving the menace of mob rule in the South was as important as finding steady work with better wages.

Between 1920 and 1930, black migration continued even as employment in northern war industries ceased and the availability of steady work diminished. Still, many migrants found unskilled work in auto plants in Detroit and meatpacking in Chicago. Black women found work in private or industrial service. While these jobs had little mobility, employers paid rates significantly higher than agricultural and industrial jobs in the South. Yet, blacks moved north for more than higher wages. The prospect of leaving segregation, the opportunity to vote and educate their children, and the new cultural opportunities became entwined with the desire to reestablish households and communities. Individuals may have departed southern towns for northern jobs in 1915, but by 1930, whole families and communities sought a better life outside the South, creating what sociologist St. Clair Drake described as the *Black Metropolis* in Harlem, Cleveland, and Chicago.

In the decade that followed, the faltering economy eventually curtailed blacks' mass departure from the South. Instead, African Americans generally confined their moves to the South, or they moved from one city to another outside the South. Despite the grave economic depression of 1930 to 1940, blacks' net out-migration from the South surpassed 400,000. The decade marked other demographic changes as well. Wherever they resided, as a group, the majority of African Americans no longer labored as agricultural workers or lived in rural areas. The majority of African Americans identified themselves as wage earners living in small towns and cities. And the overwhelming majority of African Americans living outside the South labored as unskilled and semiskilled workers in urban industries and service employment.

After 1942, the availability of jobs in wartime industries accelerated and African Americans made determined choices about where to work and live. Wage opportunities in airplane industries and shipyards drew tens of thousands of young women and men to Los Angeles and Seattle. As shipyards and military bases appeared in and around Baltimore, Philadelphia, and Newark, African Americans considered these cities important destinations. While the Army set quotas on the number of African Americans that could enlist—and severely restricted black enlistment in the Navy and Marines—African American men nonetheless pressed to volunteer. By 1944, black women volunteered for the WACs and WAVES. Tens of thousands of others were drawn into the ancillary labor opportunities of construction, road building, and transportation that the military needed for the millions of Americans in uniform.

Variously called the *Second Migration* or the *Second Great Migration*, many more African Americans migrated in the three decades after the war than had in the previous four decades. Again, more white southerners left the South during and after World War II, but as a group they were far more likely to return to the South. In contrast, African Americans made permanent departures. Yet, the postwar economic expansion was both discontinuous and occurred outside urban areas. The majority of cities that drew large black populations experienced significant declines in their industrial sectors. Between 1950 and 1970, this deindustrialization in the large cities outside the South coincided with the evaporation of skilled and semiskilled wage work. In southern industries such as in lumber, coal, and canneries, African Americans found far fewer jobs than in the pre-World War II era. Overall, black men faced higher rates of unemployment, part-time work, and underemployment than did other groups of male wage earners. By the late 1950s they had higher rates of withdrawal from the workforce. Black women's wages remained the lowest of any group of industrial and service workers. As historian Manning Marable has concluded, black labor "became less essential than at any previous stage of its development." The industrial black work class that formed between 1915 and 1945 began a slow contraction in the two decades that followed.[3]

The significant shift in blacks' residency and labor from the South to the North continued alongside a period of equally high immigration rates of blacks from the Caribbean and nations in Central America, Latin America, and, later, Africa. While large before 1940, the demand for wartime labor fueled the immigration of blacks from the Caribbean and many of these new arrivals settled in East Coast cities. Though diminished by immigration restrictions in the 1950s, migration from the Caribbean continued and then grew when these restrictions were somewhat relieved in the 1960s. Employers, particularly the fruit, sugar, and service industries pulled blacks from the Caribbean into migration patterns that continued into the second half of the 20th century.

DIASPORA AND MIGRATION

The overlapping demographic and geographical dynamics of black migration and immigration transformed the political, cultural, and economic life of black communities and American cities generally. These new urban residents from the South and the Caribbean considered their arrival as part of blacks' collective movement for freedom and full citizenship, ideas that had been at the heart of black thought since the late 17th and early 18th centuries. Blacks' movements to acquire more freedom and challenge racism and injustice had antecedents in their enslavement, which had displaced millions of Africans, caused untold suffering, and required new adaptations and new forms of resistance. At the same time, their efforts to leave the segregated South and colonialism in the 20th century emerged as a collective resistance to the draconian racial hierarchies that each system espoused and practiced. The mass migration out of the South and the significant immigration out of the Caribbean were part of a global push for full citizenship. Yet, blacks' migration and immigration were more than another stage in their efforts to escape racial oppression. Whether arriving from Birmingham, Alabama, or Kingston, Jamaica, blacks' migration and immigration propelled many into political and cultural activism, self-determination, and the search for equal participation in daily life.

These migrants and immigrants encountered resistance to their presence and aspirations. Institutions in the North that had little contact with blacks balked at sharing public space, access to jobs, and participation in leisure. Even prior to mass black migration, private and public institutions established barriers based on race. After migrants arrived in significant numbers, these extralegal and covert practices of exclusion became more overt. Many landlords refused to rent to blacks or sell them homes. Owners of amusement parks, movie theaters, and department stores established segregation policies, or they excluded blacks all together. Many employers simply refused to hire African Americans, or they offered them only intermittent and low-wage work. Unions barred black membership, while others relegated them to separate auxiliaries. Local officials confined African American children to the most dilapidated and underfunded schools.

Faced with these restrictions in their daily lives, black migrants and immigrants created a variety of institutions to challenge these cultural and legal barriers. The National Association for the Advancement of Colored People (NAACP), organized in 1909, emerged as a response to the political and economic oppression that all nonwhites—defined as *colored people*—faced in the modern world. Its organizers, which included W.E.B. Du Bois, Mary Church Terrell, and Mary White Ovington, intended to mount a national and international struggle against segregation and colonialism. Marcus Garvey, an immigrant from Jamaica who advocated blacks' self-determination, formed the Universal Negro Improvement Association (UNIA) that soon attracted millions of members in the United States and around the world. Black churches, unions, and newspapers captured the urgent, yet vibrant, encounter of black migrants and immigrants seeking full citizenship.

African Americans responded to their family and community needs by creating and using new political organizations and strategies to meet their daily needs and seek fulfillment of their collective aspirations. Churches and communal organizations provided information about jobs and access to health care. Clubs provided leisure, from films to reading clubs. Severely restricted or excluded from voting in the South, migrants became new voters in the North and their participation in politics reshaped the traditional political parties, infusing new agendas, changing party dynamics, and creating new alliances. Beginning in the 1920s, African American voters in Chicago elected a representative to Congress. Voters in Harlem did the same in the 1940s. In the border cities of Baltimore, Richmond, Louisville, and St. Louis, black Americans voted, altering the dynamics of local and state politics. By the 1930s, black voting in the North changed national politics. As a group, they continued to vote for Republicans in local elections and for the Democratic Party in national elections. After World War II, congressional representatives and Presidents Harry S. Truman, John F. Kennedy, and Lyndon B. Johnson drew on coalitions of white and black voters—many recent migrants—in northern cities. The steady election of black congressional representatives and mayors after the passage of the Voting Rights Act in 1965 demonstrated blacks' desires to participate in the daily politics of the nation. Many of these elected officials migrated from the South; others, including U.S. Representatives Mervyn Dymally and Shirley Chisholm, were immigrants or children of immigrants from the Caribbean (respectively, in this case). In the 21st century, this concentration of black urban voters in the North, and coalitions of black, white, and Hispanic voters in the Upper South helped elect the first African American president, Barack Obama, the son of an immigrant from Kenya.

The confluence of blacks' migration and immigration and their permanent settlements elsewhere demonstrates one of the important social and political phenomena in the United States, but this African Diaspora has also had important cultural implications in the nation's history. Blacks' century-long departure from points south—from New Orleans to Havana—and their resettlements elsewhere engendered significant changes in American cultural life, from the sound and beat of the nation's music, to the taste of its food. The nation's religious and cultural life underwent seismic shifts as millions of black Americans created new communities to meet their daily cultural, social, and spiritual needs. Religion was important to blacks in the South and the Caribbean, but the moves north reshaped church affiliations and denominations. Black participation in Islam grew significantly. American culture, from popular music to language, has been reshaped by blacks' participation as producers and consumers in every part of America.

Observers of these migrations agreed that blacks' moves out of the South and across the Atlantic altered the culture and politics of the United States. As African Americans left the rural South in the late 19th century, first cities then towns in the South were transformed. By 1920, more black southerners lived in towns and cities than did not, and for the first time, nonagricultural workers outnumbered those who earned a lively solely on the land. Three decades later, half the black population of the nation lived outside the South. These southerners lived among the concentrated presence of Bahamians, Trinidadians, Jamaicans, Haitians, Afro-Cubans, and Dominicans, who also significantly impacted black urban life. Cities outside the South changed as the result of the southernization and Caribbeanization of space, culture, and religion.

Every area of black cultural production, from music, art, and literature, to religion and street life demonstrated the influence of blacks arriving from various areas of the African Diaspora. The life and art of Jacob Lawrence illustrates the process. Lawrence, the son of two migrants from the South, grew up in Harlem in the 1920s and early 1930s. Harlem had become a place where black migrants had settled in significant numbers but it also included a growing population of artists, writers, and political activists from all areas of the diaspora. The creative outpouring from this multivariable presence of African Americans nurtured Lawrence's interest in art, and throughout the 1930s he took art lessons from Charles Alston at the Harlem Federal Art Project. He was an avid researcher at the famed archives on black life organized by Arturo Schomburg, a migrant from Puerto Rico. Aware of other families in his neighborhood with similar histories of migration, Lawrence began to communicate on canvas the collective story of black freedom struggles, including the Haitian revolution led by Toussaint L'Ouverture and the life of Harriet Tubman, who led legions of escaping slaves out of the South. In 1941, his body of work included a 60-panel series on black migration, which he based on what he heard, witnessed, and read about daily from other migrants.

The six chapters in this book consider the century-long relationship between blacks' aspirations for freedom, migration, immigration, and the construction of communities outside the South. Each chapter addresses a distinct period of these intertwined experiences. Chapter 1 examines the links between blacks' emancipation from slavery, the desire for mobility, and the search for safety and work within the South. Chapter 2 maps how African Americans linked their daily experiences with migration in the South to the new opportunities for work in northern industries during World War I. Chapter 3 considers how new black migrants and immigrants made northern cities home during the tumult of war and the rapid expansion of neighborhoods with too few options for homes. Most important, this chapter considers how African Americans made northern cities home. Chapter 4 explores how the Great Depression and World War II impacted black migrants' daily lives. By examining migrants' efforts to meet their everyday needs, this chapter highlights how they came to link the aspirations that precipitated their departures from the South with new ones shaped by their experiences of living in northern cities with a confluence of opposites: racial barriers and cultural and political opportunities. Their struggles to participate in unions and war industries laid the foundation for post-World War II struggles for civil rights. Chapter 5 compares the larger postwar migration to the prewar migration, especially as migrants expanded their movement to new cities in the Southwest and West Coast. At the same time, this chapter considers how the struggles against segregated transportation in the South accelerated and shaped blacks' experiences with migration. Chapter 6 links this migration with northern blacks' longtime struggles against segregation, and it compares, contrasts, and connects the northern and southern black civil rights movement. A short epilogue examines the overlapping dynamics of African Americans' return migration to the South and the large population of African and Caribbean immigrants who arrive everyday into U.S. cities. The bibliography identifies significant books and online resources about black migration and the diaspora.

Since 1865, African Americans have been in motion and their migration has had a significant impact on the history of the United States. As the influential writer Ralph Ellison noted, America would not be America without black people, but the vibrant political, cultural, and religious life that emerged as uniquely American was significantly shaped by the mass movements of black people from other areas of the globe. Many black migrants and immigrants considered resettlement in regions away from their birthplaces and communities as moving from inequality to opportunity. Yet, many also quickly discovered that their movement was just the beginning of their search for freedom.

NOTES

1. Sarah Rice, *He Included Me: The Autobiography of Sarah Rice* (Athens: University of Georgia Press, 1989), 12.

2. Langston Hughes, *The Collected Poems of Langston Hughes*, Arnold Rampersad, ed. (New York: Alfred K. Knopf, 1994), 27.

3. Manning Marable, *Race, Reform, and Rebellion: The Second Reconstruction in Black America, 1945–1990* (Jackson: University of Mississippi Press, 1991).

Chronology

1861–1865   American Civil War

1862   President Lincoln issues preliminary Emancipation Proclamation, effective January 1, 1863, freeing slaves in states in rebellion against the United States

1865   General William T. Sherman issues Field Order 15 and orders up to 40 acres to be given to each African American household; Thirteenth Amendment passed; Freedmen's Bureau established; Ku Klux Klan organized in Tennessee

1866–1870   Congress passes Civil Rights Act that establishes birthright citizenship; Congress passes First Reconstruction Act, granting suffrage to African American men in former Confederate states; Congress passes and states ratify the Fourteenth Amendment, which grants African Americans equal citizenship and civil rights; Congress passes and states ratify the Fifteenth Amendment, prohibiting bans of male voting based on race

1867   Federal troops occupy former Confederate states

1875   Congress passes Civil Rights Act of 1875

1877   Last of federal troops leave the South and Reconstruction officially ends

1878	Thousands of African Americans depart Deep South states for Kansas
1883	Supreme Court overturns Civil Rights Act of 1875
1890	Mississippi becomes first state to enact legislation that limits the franchise, which sets precedent for other laws to limit voting
1895	Ida B. Wells-Barnett writes *A Red Record*
1896	Supreme Court establishes "separate but equal" doctrine in *Plessy v. Ferguson,* which established base for legal state-mandated racial segregation
1905–1909	*Chicago Defender* is first published in 1905 by Robert S. Abbott; the *Pittsburgh Courier* is published in 1907 by Edwin Harleston; and the *New York Amsterdam News* is published by James Henry Anderson in 1909
1909	National Association for the Advancement of Colored People (NAACP) is founded in New York City
1910	Great Migration begins
1914–1918	World War I; United States enters war in 1917
1914	Fellowship of Reconciliation organized by A. J. Muste
1916	Marcus Garvey, an immigrant from Jamaica, establishes the Universal Negro Improvement Association (UNIA)
1917–1923	Riots erupt in northern and Upper South cities, including East St. Louis, Chicago, and Tulsa
1922–1933	Harlem Renaissance
1922–1941	African American workers and civil rights activists organize boycotts known as "Don't Buy Where You Can't Work" to end employment discrimination in northern cities
1930	Great Depression begins; Great Migration ends; W. D. Fard organizes the Nation of Islam in Detroit
1939–1945	World War II; United States enters war in 1941 after Japan bombs Pearl Harbor
1941	Second Great Migration begins
	Labor and civil rights activist A. Philip Randolph organizes March on Washington Movement to end segregation in the military and employment discrimination in war industries

1942–1943	Hundreds of race riots occur in cities, workplaces, and military bases
1943	Congress of Racial Equality (CORE), founded in Chicago by James L. Farmer, George Houser, Bernice Fisher, and James R. Robinson (Bayard Rustin becomes critical participant), organizes its first successful sit-in
1943–1965	In cities across the United States, African Americans organize boycotts, marches, and demonstrations against discrimination in housing, employment, and public accommodations
1946–1948	Supreme Court bans segregation in interstate busing *Morgan v. Virginia* (1946) and bans racially restrictive covenants in *Shelley v. Kramer* (1948)
1953	Malcolm Little joins the Nation of Islam and changes his name to Malcolm X
1954	Supreme Court declares segregated public schools unconstitutional in *Brown v. Board of Education,* which challenges, but does not technically overturn *Plessy v. Ferguson*
1963	March on Washington for Jobs and Freedom attracts over 250,000 participants
1964–1973	Vietnam War
1964	Civil Rights Act passed; riots erupt in Harlem, Rochester, New York, and Philadelphia, Pennsylvania; President Lyndon B. Johnson begins Great Society programs
1965	Malcolm X assassinated in Harlem; Voting Rights Act passed; Immigration and Nationality Act passed, which abolishes "national origins" quotas; first year more African Americans return to the South than leave
1965–1970	Hundreds of riots and rebellions occur, including the Watts area of Los Angeles (1965), Detroit and Newark (1967), and Cleveland (1968)
1965–1975	Amiri Baraka begins Black Arts Movement in Harlem
1966	Black Panther Party founded in Oakland, California
1968	Martin Luther King Jr. assassinated in Memphis; Shirley Chisholm becomes first black woman to be elected to the U.S. Congress; President Johnson signs the 1968 Civil Rights Act that bans discrimination in the sale, rental, and financing of housing

1972	First Haitian boat people arrive in South Florida
1983	Harold Washington is elected the first African American mayor of Chicago
1986	Immigration Reform and Control Act passed
1987	August Wilson wins Pulitzer Prize for Broadway play *Fences*
1990	African American population reaches 12 percent of the U.S. population with 50 percent residing in the South
2005	Hurricanes Katrina and Rita hit the Mississippi Delta

1

African American Migration after 1865

Born 20 years after the end of the Civil War, Nate Shaw heard stories from his grandmother and father about slavery, how some blacks owned land after its end, and that black men voted. Like most African Americans in Tukabahchee County, Alabama, who could no longer vote, Shaw's father worked for shares on land owned or rented by white farmers.[1] Because Nate Shaw and his siblings helped their parents with the myriad demands of growing cotton, they had no time to attend school or learn how to read. Despite the relentless and hard work, Shaw's father earned too little money as a farmer and he could not provide for his family without additional wage work. He farmed for others, and he cut crossties for the new railroad lines that traversed the South. Every year after the cotton harvest, he and other black farm families learned they owed more to the landowner for supplies than they had earned growing cotton. By the time Nate turned 20 in 1905, other young black men in his county had abandoned farm labor and searched for jobs in nearby rural industries and small towns. Shaw occasionally joined these men, but he hoped that through hard work and thrift, he might some day own his own land and acquire the independence that had eluded his father.

Shaw's family, like the other African Americans newly emancipated after the Civil War, considered the right to own land, vote, and move wherever they pleased as critical markers of their new freedom. Between 1865 and 1900, these men, women, and children attempted to acquire these and other aspirations of freedom, which they defined as key to controlling their labor, time, and community. Blacks understood that their efforts to create their own communities and establish boundaries over how, where, and when they intended to labor depended on their equal participation in politics and the right to vote. As African Americans pursued these goals in the two decades after the Civil War, they faced resistance from former slaveholders and many white nonslaveholders who insisted that blacks' efforts to acquire economic independence and political equality violated the racial regime whites established in slavery and meant to maintain regardless of blacks' legal status.

By the 1880s, a new business and political elite emerged in what many observers called a New South that emphasized industry over agriculture, but this new elite used violence and intimidation—practices that harkened back to slavery—to seize control of state politics and impose a new racial and economic order. Along with laws that segregated and disfranchised blacks, this New South elite regulated blacks' mobility into rural and urban industries as low-wage workers. By the turn of the century, African Americans in every state of the former confederacy faced a suppression of their political rights, violence, and an economic system that relegated them to the margins. The daily sedimentation of this new racial and economic order did not diminish African Americans' quest to be free and equal citizens, but as they encountered organized political, social, and economic repression in rural areas, they moved to nearby towns and cities in search of better work conditions and a modicum of safety. When violence and segregation laws became common and work opportunities diminished, blacks responded with a mass and permanent departures to other regions.

DAILY LIFE AND LABOR AFTER SLAVERY

In the immediate months following the war's end, the former slaves shared a collective understanding of freedom as the ability to control their labor and mobility in order to protect their families, worship as they pleased, and establish communities on their own terms. After slavery, blacks legally married, formed households, claimed authority over their children, and demanded fair wages. As important, they asserted their right to move where they pleased. Just as northern workers demanded time for leisure and family,

African Americans insisted on their right for their own time. When Union soldiers pressed to return them to the cotton, rice, sugar, and tobacco fields in nearly ceaseless toil, the ex-slaves insisted that freedom included an end to the workday and the workweek. Assaulted and raped during slavery, freedwomen brought suits against white men who attacked them. In these everyday claims of individual, communal, and political rights, African Americans meant to establish and assert clear legal and moral boundaries between enslavement and freedom.

A broad coalition of Radical Republicans, ex-Union soldiers, and ex-slaves advocated for the land abandoned by former slaveholders to be given to the freed people and landless whites, which would be redistributed and parceled out in small plots. Many newly freed African Americans argued in letters sent to the federal government or to nearby Union officials that they had worked hard during slavery, but that the system had prevented them from earning money or accumulating land and other wealth. Men who served in the United States Colored Troops (USCT) suggested they should receive land for their loyalty to the Union and for saving democracy. At the same time, the ex-slaves heard or read about land offered in the 1862 Homestead Act, which the federal government would eventually

Alfred Waud's illustration of African American soldiers being mustered out in Little Rock, Arkansas. (Library of Congress)

redistribute (approximately 80 million acres of land in Kansas and other states and territories).

These advocates had allies in the new Freedmen's Bureau, the agency established by Congress in March 1865 as the Bureau of Refugees, Freedmen, and Abandoned Lands to distribute food, clothing, and other supplies to the newly freed slaves, but some officials expanded its duties to include the redistribution of abandoned land. Under the purview of the War Department, the Freedmen's Bureau sent agents who were typically Union veterans to coordinate the redistribution of land and oversee the resumption of agricultural labor, frequently by encouraging blacks to labor for wages on their former plantations. At the same time, General Oliver O. Howard, director of the Freedmen's Bureau, and other bureau officials, including General Clinton Bowen Fisk in Tennessee and General Rufus Saxton in South Carolina, organized the dispersal of abandoned and confiscated lands to the freed people. Saxton believed landownership would provide blacks with autonomy and independence. In some areas of the South, especially in South Carolina, federal officials claimed the abandoned land and plantations of departed confederates and reapportioned them as small plots for the former slaves. Such distribution occurred in limited areas and was conditional on governmental approval. The new president, Andrew Johnson, vetoed the legislation in September 1865.

Over the last months of 1865, Freedmen's Bureau agents received orders to return the land to the former owners. Soldiers who had earlier helped blacks move onto land now evicted them and insisted they sign labor contracts with their former owners. In Norfolk County, Virginia, and on the Sea Islands, South Carolina, blacks mounted an armed resistance to the forced removal. As Congress passed legislation allowing for redistribution of lands in the western territories to settlers under the Homestead Act, a broad coalition in Congress and the federal agencies determined that providing free land to the former slaves was contrary to the values of free enterprise and private property. While blacks pursued a variety of economic endeavors, the cessation of land redistribution meant that few of them owned land or achieved any economic independence.

The freed people's dream of owning land as recompense for involuntary slavery and uncompensated labor—their own and generations before them—and service to the federal government during the Civil War dissipated further as southern legislatures in 1865 and 1866 quickly passed laws that returned African Americans to labor and social conditions that resembled slavery. Collectively known as Black Codes, these laws drew on prewar slave codes and laws used to regulate black political and social behavior in northern states. Though the provisions varied, overall the former confederate states used the new Black Codes to force blacks into year-long labor contracts, denied them the right to quit and seek better work conditions, and limited their right to negotiate the terms of the contracts. In order to enforce these labor conditions, these codes defined blacks' efforts to work for themselves as vagrancy and, therefore, illegal. Blacks had to prove they worked for whites. In order to impede their ability to be self-sufficient—and force them to labor for whites—the laws forbade blacks from owning guns to hunt for food; some states prohibited blacks from renting land. These new laws allowed landowners and employers to claim control over the labor of women and children, which prevented them from attending schools. Along with laws that granted them rights over blacks, planters organized vigilante groups to terrorize and threaten blacks who insisted on their right to control their own time and labor.

Republicans who controlled Congress reacted to white southern efforts to re-enslave blacks by empowering the Freedmen's Bureau to negotiate labor contracts, enacting the Civil Rights Act of 1866 that effectively struck down the Black Codes by defining civil rights and promising protection of those rights, and by passing the Fourteenth Amendment that established birthright citizenship and required states to ensure due process and the equal protection of the laws. These legislative interventions immediately allowed African Americans to participate in the creation and approval of new state constitutions. Congressional Reconstruction further mandated that the state constitutions in the former confederate states be rewritten to overturn the constitutions written immediately after the war. Once approved, the state could create a state legislature. If the legislature passed the Fourteenth Amendment, it could be readmitted to the Union. By 1868, all the former confederate states had done so. Congress passed the Fifteenth Amendment in 1869, which it intended to protect black men's right to vote, and the states ratified it in 1870. Through this process, many of the new southern state constitutions emerged as some of the most egalitarian as they mandated funds for public education, the construction of railroads, and services for the disabled and indigent. These constitutions abolished imprisonment for debts and public whippings, a common punishment especially directed at slaves and free blacks before the Civil War. While many of these state legislatures blunted or overturned the Black Codes, the impact of these unequal laws lingered into the 20th century.

BLACK POLITICS

The Fourteenth Amendment and the Reconstruction Acts, which allowed for the registering of black voters, instigated blacks' widespread participation in the political process. They immediately sought ways to shape a more equitable political and economic life for themselves and their communities. Significant numbers of black men voted across the South and black women participated in the creation and organization of political clubs that informed the ex-slaves of their rights. Men who had served in the military or participated in the efforts to create state constitutions in the late 1860s offered important experience as they discussed the issues that mattered to their communities. African Americans typically nominated and then elected candidates with education, service in the military, or who were skilled workers; others had already acquired land and other property. In every southern state except Tennessee, the Republican Party, which included blacks, won the elections and controlled the new state legislatures. Except in Louisiana and South Carolina, black elected officials at the state level were in the minority. These delegates disagreed over some economic issues, but across the South they voted for equal access to schools, women's rights, and the 10-hour day. They insisted blacks should have full political rights and equal access to public space.

African Americans were immediately elected to state offices, including 16 to national offices, and many more to serve in local offices. One conservative estimate suggests that blacks held up to 1,500 elected and appointed local offices in the decade after the passage of the Fifteenth Amendment. They served as coroners, surveyors, treasurers, tax assessors and collectors, jailors, solicitors, justices of the peace, clerks of courts, sheriffs and marshals, fire fighters, and mayors. In these roles they established and enforced county and municipal regulations; levied and assessed taxes; imposed and collected fines; controlled appropriations; and established and adjudicated boundary disputes. As elected officials, they replaced former slaveholders who had regulated local economic and social relations through arbitrary practices and violence. Between 1870 and 1880, at least one black man held local office in 200 counties of the former confederacy, and in more than 80 counties, at least 3 black men

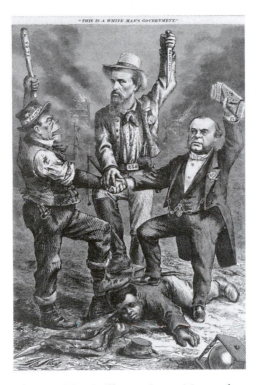

Thomas Nast's illustration critiques former Confederate responses to the Reconstruction Acts, "This is a white man's government." (Library of Congress)

held office. At the same time, in some states, they created biracial political organizations.

After their efforts to recreate the conditions of slavery were quashed by the new state constitutions and the elections of biracial legislatures, former confederates and slaveholders established paramilitary organizations to counteract blacks' new political mobilization, control their labor, and defeat federal and Republican Reconstruction. Vigilante groups like the Red Shirts and paramilitary organizations, which included the Ku Klux Klan and the Order of the White Camelia, used violence against blacks and whites who nominated and supported black candidates and then voted for Republicans, regardless of race. With too few agents and troops to ensure voters' safety during elections, these organizations escalated their terror and murdered black voters and officeholders. They also attacked interracial political organizations, such as the Republican Party's Union Leagues. The cumulative impact of these tactics resulted in blacks' diminished participation in elections and the end to biracial politics. In nearly every former confederate state—Virginia remained a notable exception until 1896—former slaveholders returned to political power in the elections held between 1876 and 1884.

In states across the South, Democratic politicians and their allies presented themselves as saving the South and they promised to wrest control away from Republicans committed to biracial politics. Presenting their party as the Redeemers or the Redemption Party, Democrats dominated the state legislatures and overturned the egalitarian laws that had promised basic civil and economic rights. The Redeemers immediately passed laws to regulate or prevent blacks' ability to move from one job to another. Southern planters used these new laws to hold the former slaves on the land as tenants and sharecroppers bound by contracts; industrialists in the region confined some black men to labor in the menial, heavy, and least desirable jobs of factories and service work. Black women not bound to the land found work only in domestic service or as laundresses.

State legislatures dominated by Redeemers overturned laws that protected sharecroppers. Legislators passed new vagrancy laws and contract laws, many resembling the infamous 1866 Black Codes. In North Carolina, for example, the Landlord and Tenant Act of 1877 defined sharecroppers as a wage earner bound to the authority of the landowner; in addition, these workers had no ability to question the terms of their shares. When blacks settled at the end of the harvest of their crops, planters either short changed them or they faced claims that they owed more than they earned from their crops. Most families sank into debt, and few broke even. Blacks who attempted to break their contracts with unscrupulous planters and seek more favorable arrangements with other landowners typically faced vagrancy laws that forced them into prisons. Employers then leased these prisoners from southern states through the convict lease system. The collapse of cotton prices and most usurious credit rates trapped farmers and sharecroppers in a cycle of debt that most could not escape. The crop-lien system, which required indebted farmers to pledge their crop and labor to merchants and landowners extending credit, left poor blacks, and many whites, hopeless. By 1880 close to 80 percent of African Americans in the South worked as sharecroppers, so these new laws had an immediate and devastating effect. Unable to escape debt and exploitation, the number of black sharecroppers increased from 429,000 to 673,000 over the next three decades; the percentage of cash tenants rose too.

Black landowners fared little better. While the amount of land they owned increased to an estimated 12 million acres in this period, they owned only a small percentage of land overall in the South and, on average, the size of farms for all southern farmers had dropped by more than half from 346 acres per farm in 1865 to 156 acres in 1900. Black landowners, like sharecroppers and tenant farmers, worked harder on fewer acres and for diminishing returns.

The few remaining federal troops in the South after the 1876 elections departed, and local police and militias ignored planters' assaults on workers. Unimpeded by any federal interventions, planters treated rural workers with no respect and kept them intimidated with physical assaults, including pistol whippings, verbal insults, beatings, and arrests. Sexual assaults against black women rose. Even as many blacks continued to insist on their rights, local customs and then the laws passed by the Redeemers determined these actions as illegal and violations of the racial order. Those African Americans who insisted they owned land, claimed they had the right to walk on the sidewalk, or who demanded their wages at the end of their terms, were arrested and charged with disorderly conduct. Blacks who asserted their legal right to quit a job, or who failed to prove they worked elsewhere, were arrested for vagrancy. Black women who worked in their own homes and not in a landowner's field or home, too, were arrested for vagrancy. After these arrests, courts sentenced black men to unpaid labor gangs that worked for the state or for white landowners.

These unfavorable conditions led increasing numbers of African Americans to consider emigration from the South. When the labor and political opportunities narrowed, especially in the Deep South states, blacks formed dozens of emigration societies with the intention of moving west. Without cash and other resources, however, blacks' desire to migrate was repeatedly thwarted.

Tennessee provides a representative case. Discouraged by the poor living and work conditions and alarmed by the violence against black Republicans in the 1869 election, many blacks in Nashville resolved to migrate, however, few blacks had the means to leave the state, so the society did not get established. Yet the desire for land continued, and African Americans sought various strategies to emigrate.

Benjamin Singleton responded to the initial impetus to leave Tennessee and when the emigration society failed to materialize, he nonetheless persisted in his efforts to find land elsewhere. Trained as a cabinetmaker, Singleton escaped from slavery in Tennessee and traveled first to Detroit and then to Canada. After the Civil War he returned to Tennessee. Between 1869 and 1875, he mounted various efforts to establish black communities in Tennessee. Though all of these efforts failed, the worsened conditions for blacks led to the creation of the Tennessee Emigration Society in 1875 with the intention to settle in Kansas. By then, homestead opportunities that were reported in Kansas drew the attention of increasing numbers of blacks from Tennessee to Louisiana.

THE EXODUSTERS

In a letter sent to the federal government in late 1879, Civil War veteran Henry Adams urged officials to give him and other blacks some territory of their own. "Let us leave these Slave holders to work their own land," he pleaded, "for they are killing our race by the hundred every day and night."[2] Adams's urgent appeal for aid and land addressed two tragedies that had created terrible and swift consequences for African Americans in his Louisiana parish. The first began on the docks of New Orleans as the mosquito-born disease of yellow fever felled dockworkers of all races during the summer months of 1878. Within weeks, the disease spread through the Mississippi Valley and into Memphis with devastating consequences. As in other natural disasters that occurred after the Civil War, African Americans found that their race and former status as slaves hindered their efforts to find medical care or resources to care for the orphaned children and the elderly.

The second tragedy erupted when white Democrats used shotguns and rifles against Adams and the other black men who voted during the fall elections. In one rural Louisiana parish determined white men threatened black voters with a cannon. Despite the Fifteenth Amendment, Adams and others found they were disfranchised in the new political order. Faced with the unchecked yellow fever and the political violence, Adams decided that he could not make a life in the current conditions of the South after Reconstruction's end. Thousands of other African Americans agreed that emigration provided an important opportunity to escape the poverty, the limited work opportunities, and the violence. Some looked to Liberia, but by 1879, many southern African Americans set their sights on Kansas and the West as the destination for their mass escape.

Exodus! (Library of Congress)

Observers described blacks' mass departure that spring and summer of 1879 as a "flood" and a "tide," but participants considered
their migration as people in flight from the wrath of former slaveholders, which had "erupted like a volcano." These vivid metaphors
describing black migration borrowed language typically used to describe the spontaneous acts of nature. Crowds of blacks—some
gatherings numbering in the hundreds—suddenly appeared on the
banks of the Mississippi River. Hungry and with few assets, they
waited for steamers to take them to St. Louis. They had no money for
their passage, but when asked by observers, they claimed they
planned to travel for free. As these groups of families clustered,
reporters from local papers amplified the millennial tone that the emigrants conveyed. Some would-be migrants explained their departures as biblical. They were "like the children of Israel" escaping
bondage. African Americans had frequently used similar language
to describe their enslavement; in its current iteration, these were
families leaving the South, much like how the Israelites fled Egypt.
They called themselves *Exodusters* because they considered their
departures to be a flight from re-enslavement to freedom.

As thousands of African Americans left the South between March
and May, landowners' efforts to stop them increased. Steamboat

captains reported receiving orders from local officials not to allow blacks onto boats. The cost of the trip and settlement kept most rural families from joining the exodus, as many lived on credit most of the year. Once they settled their accounts at the end of the year, few had any profit from their labor and most were further indebted to merchants and planters. While many blacks found it increasingly impossible to secure the resources to pay for their transportation, the yellow fever epidemic that swept through the South and the organized efforts to keep them from leaving slowed and, eventually, impeded their emigration.

In contrast to whites in Kansas who viewed the arrival of significant numbers of blacks with alarm, Arkansas planters considered former slaves as a docile, steady, and stable labor force. These planters circulated their appeals for black workers through broadsides and newspaper announcements. They sent labor agents into the Deep South. Black emigration societies helped broadcast the news and blacks who were anxious to find more favorable work and living conditions immediately departed for the state. Migrants' success in finding higher wages in Arkansas—some earned wages 33 percent higher than elsewhere in the nearby states—fueled further departures. The release of nine million acres for homesteaders and the potential for black men to vote with little resistance provided additional lures. While only a few hundred blacks secured land in this period, migrants continued to arrive in the state. Between 1870 and 1900, the Arkansas's black population rose from 25 to 28 percent. The opportunities for land and political participation dimmed late in the century, however, as the suppression of blacks' political and labor rights elsewhere reverberated through the state. By 1891, the Arkansas legislature established the poll tax, grandfather clause, and the white primary. Violence against black voters and the few black state representatives drove many blacks farther west or into all-black towns, with a dozen established by the start of the new century.

In this context of narrowed economic opportunities and greater physical danger, increasing numbers of African Americans looked to migration as a personal and collective effort to pursue better opportunities. Along with migration to Kansas and Arkansas, African Americans departed from rural and urban areas in the Deep and Upper South for Oklahoma, Indiana, and the far West, which included the North and South Dakota, Nevada, and California. Black organizations and churches endorsed their emigration. The episodic violence that became commonplace throughout the South precipitated other departures of African Americans in sizeable groups. When South Carolina passed legislation to curtail black farmers' access to common grazing rights, thousands of blacks in Edgefield County departed for Arkansas. That so many blacks moved with such suddenness attests to their acquisition of resources, but many had discussed and planned such departures in emigration societies and other black organizations. In the mid-1880s, for example, a spate of violence in South Carolina sent 20 or 30 wagons of black families from the hill country to the river bottoms. The departure was significant and orderly.

SUGAR: BLACK AND IMMIGRANT LABOR, 1880s–1890s

Blacks' mass departure from Louisiana and other areas of the Mississippi Delta struck a particular blow to sugar growers. Sugar required a long growing season where a small cadre of workers tended to the crops, but the harvest of the crop had to be done quickly, which demanded a much larger work force of temporary workers to cut, haul, and rapidly grind the cane in order to extract the raw sugar juice before the oxidation launched fermentation that irrevocably changed its chemical content. At every stage of the growing, harvesting, and milling process, sugar workers faced harsh conditions. The need for a large cadre of temporary workers who required immediate pay increased the planters' labor costs. Along with the need to hire workers who easily found work in other industries, planters in Louisiana faced increased competition from sugar planters in the Caribbean and South Africa, who paid lower wages and used harsher labor practices, which rapidly diminished the profits Louisiana growers earned. The emergence of alternatives to cane sugar, particularly beet sugar grown in Canada, also presented competition to these growers.

Finding workers who would accommodate to the onerous demands of sugar and lower wages proved difficult for southern planters who had relied on slave labor through the mid-1860s and then coerced the freed people into gang labor after emancipation. In the late 1870s, planters attempted to stop blacks' departure for Kansas by threatening to shoot them. Even as their control of black labor increased after Redemption, planters learned that using force to halt blacks' departure deterred other workers from coming into the cane fields. As other industries, including lumber and railroad companies, offered higher wages and better work conditions, sugar workers launched strikes for similar demands. When workers' organization flared into a strike in LaFourche Parish in 1887, the planters massacred workers. The Thibodaux Massacre squashed similar protests, but blacks left the area in droves. By the late 19th century, blacks' insistence on owning land or remaining mobile and earning fair wages challenged the sugar planters, who increasingly considered black workers "unreliable" and "unsuited" workers. Such claims revealed planters' desire to return blacks to work conditions similar to slavery and they sought to recruit labor that would compete with black workers and force them to accept a landless existence defined by low wages and coercive conditions.

Louisiana planters responded to blacks' assertiveness and departures in the 1880s by attempting to import indentured labor similar to employers' practices in the Caribbean. Earlier attempts to bring in indentured workers from Sweden and Germany failed as these workers refused to "be treated like negroes." Some planters imported Chinese workers, some of whom had arrived during the Civil War, to labor for $14 a month and rations of meat and rice. After the war, labor contractors brought in 30,000 Chinese workers into the South. The experiment failed as many of the men wanted to farm for themselves. Other Chinese workers joined with black workers in the labor rebellions and demands for land, fair wages, and an

Sugar workers in Baton Rouge, Louisiana. (Library of Congress)

end to the violence—including murder. When these efforts proved fruitless, they departed with other groups of workers forming inter-racial labor gangs in search of better conditions elsewhere. Some of these workers traveled west to work on the railroads and in mines.

By the early 20th century, growers looked to workers from Sicily. Increasing numbers labored elsewhere in the Mississippi Delta. Treated as not white, Italians were subjected to racial restrictions similar to those African Americans faced, including lynching and assaults. Relying on a variety of stereotypes, planters believed that in contrast to African Americans, Italians ate less, worked harder, and forced women to labor in the fields. Unlike blacks, however, sugar owners used Italians as supervisors and assigned them techni-cal tasks. Outraged by the segregation and violence against these workers in Louisiana and reports of peonage in the Mississippi Delta, the Italian government protested, demanded investigations, and dis-couraged other workers from migrating into the Deep South. As devastating to the planters' experiments, these workers left, too, for better labor conditions. Planters' intentions to provide black work-ers with competition from other groups deemed more pliant and like blacks did not succeed, and planters were forced to return to negotiating with the group they hoped to control.

Between 1890 and 1910, many sugar workers switched plantations as they sought the highest bidder for their labor in both the cultiva-tion and harvest seasons. In turn, employers competed for the best workers, especially during the grinding season. Wages did rise, espe-cially in areas where there was limited production. Women typically earned $.10 to $.20 less a day than men, but skilled women could sometimes earn higher wages too. Competition for these workers was intense at times. Over time, labor market conditions forced some landowners to make concessions, even bargain with workers. In turn, planters tried to set wages, but with little success; wages fluctuated widely in the same season. In 1894, for example, wages dropped from $1.00 per day to $0.85. Rumors about planters' plans to lower wages spread amongst workers and included reports that they explicitly sought unskilled workers to drive wages down.

The reports of abuse impeded planters' retention of workers, forc-ing some to search for workers in nearby plantations and towns, or as far away as the Mississippi and Alabama cotton fields. Some planters hired labor agents to lure workers in nearby cities, such as dockworkers in New Orleans. Cotton workers were disinclined to switch from hard labor for more intensive labor, especially during periods when cotton prices were high. Other times, they moved to sugar fields for short periods of time. Agents complained about the scarcity of labor, and owners decried the independence of laborers generally. Mindful of the impending harvests, some employers offered workers rough shelter, food, and small plots to encourage them to stay. Others encouraged the presence of women and children by establishing schools, libraries, and churches. By then these planters found it increasingly difficult to compete in the global sugar production.

Labor recruiters for other extractive industries competed for these transient workers, a population that included large numbers of African Americans and increasing numbers of European and Caribbean immigrants. Most were young men who found work cutting logs, digging ditches, hauling freight, or doing general heavy unskilled work. Such opportunities meant they did not have to yield to the coercions of full-time agricultural labor, but the work was intermittent and backbreaking. When they picked cotton or cut cane, they had some leverage with employers bound by the demands of the harvest and the market. They negotiated to work in gangs for better wages. This collective behavior sometimes provided protections from the sorts of massacres in the 1880s. More often, the only right workers possessed was the ability to quit and look for work elsewhere.

NEW SOUTH

African Americans labored within the dominant ideology of white supremacy that shaped the racial, class, and gender relations in the South beginning in the late 19th century. While this ideology drew from older ideas about blacks' supposed inferiority prominent during slavery, new ideas emerged within the industrial age from a collective belief about a global racial hierarchy that placed Anglo Saxons at the top and the darker races—specifically Africans—at the bottom. In the American construct, blacks were biologically, morally, and spiritually inferior; and such traits were considered immutable. This idea about racial hierarchy coincided with American and European efforts to extract and export diamonds, rubber, and gold from Africa and other places then subjected to European colonial ambitions.

The racial ideology of white supremacy legitimized popular arguments that an industrial and financial elite should control the resources of the state. This new elite viewed the New South as interconnected regions where raw material such as lumber, iron, and cotton would flow into nearby cities and small towns where a powerful business class controlled not only the manufacturing process, but the distribution of the final products as well. The production of paper, steel, and textiles represented this new industrial elite. In this New South, rural and urban manufacturers and captains of industry replaced the older planter class; wage workers, not slaves, provided inexpensive, available, and mobile labor. Low-wage workers, regardless of race, were critical to the profitability and competitiveness of these industries.

Lumber became one of the first new industries to utilize the ideas and practices of white supremacy as a way to encourage African Americans to pursue wage work while they were also subjected to limited social and political rights. The lumber industry, which ran from the so-called pine belt that spanned from southern Pennsylvania to eastern Texas, sought the most valued of the wood in the plantation and Piedmont regions of the South, but it also required a mobile and inexpensive labor supply. Employment in lumber began as a seasonal employment for black farmers, but over the course of the last three decades of the 19th century, the industry expanded its production and claimed more workers in the South than any other industry. It outpaced lumber production in other regions. Unlike other industries that excluded African Americans, lumber employers hired them at a fast rate. By 1910, 83,000 black men were cutting trees and logs in southern sawmills, more than the combined population of workers employed in cotton textiles and four times the number of workers who labored in iron and steel. By the end of the 19th century, blacks claimed the majority of positions in lumber camps and sawmills.

Many African Americans did not leave the South in high numbers in the late 19th century because new industries in the region promised alternatives to agricultural labor. African Americans were relegated to the least skilled and stable work. While blacks had held the majority of skilled work in the South before the Civil War, they rarely found such work after 1870. Only a small population owned businesses, with barbershops and grocery stores the most prevalent. Some industries did employ some African Americans, but only for the most poorly paid and unskilled positions, such as tobacco stripping; other industries offered access to a variety of unskilled and semiskilled positions, including the steel, iron, coal, tobacco, and railroad industries. In cities and towns, black men found day work such as hauling, lifting, and loading material. In some cities, they found work in construction, but typically as helpers. Black women had the fewest choices of any group. Most labored in domestic and laundry work. They often worked on the margins of these new industries as janitors and domestic workers.

Many in the generation born during and after slavery considered the ownership of land and other property vital to their independence and stability, but as many found these goals elusive, increasing numbers of African Americans considered seasonal work in the emerging southern industries vital to economic mobility. Black women joined their brothers, husbands, and other male kin for extended periods away from agricultural work.

Tobacco factories in Durham, a key city in North Carolina that emerged as the industrial center of the Upper South, experienced a rapid capitalization and growth as black and white women became the largest group of low-wage workers. Outfitted with the latest technologies, these factories attracted women to the city in increasing numbers. By 1900, black and white women were 40 percent of the workforce, but the former group of workers experienced greater labor and racial segregation in Durham than other groups. Excluded

Tobacco, a New South industry in Richmond, Virginia. (Library of Congress)

from textile mills, blacks were available and inexpensive labor to strip the raw leaf, which was the dirtiest job in the mills. More typically, employers confined African American women to cleaning positions and African American men to hauling the tobacco. Employers restricted white women to the unskilled, but far less foul work of sorting and packaging cigarettes. As more white women worked in these positions and as the tobacco industry required a white managerial class, black women found work in the city in domestic positions for whites of all social groups. African Americans earned the lowest wages, and black women earned the least of all workers. Though confined to the least desirable and the lowest paid positions in tobacco factories, many blacks found these jobs preferable to the intermittent casual and domestic labor. By 1890, black men found their economic options especially diminished in the building and blacksmithing trades. This scarcity of work, fueled by the economic depression in the 1890s, forced African Americans to seek work elsewhere.

THE NEW BLACK SOUTH

By 1890, Birmingham, Atlanta, and Durham emerged as three New South cities characterized by large industries and low-wage workers. Atlanta became a railroad center where urban and rural industries met. Planters moved cotton into the mills and then onto railroads. By the 1890s, these mills, along with cotton textiles and clothing manufacturers, drew thousands of black and white workers from rural areas. Other establishments, including paper mills, food manufacturers, industrial laundries, and railroads provided employment. The various cotton-related industries especially attracted white women workers, but black women rarely had access to these jobs. Instead, most labored in domestic work or as laundry workers. Black men hauled and loaded cotton. Some cleaned railroad tracks.

Atlanta's population quadrupled between 1880 and 1910, and the black population tripled in this period. Unlike northern cities where blacks were increasingly confined to the oldest residences in the core, black southerners were relegated to the periphery where they lived in shanties. Sewers and electricity slowly became available, but blacks in low-lying areas of Buttermilk Bottom and Dark Town did not have access to these utilities or other public services. At the same time, blacks settled in these neighborhoods to find family and familiar institutions, especially churches. Some neighborhoods mixed a variety of institutions and businesses. In South Atlanta, called Brownsville, black universities, businesses, organizations, and residences emerged side by side. As segregation and its attendant policing arose, these neighborhoods became havens for migrants. There, they found relief from the daily intrusions that the Jim Crow system imposed. Eager to avoid the arbitrary stops and arrests by white police, middle-class blacks began to build their own businesses, churches, and organizations along Auburn Avenue. Other areas became known for their cluster of beer saloons, dance halls, and overcrowded homes and flats. As the population expanded, alleyways became residences, which contributed to the congested and unsanitary conditions.

Despite the low wages and crowded living conditions, blacks, especially young blacks, saw the city as an opportunity to find new independence and leisure to dress and act as they pleased on their own time. Kathleen Adams, who was born and raised in Atlanta, recalled that women churchgoers wore "their taffetas, alpacas, and grandmothers even wore their brocades," and remembered how the women's bellback skirts "gave you that flow and as they walked down the street those skirts had a certain bounce to them." After

An industrial laundry in Lexington, Kentucky. (Library of Congress)

increasing numbers of single and young men and women arrived and sought wage work, the descriptions of the city's streets increasingly captured the vibrant night leisure around juke joints. Equally vivid accounts of Beale Street in Memphis emphasized how the "high-brown belles" strolled the street with "darktown dandies." George W. Lee noted the Saturday Night Stroll on Beale Street in the 1910s: "Golden browns, high yellows and fast blacks, some gorgeously dressed and others poorly clad, move together down the old thoroughfare. The working folks are on parade; going nowhere in particular, just out strolling just glad of a chance to dress up and expose themselves on the avenue after working hard all week."[3] Saturday nights and Sunday mornings provided a fleeting, but critical, moment for African Americans to wear what they pleased and to stroll with pride and safety in their own neighborhoods.

The rise of new industries in rural and urban areas created demands for labor, which drew increasing numbers of southerners and immigrants of all races into towns and cities. In turn, new recreation, such as cheap theaters and dancehalls, and public spaces, such as parks and beaches, emerged to attract their business. Typically young, these men and women worked and sought leisure outside the daily supervision of their parents. Many defied or ignored popular ideas of racial relations and some established intimate relationships across the color line. Although most southern states did not allow interracial marriage and other laws prohibited interracial cohabitation, some of these relationships became the equivalent of common-law marriages. These intimate contacts became intolerable to many middle-class observers, white and black. By the 1890s, southern custom and Victorian-era mores considered white women who congregated with black men to be prostitutes or depraved women. Policing these private relationships proved nearly impossible through law, but some communities used physical assaults to express their censure.

The violence that followed the 1870 elections in the South had attracted the attention of Congress and African American witnesses and victims described the assaults as a response to their political and economic assertions. With the removal of federal troops and the decreased interest in the protection of blacks' civil rights, the ongoing violence was framed as responses to black men's violation of sexual etiquette, or assaults against white women. Whites sympathetic to the extralegal violence blamed the passage of the Fourteenth and Fifteenth Amendments for granting blacks too many rights. Lynching individuals without granting them a trial ignored

due process guaranteed by the Constitution, but this vigilante justice was not peculiar to the South and it flared in the Far West and
Midwest territories as well. The victims included all races. Eventually, this practice waned in other regions, but it became part of
daily life in the South as a form of punishment meted out to African
Americans who were accused of a crime. The threat of lynching
served as a warning to any African American not to overstep the
color line.

As white supremacy linked blacks' demands for equal political
participation to a challenge to white authority, which asserted control over public and private life, black men's political and economic
assertiveness was akin to the rape of white women. Popular images
of black men voting portrayed them as uncivilized predators and
savages. Popular culture, including novels, films, and advertisements, reinforced these claims that inherent racial characteristics
made blacks violent and placed them beyond the rule of law. They
had no rights as citizens, including equal treatment in the courts.
Based on this logic that African Americans had no rights, propo-
nents of lynching argued that it served not only as a reasonable and
accepted punishment, but it deterred blacks' aspirations for political and economic equality.

In the decade after the Redeemers came to power, more than
139 people died each year from lynching; 75 percent of the victims
were black. In the decades between 1890 and 1945, African Americans were 90 percent of the 4,708 lynch victims recorded by antilynching reformers. By the early 20th century, more than one-third
of the lynch victims were women and children. Scholars estimated
thousands more probably died under similar circumstances. Many
thousands more simply disappeared, or were murdered. During this
same period, African Americans became a significant portion of the
lynchings sanctioned by the courts, a punishment typically meted
out after fast trials.

African Americans' investigations into the allegations of rape
challenged the popular justifications for lynching. Ida B. Wells-
Barnett, a journalist from Memphis, compiled an extensive record
of these victims and published it as a one-hundred-page pamphlet
in 1892 titled *Southern Horrors: Lynch Law in all Its Phases.* Her evidence revealed that many of the victims had long advocated blacks'
civil and political rights; many had called for blacks' economic advancement. Others had been lynched because they demanded the
wages they were promised or they refused to sell their land to
whites. Wells-Barnett began her investigations after the lynching of

two men she knew in Memphis. Both had advocated black political activism, and each had tried to establish stores that competed with a white man's efforts to monopolize the store trade in the black neighborhoods. The men refused to yield, and a mob lynched them. Others were lynched because of interracial political and labor alliances. Her 1895 pamphlet, *A Red Record,* provided additional research and statistics that demonstrated the widespread practice of lynching, including outside the South.

This effort to challenge the justification for lynching held little sway in Georgia. Between 1890 and 1899, at least 115 blacks in the state had died through racial violence. After lynchings occurred in some towns, participants created a celebratory atmosphere. Others made public displays of the victims' mutilated bodies and took pictures, which they later collected or mailed as postcards. Charged with crimes, the victims did not have the opportunity for a trial by their peers. In late April 1899, for example, thousands traveled by train to Newman, Georgia, to see the lynching of Sam Hose, whose guilt had not been proven in a court of law. Hose had asked for his wages from his employer, Alfred Cranford, who refused and threatened him with a pistol. In self-defense, Hose flung his ax, striking the man in the head. Newspaper accounts claimed Hose plotted his employer's murder and raped the man's wife. Some in the crowd that gathered to lynch him, first doused him with kerosene while others mutilated and skinned his face. In separate investigations, the eyewitnesses to Hose's encounter with his employer agreed that he had flung his ax in self-defense. Mattie Cranford, Alfred's wife, repeatedly insisted Hose did not attack her.

These racial tensions over disputes about wages increased in the late 1880s as signs of an economic depression began in the Midwest wheat industry. By 1890, it spread to the southern cotton industry, where the decline in prices and wages lasted to the end of the century. Many railroads failed and banks closed, creating upheaval in other sectors of the U.S. economy. Urban unemployment rose to 25 percent. Strikes broke out in northern cities, which included a steel strike in Homestead and a railroad strike in Chicago. In response to the deplorable working conditions, frequent layoffs, and low wages, working-class men created labor unions. In some areas of the upper South, especially North Carolina and Virginia, some African Americans sought to join unions. In West Virginia, blacks successfully pressed to join the new United Mine Workers and the interracial union elected Richard Davis, an African American, as vice president. As the depression worsened, some blacks and whites supported the Populist Party because of its pro-worker rhetoric, but these alliances did not temper racial tensions as many whites in the party believed in the necessity of segregation. Blacks who could still vote in North Carolina joined with whites to end the rule of antilabor Democrats in the 1894 state elections and replaced them with Republican and Populist candidates. In some towns and cities in North Carolina, blacks returned to municipal offices as Republicans.

The severe depression that launched the Populist revolt and labor activism, which challenged the political order established by the Redeemers, instigated a countermovement that impacted the presidential election of 1896 and local elections in 1898. In the South, alliances of white men used threats of violence to discourage black and white voters who favored Republican candidates. In Wilmington, North Carolina, Alfred Waddell, who organized the White Government League, boldly announced he planned to rid the city of black politicians and voters "even if he had to chok[e] the Cape Fear with the bodies of negroes." Women in the state applauded the charged language and encouraged the men to use their shotguns at the polls. On the day before the election, Waddell urged his supporters "to do your duty. . . . Go to the polls tomorrow, and if you find the negro out voting, tell him to leave the polls, and if he refuses, kill him."[4]

Though Democrats in support of white supremacy won, the violence around the election continued the following day. Waddell and others in the White Government League armed themselves, and their arsenal included a Gatling gun—a rapid-firing gun. On November 10, 1898, Waddell led a mob of armed men through the city. They shot black men and chased others out of the city. The city's militia, the Wilmington Light Infantry, had just returned from fighting in Cuba during the War of 1898 and the troops joined Waddell. Its reinforcements and two cannons increased the number of African American fatalities to 10. Waddell removed the mayor and declared himself the new one. One eyewitness reported that black men were "shot down like dogs" in the days after the election as a way to prevent other blacks from voting in future elections. Again, where ordinances and heated racial rhetoric failed to discourage black voting, organized violence proved to be more effective. In the month after the riot in Wilmington, nearly 2,000 African Americans left the city. The exodus continued for months after blacks' appeals to President William McKinley for an investigation and justice failed to elicit a response. Instead, Republicans endorsed southern states' amendments to disfranchise black voters through literacy tests, property qualifications, poll taxes, and other impediments. In a region where more than one-fifth of the white male population could not read, did not own property, or could not pay taxes, many white voters found themselves excluded as well.

Inflamed by the rhetoric of white supremacy, lynching became more public and elaborate. Lynchings typically attracted hundreds and thousands of spectators. The process included torture, mutilation, and burnings. Women and children were lynched. Sometimes communities spent their fury on an entire family, or anyone associated with the accused. The press stoked the events by including false claims, rumors, and hearsay; others called for the lynchings to assuage people impatient with investigations, laws, and courts. These men may have described black men as savages and brutes, poised to rape white women, but southern newspapers more frequently described blacks as recalcitrant workers and demanding voters. The articles that reported the details of one lynching after another, informed readers that "the best men of the South" attended these events. These participants included business and political elites. Many sent reporters to witness and document the murders. Others published photographs of the lynched men, women, and children. By the turn of the century, lynching became more than communal vigilantism—it became a form of ritual and entertainment.

The first sustained legal efforts to manage racial contact emerged in cities as the response to the growing population of African American residents. As increasing numbers of blacks of all classes traveled on trains that challenged older ideas of blacks' subservience, some white elites questioned the new social and economic relations that swept aside the older distinctions of black slaves and free whites, regardless of class. In the New South, well-dressed black wives of black businessmen and landowners sat beside the well-dressed wives of white business owners and landowners on streetcars or in the ladies cars of trains. They jostled each other in stores and sidewalks. On weekends, black maids wore their best clothes and strolled the streets. In the theaters, black porters sat next to white owners of businesses. While some white southerners welcomed the new economic order that required blacks to labor in cities, others believed firmly in the inherent inferiority of blacks and they moved swiftly to establish new ways to make distinctions between blacks and whites, regardless of class.

Along with their criticism of the nighttime mayhem of interracial conviviality, middle-class and elite white men and women objected to the daily sight of blacks walking freely on sidewalks, or traveling alongside them in streetcars and trains. Despite the end of slavery, many whites urged blacks to behave like slaves, cease the clamor for civil rights, and remove themselves from whites' spaces. Whites' repeated lament about crowded sidewalks and streetcars where blacks and whites mingled and jostled each other became a metaphor for the larger struggles over political and economic equality. Many of the first laws intended to govern blacks' behavior in public space after their emancipation and later in the 1870s demanded that they remain off the new sidewalks and public walkways. Reports appeared in the white press about black women's boisterous public behavior. Others claimed that black women jostled white women on sidewalks, and poked them with elbows or umbrellas. These street confrontations correlated with increased black political and economic gains. In Virginia in the 1880s, for example, blacks retained the right to vote and whites frequently insisted blacks yield the sidewalks. When black pedestrians refused, whites repeatedly bumped or pushed against them and then demanded that blacks apologize or face arrest. By the 1890s, blacks no longer held public offices in the state or on city councils and they could not vote. Without representation, all-white city councils in many towns and cities passed new ordinances that prohibited blacks' use of the sidewalks. Instead, they had to walk in the muddy or dusty streets alongside horses and mules.

As the South became more urban with diverse populations simultaneously walking, shopping, and working in the same spaces, segregation laws established lines of social control that mapped out new racial, class, and gender hierarchies. These new laws—commonly known as Jim Crow laws—provided broad and coercive means to punish those individuals and communities that violated them. Although lynching had emerged as extralegal and sometimes hidden, segregation laws allowed for visible and draconian means to govern every encounter between blacks and whites. These laws dictated punishments, such as fines and imprisonment, but they also allowed whites to physically assault blacks perceived as violating these laws. African Americans who defied—or were perceived as having defied—segregation laws on streetcars, for example, faced immediate punishment from drivers who carried clubs used to beat riders who violated the laws. These public and sanctioned assaults spread into other areas of daily encounters between blacks and whites. Those African Americans seeking their right to vote or speak freely were considered "uppity," a common description used to justify lynching or brutal attacks. The allowance for such physical ferocity permeated every social encounter between blacks and whites; blacks feared for their safety and many voluntarily removed themselves from contact with whites.

NEW BLACK SOUTH: PROTESTS

Yet, blacks fought back against segregation and lynching. The Jim Crow laws regulating blacks' use of streetcars in the South began to appear as early as 1884, but did not solidify as a regional practice until after the 1896 U.S. Supreme Court decision in *Plessy v. Ferguson* that determined separate but equal accommodations did not violate African Americans' constitutional rights. Social equality, the majority of the justices argued, differed from political equality. Many of the first laws were municipal ordinances for private businesses, such as streetcars. Others, such as laws passed in Richmond, Virginia, called for voluntary segregation, but as early as1905, many state legislatures passed laws that mandated segregation on streetcars. Virginia passed state-wide legislation in 1906; over the next year, legislatures in North Carolina, Texas, and Oklahoma crafted laws requiring streetcar companies to operate segregated streetcars. Municipal and local Jim Crow ordinances, along with streetcar company regulations, remained the standard in Alabama and South Carolina.

As whites pressed companies, city councils, and state representatives to enact more laws after 1896, black customers organized dozens of boycotts against these regulations in nine of eleven southern states. Protests, mass meetings, and petition drives took place in every southern state where such laws had been passed, or where companies had policies of segregation. Few boycotts succeeded in overturning either state laws or local ordinances, and the five that prevailed—Jacksonville in 1901; Mobile and Montgomery in 1902; Richmond, Virginia, in 1904; and Jacksonville and Pensacola in 1905—were temporary. In some cities, owners of streetcar companies resisted the legislation and claimed creating separate cars added expenses to their operating costs. In Savannah, Georgia, some whites found the practice "distasteful" and resisted the ordinance when it first appeared in 1901. They sustained this effort each year until 1906. Black Richmonders organized a streetcar boycott in April 1904, as much to protest their diminished political rights and the sixty victims lynched in Virginia since 1880, as it was to express dissent against the Jim Crow laws on transportation. Blacks of all classes stayed off the streetcars, though working-class women participated

more than any other group. Hundreds of black wagon drivers transported passengers—frequently without charge—up the city's many
hills. The boycott lasted into 1906, but by then the Virginia General
Assembly passed laws mandating segregation on all transportation
in the state making it impossible to challenge the streetcar company's policies.

The spread of segregation laws from private practice on transportation to a state mandate in every area of transportation became
common across the South after 1906. African Americans described
the plethora of new laws that designated waiting rooms, ticket windows, and toilets as *colored* and *white* as humiliating and shameful.
Some stations did not have separate facilities for blacks and certainly not separate toilets. Instead, owners of these stations required
blacks to wait outside in the heat, cold, and rain. If black passengers
asked for toilets, they had to wait or use the woods. The curtail-
ment of access to public facilities restricted blacks' movement in
and around cities, from one city and town to the next, and from one
state to the next. Black women found boarding trains and streetcars
dangerous, as the policing of the new ordinances encouraged conductors and trainmen to insult and strike the women if they did not
immediately comply to the conductor's satisfaction. Frequently,
women paid for tickets in the front of cars and then they had to
climb down steps and board at the back of trains. Women reported
that the trains and streetcars pulled away, leaving them stranded.
Some ordinances gave conductors the power of police, allowing
them to arrest, fine, and club black passengers who refused to comply with the laws. The rapid expansion of segregation laws in every
area of public and private life meant that regardless of class, black
men and women shared the surveillance, violence, and humiliation
that these laws imposed on their daily lives.

Blacks' use of boycotts to challenge segregation continued, but
these efforts rarely stopped southern state legislatures or city councils from passing more restrictive laws. By 1906, the Georgia state
legislature passed laws that prevented blacks from serving on juries,
disallowed their right to vote, and limited their access to employment. State newspapers called for "a thousand men to hunt the
Negro criminal."[5] Leaders in the state, including Max Barber, editor
of the *Voice of the Negro* and W. E. B. Du Bois, sought to ameliorate
these legislative efforts through the creation of the Georgia Equal
Rights movement that called for equal rights.

Eager to use the popular appeals to quash blacks' political rights
as a way to sell newspapers, editors of the *Atlanta Evening News*

alleged a wave of black crime and urged whites to respond. A crowd of 10,000 arrived in downtown Atlanta on September 22, 1906, determined to arrest and harm any African American in sight. Crowds of white men, women, and children destroyed black-owned stores. They attacked and murdered blacks, including a child. Throughout the five-hour rampage, the crowd left mutilated corpses on display. A new mob gathered the next day and joined a well-armed militia preparing to enter black neighborhoods, but they encountered residents determined to protect themselves and their property. In the violence that followed, dozens of residents were assaulted and four were murdered. In addition, a police officer was killed, his assailant unknown. Still, the militia and its accompanying mob arrested hundreds of blacks and charged them with his murder. After this latest riot, dozens were dead, hundreds wounded, and blacks' property lay in ruins.

Black religious, civic, and labor leaders moved quickly and appealed to progressive whites, and together they organized efforts to calm the city. In the wake of the riot, these interracial alliances were forged on the shared rhetoric that the "better classes" had to unite against the "riffraff" that had moved into the city. These leaders insisted that poor blacks and whites committed crimes because they labored intermittently, roamed the streets, and congregated in bars and dives.

ALL-BLACK TOWNS

Many African Americans believed creating all-black towns might temper the violence and the diminution of blacks' political rights. All-black towns appeared rapidly in the western territories; 50 emerged in Oklahoma alone between 1890 and 1910. These towns attracted migrants from nearby southern states. Many emerged as a response to the violence against blacks, but some blacks supported the creation of all-black towns for entrepreneurial and religious reasons. Other African Americans saw Oklahoma as the place for the redistribution of land that had eluded them after the Civil War. Many African Americans who had relocated to homesteads on assigned lands in the Oklahoma Territory moved to form all-black towns because, like many Americans, they considered the West a place of opportunity.

Langston, Oklahoma, emerged on these formerly Indian lands under the aegis of Charles H. Robbins and Edward P. McCabe. Robbins bought and plotted Gutherie, a town that had quickly attracted whites moving into the territory. McCabe, who launched a newspaper in Oklahoma, had surveyed and sold land to African Americans in Nicodemus, Kansas, in the aftermath of the 1878 influx of Exodusters. In addition to Langston, McCabe also helped form the all-black town, Liberty, and indirectly supported the creation of several other all-black towns in the territory.

These migrants tended to have more resources as individuals and as a collective than migrants typically possessed in this period. Observers remarked that some of these migrants appeared to be middle class. McCabe used the pages of the newspaper he owned and edited, the *Langston City Herald,* to urge blacks to move to all-black towns like Langston where they could establish their own economic institutions and political institutions. Some of these migrants subscribed to Booker T. Washington's idea of self-help and social segregation.

Regardless of resources, settlement in these towns proved difficult. The push for these towns came as blacks faced a flurry of laws establishing segregation. These laws and practices appeared in the territories, as some whites feared Oklahoma might become an all-black state. Blacks were asked to leave and in some areas, including Norman and Tesumsek, they were forced to leave. In other areas, vigilante groups terrorized the new arrivals. Black leaders and newspaper editors, including Ida B. Wells, editor of the *Memphis Free Speech,* considered the responses to migration into these towns and territories indicated further difficulties blacks would encounter. No such violence occurred in Langston during this period. As segregation and violence escalated elsewhere, blacks continued to migrate to Langston and other all-black towns in Oklahoma for their relative safety. They established businesses, schools, and a college, the Colored Agriculture and Normal University of Oklahoma (later changed to Langston University, which is still in existence). Langston and other towns demonstrated blacks' efforts to realize aspirations of independence free from violence and racial proscriptions.

MIGRATION OUT OF THE NEW SOUTH

Despite the diminution of their political and economic opportunities, the overwhelming majority of African Americans considered their options, either to remain in the South or depart for cities and work in other nearby regions. Even as the various laws and practices that kept many blacks bound to the land in the 1870s and 1880s loosened to accommodate employers of New South industries, black workers found little economic and social mobility. The unskilled and low-wage work available to black men in the lumber, turpentine, and railroad was intermittent. Black women found little beyond domestic work. With little access to land for independent farming or limited choice for steady work in towns and cities, increasing numbers of African Americans cobbled together temporary work as they moved between rural and urban areas. By 1910, cotton, tobacco, and sugar prices plummeted while wage work in the new industries and urban domestic markets demanded African Americans spend extended time away from farms. As they searched for steady work, many African Americans began to move farther and more permanently away from rural homes. Encouraged by employers in the new rural and urban industries, increasing numbers of these itinerant workers made these low-wage and intermittent jobs the focus of their search for work.

Paradoxically, the demands of this geographic expansion and diversification of labor were coincident with a widening segregation in the New South that relegated blacks to the margins of the region's political, social, and economic relationships. This combination of the constant search for work within the humiliating and dangerous conditions of segregation provided the foundation for blacks' mass migration to the industrial urban North between 1910 and 1930. While African Americans' travels and labor experiences beyond the South had been limited, the institutions and communities they created in the South made them attuned to the possibility of life and work outside the region. In this context of Jim Crow politics, limited wage opportunities in the South, and dreams of more freedom in the North, African Americans acquired individual experience and the collective reason to leave the South permanently.

NOTES

1. A pseudonym for Nate Shaw's county in Alabama. See: Theodore Rosengarten, ed., *All God's Dangers: The Life of Nate Shaw* (Chicago, IL: University of Chicago Press, 1974).

2. Quoted in Nell Irvin Painter, *Exodusters: Black Migration to Kansas after Reconstruction* (New York: Norton, 1986), 98.

3. Shane White and Graham White, *Stylin': African American Expressive Culture from its Beginnings to the Zoot Suit* (Ithaca, NY: Cornell University Press, 1998), first quote, 164; second quote, 161.

4. Glenda Gilmore, *Gender and Jim Crow: Women and the Politics of White Supremacy in North Carolina, 1896–1920* (Chapel Hill: University of North Carolina Press, 1996), 109.

5. Quoted in Dominic Capeci, "Reckoning with Violence: W.E.B. Du Bois and the 1906 Atlanta Race Riot," *Journal of Southern History* 62 (November 1996): 739.

2

Going North: The Great Migration, 1910–1930

While landowners in nearly every southern state pressed legislatures to pass laws that would control blacks' mobility, limit their
wage opportunities, and minimize their ability to buy and own land,
industrial and urban employers showed little interest in laws or policies that limited workers' ability to move from one job to another.
Landowners used coercive efforts to keep blacks at the plow, and over
the next decade and a half, black involuntary servitude increased;
industrial employers used a variety of policies to confine blacks to
the lowest paid and least desirable labor. The New South's industries, these advocates argued, required available and cheap labor.
The region's burgeoning steel, coal, lumber, and railroad industries
needed a more diverse and mobile working class. But these differing approaches to ensure an inexpensive laboring class did not
challenge the doctrine of white supremacy, which was increasingly
codified in segregation laws. These new laws, popularly called *Jim
Crow* laws, policed public spaces, including workplaces; most important, they offered mechanisms to monitor and limit black mobility.
When, or if, blacks overstepped "their place," these laws provided
myriad forms of punishment. If laws did not adequately and immediately punish blacks, popular culture sanctioned lynching and
other violent reprisals.

Workers on a cotton plantation. (Library of Congress)

Despite the legal and extralegal efforts to limit their mobility, African Americans migrated. Paradoxically, the very efforts used to control their movements to find work in the South also compelled them to move greater distances; for many blacks, this movement included extended stays away, or permanent departures, from rural homes. After 1900, increasing numbers of African Americans found unskilled and semiskilled work in the mines in West Virginia and Tennessee, steel mills in Alabama, and in the lumber camps of East Texas. New South industries in cities like Birmingham, Alabama; Durham, North Carolina; and Atlanta, Georgia, drew black workers into unskilled jobs. This new employment, especially work in towns and cities, provided blacks numerous opportunities to create large and stable communities where organizations, newspapers, and churches thrived. By 1910, the greatly expanded black population in cities and industries of the New South attested to their diminished ties to the land and by the second decade of the 20th century those who labored in agriculture became the minority among all black workers. The large-scale and rapid movement of blacks off the land and out of rural areas for towns and cities and for longer periods of time widened to include movement into cities on the border of the South, especially Baltimore, Louisville, Memphis, Nashville, and Richmond, Virginia.

Despite blacks' frequent and widespread movement within the South, few made permanent or even temporary moves beyond the South. Until 1914, northern employers' demand for labor was met by the large influx of European immigrants. Many northern employers, especially industrial manufacturers, did not hire African Americans for work in factory jobs. The outbreak of the Great War in Europe greatly reduced the availability of newly arrived workers from abroad. With demand for war goods in 1915, northern employers looked south for workers. Many companies had affiliated plants and industries in the South, and first white and then black workers provided immediate populations for new recruits. When the United States formally entered the war in 1917 and mobilized men for the military, new, but temporary, workers were needed to meet acute labor shortages. And these employers stressed they planned to pay higher wages.

Influenced by, or experienced with, migration in the South, hundreds of thousands of African Americans responded to opportunities in a Great Migration north for better jobs and wages, but it also became apparent that other, equally pressing reasons motivated their departures. Many wanted to leave behind segregation and live, as many migrants expressed, "as full citizens." The earlier pattern of individual and temporary labor migration became one of a collective and permanent migration that rejected the economic, social, and political restrictions they found in the South. At the same time, African Americans hoped to find better opportunities in cities outside the South.

As early as the 1890s, increasing numbers of black men found intermittent and, on occasion steady, work in southern cities and towns near their rural homes. Mostly, the work was the least desirable work. In Birmingham, men worked in the steel mills where employers consigned them to the most dangerous and physically demanding jobs. Black men labored in the most dangerous and arduous positions in the blast furnaces where they produced molten iron. Despite the circumscribed nature of the work, by 1910 blacks held 90 percent of unskilled jobs in the Birmingham steel district, making the city and the surrounding areas one of the largest black urban communities of industrial workers in the New South. Despite the opening of industrial jobs to blacks, workplace segregation limited their occupational mobility and wage opportunities. Aware that white workers generally refused the most arduous work, black men leveraged their positions in the labor market. Unable to lure eastern and southern European workers into the South in any great numbers, employers sometimes had to pay black men higher wages, especially during the boom times. In the first decade of the new century, black men built railroad tracks, labored in coal mines, and did the rough work in turpentine camps. In New Orleans and Mobile, they held the majority of unskilled jobs on the docks; in every large and small city in the South, they predominated as teamsters.

A much smaller population of African American women found employment in southern industries. Segregation laws in some areas precluded their access to jobs as unskilled workers and machine tenders, but some employers hired them to work in a variety of menial capacities. They did the rough work in the tobacco mills, box factories, and paint and varnish factories. Most black women labored in domestic service as cooks, nurses, and household servants. Many employers demanded constant service and subservience from black household workers; some workers faced sexual harassment and other forms of abuse. Nonetheless, many women insisted on working by the day, which allowed them to return home to families. Whenever possible, women quit jobs they considered dangerous and demeaning. In some cities, officials refused to extend electricity and sewers into black neighborhoods. Forced to wash clothes by hand in unsanitary conditions for limited wages, black women demanded better services for their neighborhoods and higher wages. In Atlanta, women in the Washing Society launched a strike in July 1881 and demanded higher wages.

Many black women recognized the constriction of their wage opportunities because of their location at the bottom of the occupational and social ladder. Sara Brooks, who moved from rural Alabama to the outskirts of Mobile, noted that the "coloreds" had "the heaviest and hardest job all the time." And black women were especially disadvantaged. "When I went to Mobile, to me it seemed that we wasn't gonna get nowhere no how past the farm because Colored women could mostly do fieldwork or babysit or cook and clean house in the South." In Mobile, Brooks, along with her sister and other black women in their neighborhood, labored in a variety of poorly paid jobs. During the fall the women cobbled together domestic work—daywork—cotton picking, and laundry work. The remainder of the year, Brooks supplemented her meager earnings as a domestic worker with yard work, picking pecans, and childcare.[1]

Despite the move to cities, black workers frequently found only marginal improvement in their individual and household incomes. When compared to the wage experiences of northern workers, workers in the southern cities earned lower wages. Black workers had more limited job opportunities than any other group of workers, and they remained economically vulnerable, especially during downturns in the regional economy when employers replaced them with white workers. Because black men's income fluctuated as they lost jobs or moved between jobs, black married women worked in greater numbers than did other groups of married women.

Establishing new households in cities and maintaining households in rural homes meant both black men and women worked for wages, but with the fluctuation in blacks' incomes generally, men and women turned to other resources. Migrants who came to Mobile in 1910 supplemented intermittent work in the cotton presses and domestic work with food grown in gardens. Many women took in boarders and domestic workers brought leftover food from employers. In Memphis and Savannah, Georgia, new migrants collected rags, some performed in bars, and others gambled as temporary ways to earn extra income.

Many migrants working in towns and cities maintained ties to family in nearby rural areas, which stabilized urban households and eased their transition to new jobs and homes. Many new migrants did not travel far from home, and their proximity to rural areas provided them with financial and emotional support. Sara Brooks's older brother encouraged her to leave an abusive husband and a precarious financial situation and join him in Mobile, Alabama. Because he found greater wage-earning opportunities, he frequently provided his sister with a place to live and contacts with potential employers. Older African Americans, especially women, maintained rural residences and took care of grandchildren while parents took advantage of distant labor opportunities. Older women's care of children was especially critical for single mothers, allowing them greater mobility for extended periods of time. Brooks's brother had neither the money nor household space to include her two children; three of her four children remained on the farm with her parents. The children, in turn, provided much needed labor on farms or as wage hands for others. Older women's chickens and rural gardens supplemented urban diets with eggs and familiar vegetables, such as pole beans and greens. And these rural and urban households remained important during the Great Migration and the decade after. When unable to move wives and children north, black men relied on their families in the South to support and maintain wives and children.

These calculated labor migrations to southern towns and cities accelerated as floods and vermin swept through the South. First, the infestation of the boll weevil that began in southeastern Texas in the late 1890s slowly spread eastward and by 1913, the boll weevil had infested nearly 20 counties in southeastern Georgia. Over the next three years, the boll weevil moved like fire through the crops of the Deep South, wrecking havoc in Alabama and Georgia. Despite the use of chemical and home remedies, such as a mixture of sulfur and molasses, the worms ruined crops. Many black farmers discovered the power "of the ashy-colored rascal." Nate Shaw "soon learnt he'd destroy a cotton crop. Yes, all God's dangers ain't a white man. When the boll weevil starts in your cotton and go to depositin' his eggs . . . that's when he'll kill you."[2] Along with the boll weevil, hurricanes and prolonged rains and floods in Alabama and Georgia precipitated blacks' steady departure from the Black Belt and the Mississippi Delta.

A decade of infestation had caused many black and white rural workers to move to cities for employment, but the intensification of the infestation between 1910 and 1915 pushed many more workers out of rural areas and exacerbated an already precarious southern urban labor market. As they faced competition from whites in many jobs, blacks' urban unemployment in the South rose from 13 percent in 1910 to 20 percent in 1920. Finding so little wage work, they migrated out of the South. Yet, observers cautioned against simple conclusions about these twined events as the primary reasons for the mass departure. Despite the drama of the infestations and floods, some contemporary investigators noted that the possibility of higher wages in northern industries and households contributed the most to blacks' collective decision to migrate. Sociologist Emmett Scott concluded blacks primarily responded to the lure of job opportunities and higher wages in northern industries. He observed that the patterns of blacks' migration and the boll weevil infestations were not necessarily in synch:

The general direction of the spread of the movement was east to west. While efforts were being made to check the exodus from Florida, the good citizens of Texas are first beginning to note a stir of unrest in their sections. On the other hand, the march of the boll weevil, that stripped the cotton fields of the South, was from west to east.[3]

Historian Carter G. Woodson, another observer, conceded "what the migrants themselves think about it goes to the very heart of the trouble."[4] As local newspapers documented the steady departures of African Americans, editors marveled that migrants left en masse as much for personal and familial reasons as they did for social and economic aspirations.

Other contemporary observers noted that decades of segregation and violence against African Americans played significant roles in their willingness to see migration as a collective opportunity. Many young men and women wanted to escape the racial proscriptions that had limited their economic, social, and cultural opportunities. Investigators queried the departing men and women and discovered that their desire for better treatment and daily dignity was as important as their search for higher wages. These men and women mentioned that the constant threat of violence significantly informed their decision to leave. They saw other, better options beyond the South, and they decided to depart. In Georgia and Alabama, for example, the number of lynchings rose between 1910 and 1919 and served as a critical incentive for the migration. Jeff W. had initially rejected the decision to leave Ansley, Alabama, for Cleveland because he planned to become a minister like the other men in his family. After a cousin disappeared as a result of Ku Klux Klan violence, he decided to migrate.

Black newspapers heightened readers' awareness of racial violence, and this attention, in turn, played a significant role in many migrants' decisions to leave the South. Blacks' letters to the *Chicago Defender* poignantly detailed the low wages they earned, or the lack of work, but most cited how the violent treatment, along with the daily threats, and intimidation made them understand that they would not acquire their full rights in the South anytime soon. Instead, they had to migrate to find adequate work and safety. Their desire to live more freely, and not in fear, informed their decision to leave. Many contemporary observers noted that blacks had historically been subjected to intimidation, violence, and racial ostracism, but broader social changes around the war made acceptance of such abuse no longer possible. One young man's letter to the *Defender* encapsulated this widespread belief when he requested information about employment "any place" where he could be assured of "some protection as a good citizen under the Stars and Stripes."[5] In private and public ways, blacks expressed disdain for segregation and questioned its validity. For many blacks, their departure from the South was a response to, and a defiance of, the coercions used to keep them bound to segregation.

The search for more remunerative labor and the desire to escape the repressive racial controls and intimidation coincided with an unprecedented demand for labor in northern industries. The start of World War I in Europe that ended immigration to the United States also precipitated an immediate loss of available workers to northern industries when it was most needed for war production. Faced with severe labor shortages in steel, railroads, and meat-packing, employers immediately recruited black workers from the South. Railroad employers transported thousands of black men out of southern yards and moved them into the yards of Cleveland and Chicago. They also made appeals in southern black and white newspapers. James Robinson, an observer of the movement into Ohio and an interviewer of many migrants, commented: "In this great folk wandering, Cincinnati serves as a junction where migrants from different points in the South are distributed to other points in the North rather than as a terminus. It is apparently too near the South, which they are fleeing and does not offer the attractive wages afforded by Cleveland, Chicago and Pittsburgh."[6] Migrants wanted higher wages in a city as far removed from the South as possible.

Black newspapers and journals published in northern cities devoted significant portions of their pages to articles on the better life and higher wages black migrants would find in the wartime north. Sarah Rice recalled, "when anybody had a magazine or a newspaper, they'd gather round to talk about the news."[7] One woman noted how she and others waited impatiently for the *Defender* each week. She would "rather read it then to eat."[8] The *Chicago Defender* was the most eagerly awaited and widely read of these newspapers. Between 1915 and 1917, the weekly's editors' sharp critiques of segregation and violence in the South appeared alongside accounts of blacks' ability in the North to earn higher wages, vote, and send their children to school. The national edition carried reports from other cities where hundreds of African Americans arrived each day and found work, providing additional evidence that higher wages extended beyond Chicago. Pullman workers distributed the newspaper to southern black readers throughout the South and more than any other black weekly, Emmett Scott noted, the *Chicago Defender* brought "the North to them." Other journals equally influenced migrants. Willie Ruff heard black men read aloud to each other in barbershops, or on the front porches. These newspapers described African Americans' lives and communities. Most important, black newspapers schooled would-be migrants in what they might expect in northern cities. Through black newspapers and monthly magazines such as the *Crisis,* Bertha Cowan and other migrants learned "that a better world awaited us."[9] W. E. B. Du Bois, who edited the monthly journal, regularly described migration as an act of self-help.

THE GREAT MIGRATION

The ferment the black press raised for and about the migration accelerated after northern black organizations and newspapers reported they received thousands of inquiries about jobs and requests for information about train tickets. Many of these letters arrived in response to rumors that the *Chicago Defender* planned to provide train tickets to give to anyone who wanted to leave the South. Many had heard about a "Great Northern Drive" on May 15, 1916. Many of the letters explicitly mentioned that others waited to receive tickets. "Some are talking about a free train," one writer noted. Another politely asked the newspaper editor to "Please send tickets." In addition to requests for tickets, the writers wanted news about good jobs and steady wages. Some specifically inquired about work in Chicago, and others wanted to hear about fair wages in any city beyond the South. Generally, most writers asked for help in finding work. While some asked for particular jobs, others wanted information about jobs before they left the South. One man "needed more information before he took the leap." One writer wanted to leave the South to farm someplace where he might be more prosperous. "What about work on a grain farm in South Dakota," another writer asked.[10]

These letters arrived from everywhere in the South, and they revealed a collective awareness about the decline in immigration, the war in Europe, and the demand for workers in northern industries. African Americans collectively determined to fill the demand. "I believe in work and I have worked all my days," one Floridian noted, "and I mean to work until I die." This hopeful migrant intended to come alone, but other men detailed the needs and experiences of wives and children. "My wife is a laundress and so is my daughter and my son is a laborer all," one typical letter noted. Some writers included expectations about neighborhoods and communities. One man inquired about jobs and homes on behalf of himself and 200 or more good men.[11]

Women, too, detailed their desire to work wherever they might find employment. "I am no lazy girl," one 15-year-old wrote from New Orleans. "I can do any work that comes to my hand." One mother wrote for herself and her three daughters, all of them willing to do "any kind of work." One 28-year-old widow wanted a "position where I could live on places because it is very trying for a good girl to be out in a large city by [her]self among strangers." Women seeking domestic work wanted to know about wages. Writing on behalf of 15 other laundresses and cooks, one writer described how they "worked at starvation wages." And women were as likely as men to speak on behalf of others. "There is a storm of our people toward the North and especially to your city," one woman informed the *Defender*.[12] As the departures appeared to accelerate, the letters grew more insistent about particular details. What did rent for rooms and apartments cost? What were average wages? Should wives follow, or come with husbands? Should women bring their children?

Many expressed little personal knowledge about northern life, except what they read about in the news, or heard from family and friends. Despite news in the black weeklies, the North appeared far away, as if moving beyond Kentucky might be akin to emigrating to another country. Despite limited experience with the North, most emphasized the urgency of their request for news about work and places to live. Anywhere, one migrant pleaded, where a "man is a man." Despite their limited familiarity with the North, would-be migrants wrote the *Defender* because of the paper's "wide acquaintance with conditions" in numerous cities. Confident about the newspaper's advice, one writer asked for "all the particulars" as he intended to "become a citizen" of Chicago. Writing from Charleston, South Carolina, one inquiry focused on the weather: please make the job indoors as he read in the paper how the weather could be very cold.[13]

While the North represented "opportunity and advancement," writers stressed their desire to escape the economic and social repressions of the South. Miners from Bessemer, Alabama, and semiskilled union workers from Louisiana stressed the need to find jobs with the mobility that escaped them in the South. "In the north I can better my condition. I want to work [and] all I wish is a chance to make good." One woman from Mobile described how she and her family wanted to leave "their native home." She was especially anxious to get out of "this dog hold" and her husband was "crazy to get [to Chicago]." One woman linked work with her desire to leave the South. "I'm a willing working woman" and "I want to get out of this land of suffering."[14]

The labor conditions in the Deep South remained precarious, and despite news that the *Defender* claimed to have tickets as an advertising gimmick, writers continued to press for passes. "I could furnish you at least one thousand [workers] in the next sixty days," wrote one confident man from New Orleans. Another writer documented similar numbers that included women and children, all willing to do any sort of work. Workers in Mobile complained that they had been without work for weeks and they had a special claim on jobs. Conceding the arrival of a free train might be a rumor, one writer demanded the newspaper "answer at once." One woman reported, "so many women here are wanting to go that day. They are all working women and we can't get works so much now."[15]

LEAVING THIS SOUTHERN COUNTRY

The image of blacks clamoring to flee the South in May 1916 overlooks the range of choices many made about when and where to go. While the number of black men, women, and children leaving the South between 1910 and 1920 numbered more than half a million, the overwhelming majority of blacks remained in the South. African Americans who wanted to migrate made deliberate individual and collective decisions to leave the South or stay. Nate Shaw eloquently described the kind of choices he and other African Americans made as the war started, the boll weevil made its way east, and industrial jobs in the North became available.

A heap of families, while I was livin on the Tucker place . . . was leavin goin north. Some of my neighbors even picked up and left. The boll weevil was sendin a lot of em out, no doubt. I knowed several men went north, some with their families and some without; they sent for their families when they got to where they was goin. More went besides what I knowed of, from all parts of this southern country. They was dissatisfied with the way of life here in the south—and when I was livin on the Pollard place it come pretty wide open to me and touched the hem of my garment. But my family was prosperin' right here, I didn't pay no attention to leavin.

As Shaw suggests, the sense of deprivation in the South coincided with the availability of better working and living opportunities in the North. Shaw did not leave, however, because he "was a farmin man" and he knew "more about this country than [he] knowed about the northern states."[16]

Black southerners weighed their particular circumstances and resources against the widespread and daily discussions to migrate. When Nat Shaw farmed, he had acquired some assets. As the boll weevil infested nearby crops, he struggled to avoid its devastation and succeeded. Naomi Morgan's family, who lived not far from Shaw, faced different circumstances and then made a quite different choice than did Shaw. Morgan's parents considered their farm more stable than other farms. The infestation of the boll weevil wrecked havoc in their crops, and their relative economic stability abruptly ended. The family migrated to Birmingham where Morgan's father found work in a steel mill; soon after, he heard about higher paying work in Cleveland and decided to go north. Within months of his departure, he sent for his family.

The differing choices that Nate Shaw and Naomi Morgan's father made suggest that the decisions to move first rested on information they gathered and weighed about work opportunities elsewhere. Regardless of their point of departure, they based their decision on information they acquired about work and before blacks migrated, they had to figure out how to leave the South and settle in a northern city. Contemporary observers conceded that most migrants neither impulsively, nor abruptly, left the South. Most planned their departures, and they received aid and cooperation from family and friends. Geneva Robinson represents this aspect of migration when she left Hodges, South Carolina, in 1921, accompanied by her grandmother. The women's trip had been organized and paid for by other family members in the South after they learned how a cousin in Cleveland, who needed to work, also needed help with the care for her home and her children.

The majority of migrants planned how to purchase a ticket since many earned too little in wages and the cost of a train ticket was prohibitive. Regular passenger fares, which cost $.02 per mile in 1915, rose sharply within three years to $.24 a mile. Even with family in the North after 1920, the cost of travel remained a significant hurdle for those who wanted to migrate. When Allan Cole arrived in Cleveland after the war, he found only irregular work and for months he was unable to respond to his wife's pleas for a ticket so she, too, could come to the city. Eventually, the two managed to save enough money for her to purchase her ticket and pay off their debts in the South. Soon, the departure of some family members provided new resources for others to migrate later. Because so many blacks left furniture and other personal property behind with family and friends, many later migrants purchased tickets by selling these items.

JIM CROW TRAVEL

Entering a segregated southern train station to purchase a ticket required blacks to face repeated claims of their inferiority. They entered train stations through a separate door marked *colored*. W. E. B. Du Bois, who edited the *Crisis*, noted that black passengers endured "torture to buy a ticket. You stand and stand and wait and wait until every white person at the 'other window' is waited on." Buying the ticket proved equally harrowing. "The agent browbeats and contradicts you, hurries and confuses the ignorant, gives many persons the wrong change, compels some to purchase their tickets on the train at a higher price."[17]

Black passengers then waited in the cramped discomfort of the segregated waiting rooms that lacked heat in winter and little, if any, air circulation in the summer. Even in better kept spaces, they found few places to sit as they waited for the trains. In other stations, passengers found dirty rooms with broken and uncomfortable seats. Few of the colored waiting rooms had restrooms or water fountains, so most black passengers typically packed food and drink. In rural areas, black passengers waited alongside the tracks, in some instances avoiding whites out of concern they might be stopped, or prevented from boarding trains. Waiting for a train in the rural South took courage and patience. At times, people spent days and nights in train stations as they waited for connections. In the larger towns and cities, blacks waited in segregated rooms at the depot, most without restrooms. Once onboard, black passengers were confined to dirty and shoddy train cars. "There is not in the world a more disgraceful denial of human brotherhood than the 'Jim-Crow' car of the southern United States," Du Bois noted. If the abundance of train lines represented the modern South, the segregated train cars repeatedly emphasized the region's prevailing ideas and practices of its racial hierarchy.[18]

African Americans boarded these trains intending to leave segregation behind in the South. Charles Denby and a friend left Texas for Detroit in 1924. The two men "hoped we'd get to see the Mason-Dixon line. I thought in my mind that it would look like a row of trees with some kind of white mark like the mark in the middle of the highway." As the train approached Covington, Kentucky, other passengers told Denby "the bridge ahead was the Mason-Dixon line. We felt good. We were North." Just as many other African Americans noted, when Denby crossed the invisible line into the North it had important, even biblical, meanings. He described leaving legal segregation behind as passage into "milk and honey and pearly gates." Like many other migrants, he immediately tested the shattered colorline. Shaking from fear and hope, Denby and his friend walked through the train. They sat next to a white passenger

A colored waiting room at a railroad station in
Oklahoma. (Library of Congress)

"to see what he would do. We thought any minute he would tell
us to sit in the Negro coach." Instead, the man read his paper and
then asked Denby if he wanted a section to read, too. "He wanted
to know where I was going and said, 'Detroit is a nice place.'"[19]

As African Americans calculated how to save money for tickets
to leave the South, reports and newspaper articles claimed that
labor agents lured thousands of men to northern jobs, but more
often than not such rumors proved undocumented. Investigators
charged that these agents and recruiters lured away black workers through false claims about free tickets or jobs. Some northern
employers did use agents to recruit workers, but they primarily confined their search for labor to particular areas and targeted specific
populations and occupations, typically male workers with some
familiarity with industrial labor. Labor agents from the Cleveland
steel mills actively sought black workers in Alabama in the fall of

1916, with little recruitment through the remainder of the war. In at least one instance, steel owners simply shifted workers from a southern plant to a northern plant, as the case with McKinney Steel. Feeling the loss of immigrant laborers, the New York Central Railroad sent agents to recruit southern black railroad workers for their yards in Pittsburgh, Cleveland, and Chicago. Some of these men only intended temporary stints in these mills and yards, while many others decided to settle permanently and later brought families.

These offers of train tickets, higher wages, and better work conditions appealed to many men, and they left southern plants for northern companies. Agents promised, too, that workers could eventually bring their families. Instead, most men paid high sums to these agents and few, if any, of the promises materialized. Black migrants to Cleveland reported that they had been charged $3 each, of which $1 went to a labor agent for the Lake Shore Railroad. After they arrived in the city, they discovered much of their first several months' salary being paid for the tickets. Many blacks claimed that men posing as agents bilked them out of the few dollars they had. Some migrants complained of threats and intimidation if they did not respond to these agents. In Deridder, Louisiana, 1,800 men reportedly paid an agent several dollars each for tickets to Chicago and a promised job. After weeks of waiting for tickets, the men realized they had been duped.

As the large migration of the war years continued into 1917, state officials in the Deep South moved to prohibit blacks' departure. States quickly passed legislation to prevent labor agents from operating altogether or they passed high licensing fees and fines. In Alabama, nearly 75,000 blacks—8.3 percent of the population—migrated north between the spring of 1916 and into 1917. State legislators passed a law requiring labor agents to obtain a license, a process that included high fees. Those agents caught without a license faced a $500 fine and one year's hard labor. The City Commission in Montgomery, Alabama, passed an ordinance prohibiting any effort to lure away laborers to work elsewhere. Another ordinance made it illegal to publish, distribute, or post any information that might entice workers to leave the area for jobs elsewhere. Unable to stop the migration, some planters resorted to threatening, intimidating, or arresting blacks on petty charges. Many southern states and cities passed legislation in 1918 that required blacks to prove that they had jobs in the local area, or served in the military. These "work or fight" laws, originally designed to force men into the army, allowed southern landowners and other employers to stop or prevent some blacks, including black women, from migrating, or leaving one job in the South for another.

Most men paid for their own fares and relied on their own information about jobs gleaned from friends, family, and neighbors already working in northern jobs, but some men found other means to travel besides train tickets and labor agents. Black men who traveled alone had some greater flexibility in how and when they migrated. Some young men simply hopped freight trains. Gus Joiner recalled both the spontaneity and danger of leaving the South through this latter method. At the age of 17, Joiner did not want to work in a steel mill in Birmingham and decided instead to see Chicago. Without informing his parents, Joiner hopped on a freight train and headed for Chicago. With only a quarter in his pocket, Joiner was delayed by having to scavenge for food in Ohio and 30 days of hard labor in Indiana after police discovered him on the freight car. After several years of labor in the Chicago stockyards, and a short stint in the coal mines of West Virginia, Joiner eventually migrated to Cleveland. Joiner's decision to leave may have been spontaneous, but his circuitous route suggests that spontaneity could be dangerous.

Many migrants found that their earlier moves to southern cities or to border states made migration safer and less expensive. Black men who had left Alabama for the coalfields of West Virginia or to work on the railroads in Louisville, Kentucky before the war, made the decision to travel on to Pittsburgh or Chicago during the war. Because their families had accompanied or followed them to these new areas, black men found it less expensive to move their families once they found jobs and places to live. Many of these families drew extended kin from other areas of the South, creating a chain migration. Sometimes this chain migration could be unintentional, which was the experience of John Malone. In 1910, Malone joined other workers from Alabama to work for the Illinois Central Railroad in Louisville, Kentucky, as common laborers. In 1916, recruiters from the New York Central Railroad brought Malone and other black men to Cleveland. Many men eventually brought their families north, but Malone had intended to return to Louisville because he did not like the colder weather in Cleveland. His grave illness brought his wife to the city and, after his recovery, she persuaded him to stay. She, too, found a job as a cook in the railroad yards. Together they earned enough to bring their children to the city and by 1917 everyone worked for the railroad.

Women faced the threat of attacks, and many rarely traveled alone. Black women tended to travel accompanied by family or friends rather than migrate alone. Faced with potential physical harm, women rarely hopped freight trains, or roamed and rambled like men. Travel with family and friends provided protection and support. Young black women who traveled alone typically made one move and joined extended family; others migrated with other women. Along with a young friend, 16-year-old Bertha Cowan left Lynchburg, Virginia, for Cleveland, in late 1917. When single women traveled alone and did not join families already settled in the North, they made more calculated, one-time moves, leaving the South for a specific city in the North.

Some women in seemingly impossible relationships desired to extricate themselves from patterns of familial abuse and poverty and sometimes left on their own. Just how many women were abused and departed will remain unknown. Black women wanted to avoid racial *and* sexual harassment, but some women had the additional goal to free themselves from the abuse in southern households. Black men who stood up to white employers, men who quit a job rather than be subjected to the harsh confines of segregation were often admired; men who failed to adequately provide for their children, or who displayed an unwillingness to work hard, whether as a sharecropper or as a stevedore, encountered great condemnation from their communities. It was not uncommon for extended families to openly criticize men who abused women and children, or who refused to provide for their care. Raised by a hardworking father, Sara Brooks's family expected the same from her husband. When he refused to work, and then abused her, Brooks's family and other community members publicly chastised him, encouraged her to leave, and offered as much support as their limited means could provide.

ROLE OF FAMILIES

The daily social and economic needs and expectations of family influenced when, why, where, and how individuals migrated. The experiences of Flowree Robinson and her family during World War I displayed the intricate work of caring that extended across regions for over the next two decades. After her mother died in 1915, Robinson's father moved his children from the rural town of Edwards, Mississippi, to nearby Greenville. He left then 12-year-old Flowree in the care of her older sister and he took her older brothers and their young families to Gary, Indiana, where the men found work. Despite earning higher wages, Robinson's father grieved over the separation from his youngest child and constantly worried about her well-being. He returned to Mississippi gravely ill and soon died. Robinson married at sixteen and moved away from her sister; her brothers migrated to Cleveland, but the family remained connected through letters. While the vagaries of the early 1920s economy made visiting impossible, the siblings used the mail to loan money, dispense advice, and offer emotional support. When Flowree's husband suffered from alcoholism and became abusive, one of her brothers urged her to join him in Cleveland. Despite the strain on his limited resources, he shared his small home, gave her money, helped her find a job, and introduced her to a fellow worker from the South, whom she later married. Others had little more than family support, but relatives' encouragement and willingness to take care of children was enough to propel many abandoned or abused women northward. The earlier departure of other family members provided many migrants with the emotional and financial support necessary to leave the South.

The responsibilities of households and children made it especially difficult for single women with children to migrate since many found it nearly impossible to save money for fares out of their meager incomes. Sara Brooks only had enough money to take her young daughter when she left Alabama; she left her three sons with relatives and it took almost 15 years to gather her family together once again. Although she wanted them with her when she first came, Brooks explained, "I just wasn't able to support them, and then I didn't have no place for them, either, when I left and come to Cleveland."[20] Other women made similar efforts to bring their children to Cleveland. As historian Darlene Clark Hine has noted "that it is precisely because women left children behind in the care of parents and other relatives that their attachment to the South was more than sentimental or cultural. They had left part of themselves behind."[21] The care of these children, whether they migrated north with mothers or remained in the South with other relatives sustained the migration chain of individual families for decades.

Despite the potential danger, some single women "roamed and rambled" like men as they looked for employment. Better education and growing acceptance of women's aspirations for self-sufficiency and independence propelled increasing numbers of them to migrate alone. Young women especially hoped to take advantage of the higher paying jobs in the North, even if it meant continuation in domestic service. Typical examples can be seen in the actions of 16-year-old Bertha Cowan, who left Lynchburg, Virginia, with a friend and both intended to "see the world." The two young women heard about jobs in Cleveland, and they set about finding money and making plans to migrate. Once she arrived, Cowan then encouraged her family to come when labor demands of the war increased employment opportunities.

In the decade after World War I, blacks' continued departures, especially from rural areas, irrevocably altered their former communities, creating disparate assessments of the migration. As the Great Migration peaked, sociologist Charles S. Johnson studied these communities and he detailed the transformation in black households in Macon County, Alabama, as the remaining family members cared for children and older relatives left behind. For some families, rumors of the whereabouts of kin, or the photographs they sent in letters "remained as almost mocking mementoes of a separation as complete as death." For many families faced with sharp declines in farm and wage work, migration out of the South provided important options for themselves and their communities. Black farmers who had managed to eke out a living at the turn of the century, or who bought their own land, had little to offer their children and grandchildren 30 years later. One farmer admitted that he had a few good years growing cotton between 1915 and 1927, but "if it wasn't for the boll weevil, it was the draught, and if wasn't the draught, it was the flood." More than anything, the lack of mechanization, the low price of cotton, and competition from other nations growing cotton made this man's efforts yield little in return. In the end, one farmer concluded that he had little assets from farming to pass on to his children.[22]

More frequently, as the children of black farmers no longer considered self-sufficiency on a farm possible, many also found little wage work in rural areas in general. And for increasing numbers of African Americans, intermittent wage work in rural industries no longer provided much relief for farm debt. Instead, they looked to urban work as their main source of income. Sara Brooks and her older brother, like many of their peers, left rural farms for nearby towns in the 1920s to feed themselves and to supplement their parents' farms. Even as they did so, the resources of rural and town households remained tightly interconnected, but each could be devastated by the loss of a crop, or the loss of wages from nonagricultural work. Everywhere in the South, blacks had

precarious incomes. Many young men and women found it nearly
impossible to maintain households while they cobbled together
work on farms with work in saw mills, or in white households as
domestic workers.

Individual and family assessments about managing daily life in
the South expanded to include migration to nearby or northern
cities. Before migrants left the South, many recalled hearing stories about family and friends who moved north. In general, many
migrants made their way north because of the information and
support provided by the already departed. As one investigator
discovered, the most successful labor agent was the United States
mail. "The Negro's success in the North has been far more effective
in carrying off labor than agents could possibly have been." A letter
in a mailbox with news of success had the capability of bringing "a
new group to the promised land."[23] Migrants' letters and stories of
opportunities in Cleveland, Chicago, or Harlem provided powerful
evidence to hesitant would-be migrants in the decade after World
War I. In addition, the return of kin and friends already living in
the North provided critical incentives. No one in Brooks's family
migrated until the 1930s. "Well I hadn't heard anything about the
North because I never known nobody to come no further than Birmingham, Alabama."[24] When her brother left Alabama and settled
in Cleveland, he wrote his sister and urged her to move, too. The
friends, who had migrated, returned to Alabama wearing new
clothes and reinforced her brother's claims. Through these everyday interactions, from letters to visits, someone from the community had information and experiences that reassured individuals
who may have been unfamiliar with the city.

Along with the experiences of family and friends, where to
migrate was frequently determined by the availability of employment opportunities. Several studies have shown the relationship
between patterns of migration to northern cities and the availability
of employment opportunities. The steel and automotive factories of
Pittsburgh and Detroit attracted more male migrants than women.
Cleveland, Chicago, New York, and Philadelphia provided favorable employment to both men and women. Between 1915 and 1921,
these cities became a major destination for black families because
the expansion of war industries coincided with opportunities for
women to work and children to attend schools.

After 1920, African Americans left the South and followed families and friends into northern cities like links in a chain. The Hicks
family followed this pattern of chain migration. Josephus Hicks

grew up in the steel camps of Bessemer, Alabama, where his father labored as a minister and a steel worker; his mother worked simultaneously as a teacher and a domestic worker. As a teenager, Hicks, too, worked in the foundries. After he completed high school, an unusual accomplishment given the constraints of segregation and the demands of work, he joined friends who traveled the mid-Atlantic states laboring as agricultural laborers and service workers. Hicks eventually completed a degree at South Carolina State College and later found work teaching courses there, but he frequently did not receive a salary from the cash-strapped college. He returned to agricultural work and service work. As the depression in the 1930s made it harder to find work, Hicks "didn't see any differences [in] the money you could earn in New York City and the money that you could earn in South Carolina." Other reasons compelled his decision. Stymied by the restrictions of segregation, Hicks wanted the "expansiveness of the city, the advantages of the libraries, the movies and the social activities." And he wanted to leave behind the "managing of Negroes" and the "routines of subordination" dictated by Jim Crow.[25]

While the catalyst for Hick's decision to migrate was precipitated by his experiences with work and life in the segregated South, he decided to move because other family members had already traveled north. As early as 1915, Hicks's mother heard about the city from friends who described it as a "favorable place to live and work." After the war, she and her daughter moved to the city and a decade later, Josephus Hicks followed. His complicated and protracted migration north, shaped simultaneously by his constant search for work, his desire to escape the stultifying parameters of segregation, and his efforts to maintain ties with kin and friend, typified the experiences of many black men and women leaving the Deep South for northern industrial cities.

African Americans who departed the South between 1915 and the 1930s variously viewed their decision as a choice or a necessity, but their decisions included support and resources from family and friends. For many black men and women, the possibility of more remunerative labor in the North provided a powerful incentive to leave farms and towns, but the earlier departures of families and friends aided and hastened these decisions. Many migrants, like Josephus Hicks and Sara Brooks, made the decision to move north based on the presence of family and friends in the city. Whatever the reason behind individual and familial migration, African Americans left the South with the hope and the intent to make something better for themselves and their families. While they expected to leave behind the indignities and terror of the segregated South, they also drew on a southern black culture and familial ties that provided a rich reservoir for migrants to draw on once they arrived in northern cities.

NOTES

1. Sara Brooks, *You May Plow Here: The Narrative of Sara Brooks* (New York: Touchstone Books, 1986), 182.

2. Nate Shaw, *All God's Dangers: The Life of Nate Shaw* (New York: Alfred A. Knopf, 1974), 223.

3. Emmett J. Scott, *Negro Migration during the War* (New York: Arno Press, 1969, 1920), 46.

4. Carter G. Woodson, *A Century of Negro Migration* (Mineola, NY: Dover Publications, 2002, 1918).

5. All quotes are in Emmett J. Scott, "Letters of Negro Migrants of 1916–1918," *The Journal of Negro History*, 3 (July 1919): 290–340; and "More Letters of Negro Migrants of 1916–1918," *The Journal of Negro History*, 4 (October 1919): 412–65.

6. James R. Robinson, "The Negro Migration," *Social Service News* 1 (July 1917), 100.

7. Sarah Rice, *He Included Me: The Autobiography of Sarah Rice* (Athens: University of Georgia Press, 1989), 26.

8. Scott, "Letters," 333.

9. Quoted in Kimberley L. Phillips, *AlabamaNorth: African-American Migrants, Community, and Working Class Activism in Cleveland, 1915–1945* (Urbana: University of Illinois Press, 1999), 127.

10. Scott, "Letters," 304.

11. Ibid., 296, 314.

12. Ibid., 316–19.

13. Ibid.

14. Ibid., 315, 332.

15. Ibid., 322–23.

16. Shaw, *All God's Dangers*, first quote, 195; second quote, 296.

17. W.E.B. Du Bois, *Darkwater: Voices from Within the Veil* (New York: Washington Square Press, 2004), 176.

18. Ibid., 176–77.

19. Charles Denby, *Indignant Heart: A Black Worker's Journal* (Detroit, MI: Wayne State University Press, 1989), 27.

20. Brooks, *You May Plow Here*, 215–16.

21. Darlene Clark Hine, "Black Migration to the Urban Midwest: The Gender Dimension, 1915–1945," in Joe William Trotter, ed., *The Great*

Migration in Historical Perspective: New Dimensions of Race, Class, and Gender (Bloomington: Indiana University Press, 1991), 132.

22. Quoted in Charles S. Johnson, *Shadow of the Plantation: Peonage in the South* (Urbana: University of Illinois Press, 1972), 107.

23. Scott, "Letters," 100.

24. Brooks, *You May Plow Here*, 195.

25. Quoted in Phillips, *AlabamaNorth*, 15.

3

Black Migrants in the Metropolises of America

I got vegetables today,
So don't go away[1]

The new migrants bombarded newspapers, relatives, and organizations with letters, expressing their excitement, aspirations, and fears about the urban north. "I should have been here 20 years ago," one migrant in Chicago reported. "I just began to feel like a man. It's a great deal of pleasure in knowing that you have got some privilege." His children attended a neighborhood school populated by new migrants, immigrants, and whites. And he registered to vote. He ended his letter with another satisfaction about his daily experiences of greater freedom in a northern city: "I don't have to 'umble to no one, and there isn't any 'yes sir' and 'no sir'—it's all yes and no and Sam and Bill."[2]

In the streets of Harlem, Cleveland, and Chicago, migrants arrived and found neighborhoods bursting with fantastic sights, sensations, and experiences. Lil Hardin, a migrant from Memphis, found the hustle and bustle of Chicago invigorating. Every day she strolled the streets and "looked this 'heaven' over. Chicago meant just that to me—the beautiful brick and stone buildings, excitement, people moving swiftly, and things happening."[3] The tens of thousands of migrants who arrived in this and other cities encountered bewildering, yet exhilarating, urban settings. Vast industries of rail-roads, meatpacking, auto, and garment manufacturing coexisted with skyscrapers, multi-floored department stores, and the new entertainments of movie houses and baseball stadiums. To many migrants, these industries and entertainments represented oppor-tunities to make themselves into modern industrial workers and urban residents freed from the limits of southern segregation. Langston Hughes described the newcomers to Cleveland as "the gayest and bravest people possible—these Negroes from the south-ern ghettos—facing tremendous odds, working, and laughing and trying to get somewhere in the world."[4]

Some migrants expressed apprehension about living in a city far from family in southern communities. One man lamented that while he found the city "a fine place to make money," he still planned "of coming back." *He* had "no trouble whatsoever," but raising his "children like they should be" had become more difficult without the familiarity of "the surrounding friends" still in the South, all of them "more dear" now that he lived in a city filled with strangers.[5]

By the late 1920s, African Americans' hopes for greater economic and social freedoms remained elusive. Richard Wright, who was born and raised in Jackson, Mississippi, sojourned briefly in Mem-phis before he migrated to Chicago. After he arrived, he noted how his "first glimpse of the flat black stretches of Chicago depressed and dismayed [him], mocked all [his] fantasies." Whereas some migrants found the city modern and exciting, Wright found it ener-vating: "The din of the city entered my consciousness, entered to remain for years to come."[6] And it was more than the dissonance that rattled his sensibilities. Southern segregation had imposed both physical and psychic terrors on Wright, but he and many other migrants soon discovered how the northern and modern industrial city also presented similar racial obstacles. In the North, popular and insidious ideas about blacks' inferiority elicited violence and imposed barriers, some legal, others cultural, which shaped nearly every aspect of their everyday lives. Neighborhood associations created restrictive covenants on real estate; landlords and realtors colluded to confine black migrants and immigrants to crowded neighborhoods and dilapidated dwellings. Employers' and union policies barred them from the better-paid and desirable jobs. Many businesses denied them access to stores, theaters, and other recre-ation. During and after the war, race riots erupted with frequency and across a wide geography.

Yet, as the numbers of black migrants and Caribbean immigrants arriving each week increased and as they confronted barriers in their efforts to settle and live, their aspirations for equal access to jobs and homes in northern cities necessitated new cultural and political strategies. Their desire for self-determination, equality, and opportunity remained tied to the struggles in the South, but they were also energized and informed by the global struggles for full citizenship. Many northern cities, particularly eastern cities, became zones of interaction between black migrants from the South, black immigrants from the Caribbean, and longtime black residents. Each group formed part of the larger African Diaspora, and their overlapping encounters in the urban North of the United States coincided with the hardening of racial hierarchies around the world. Their desire to make the North fulfill its promises included new social and political efforts that created reverberations throughout American cultural and political life and institutions.

These migrants moving north in the first two decades of the 20th century found cramped and rundown neighborhoods. Harlem's black population from the South and the Caribbean population pushed their collective numbers from 60,000 in 1910 to 300,000

Bronzeville in Chicago, Illinois. (Library of Congress)

a decade later. These new Harlemites settled in a densely populated, yet narrow area, between 114th Street and 145th Street east of Lenox Avenue. In this same period, Chicago's black population nearly tripled from 44,103 in 1910 to 109,458; nearly 50,000 of this new population arrived between late 1916 and early 1918. New migrants settled in a thin swath of land called the Black Belt, which was located on the south side of the city from 18th Street to 39th Street and bounded by State Street on the east and the Rock Island Railroad tracks and LaSalle Street on the west. Smaller cities, too, showed steady increases in their black populations that were similarly confined to the least desirable areas.

As successive groups of migrants arrived between 1915 and 1930, they chose where to live and work based on the economic limitations and spatial barriers they encountered, but their individual needs, including the desire to reestablish households and connections with family and friends, also influenced their decisions. Many migrants arrived in a new city with information gleaned from friends, family, and newspapers about how to travel to their destinations, what to expect once they arrived, and where they might find a place to live and work. Many had used these family and friend connections—relationships that historians and other social scientists describe as migrants' networks—to gather and assess information about how and where they might work, how much they might earn, and what to expect from employers in the North. Richard Wright moved to Chicago only after extensive conversations with his mother about available work and rent for an apartment. They crafted a plan for how much money to save for travel, when to leave Memphis, and their material needs once they arrived in Chicago. After calculating their resources, Wright and his family realized they did not have enough money for all of them to move at once, so he and his aunt left for the city, first, with plans to live with another relative until they had a room of their own and more resources for other family to travel North.

Even with contacts and information, many migrants learned that finding a place to live could be a daunting task. Many migrants discovered how hard it was to navigate the unfamiliar streets and neighborhoods of a new city. Traveling with a friend, Charles Denby arrived in Detroit with a half-memorized address for a boarding house. Friends had given them the address and the two men roamed the streets knocking on doors and seeking help from unresponsive strangers. "We thought if we asked someone on the street they would surely know our friends just like we knew everybody in the country." In contrast, Richard Wright had clear and accurate information about where to live and he rented a room from his aunt's landlady, but he found the building "makeshift and temporary." Months after his arrival, he still found the city "baffling."[7] Wright and Denby faced typical hardships that other black migrants encountered.

Overall, African Americans found far fewer choices in a more circumscribed geography because of the growing number of particular restrictions landlords and neighborhood associations imposed on them. Though some landlords had refused to rent to African Americans before the war, others quickly adopted similar racial proscriptions during and after the war. Aware of the demand for better housing and the restrictive policies against black migrants, owners of buildings and properties where blacks already lived increased their rents for the new arrivals. Wartime surveys found that blacks paid a disproportionate share of their income in rent when compared with native-born whites and immigrants in similar housing in adjacent buildings and neighborhoods. In Cleveland, blacks rented five-room suites for $31 a month; in contrast, whites paid $22 for similar space. This dissimilarity led some migrants to describe the high rents as "the colored tax."[8]

During World War I, migrants began their search for a place to live as housing became scarcer and African Americans in particular found fewer choices than other groups of new arrivals. In every northern city, blacks competed with other groups for a limited number of rentals clustered in older neighborhoods where landlords had deliberately ignored the need to repair and maintain buildings. Taking advantage of the limited choices available to black migrants, property owners quickly subdivided older homes into smaller spaces. Harlem landlords began this process in 1906, when migrants arrived in greater numbers, but it accelerated in 1915. In Chicago, landlords forced immigrant renters out of larger apartments, and then subdivided the rooms into small kitchenettes. Langston Hughes watched owners take an "eight-room house with one bath would be cut up into apartments and five or six families crowded into each two-room kitchenette apartment."[9] Overcrowding became common. Despite the need and the demand for housing, property owners erected few buildings and employers did not provide housing for migrant workers, or their families.

Newly arrived migrants coped with these limited housing choices in a variety of ways. As rents increased and living space disappeared, people rented hallways, sheds, garages, and storefronts.

"Changing Tenants" sign in Chicago, Illinois. (Library of Congress)

In one of the rare instances where employers offered housing, migrants in Cleveland moved into boxcars provided by the New York Central Railroad. The company partitioned each car into three rooms and then hoisted them on top of bricks; each car had a coal-burning stove, and the families shared two water pumps and several outhouses. Despite the inconvenience, black workers chose the boxcars over the company's rundown tenements. Typically, city social welfare officials scrambled to house the new migrants in the available rentals. Overwhelmed by the appeals for housing, officials in Cleveland and Chicago urged migrants to pitch tents in the city parks. As the competition for housing continued in Cleveland, some migrants did pitch tents in an area outside the city. In Chicago, tent cities appeared in available parks and empty lots.

On average, migrants earned lower wages, which contributed to their confinement in the least expensive housing. Throughout the war, migrants typically faced precarious employment; after the war, they experienced frequent layoffs, which limited their resources and prevented the majority from moving to, or purchasing, better housing. Their irregular labor after the war meant they used a larger portion of their monthly incomes for rent in dwellings that lacked indoor plumbing and running water. By the 1920s, investigators noted that landlords knew of blacks' narrower options for rentals and they regularly exploited them. The rents in Harlem exceeded most household incomes. Many black renters paid $55.70 each month in the 1920s on average family incomes of $1,300. Whites in the city paid two-thirds of what blacks paid for housing and they earned $200–$300 more on average.

LIVING IN THE CITY

Confronted with restrictions on *where* they lived, many migrants intended to make the most of how and with whom they lived. Blacks' protracted migration and their precarious economic circumstances changed the size of black families and the configuration of black households in most cities outside the South. Many black households became elastic as they expanded and contracted to accommodate the needs and financial resources of young working adults, young children, and the older women who cared for them. Households based on marital and blood ties predominated, but the presence of nonrelated members remained high, making the average number per household higher than for other groups. Between 1920 and 1930, the percentage of female-headed households rose only slightly higher than that of other groups, and nearly equaled the percentage of second-generation immigrants with female heads. The percentage of northern black female-headed households remained equal to, or lower than the percentages in the urban South. Regardless of region or social class, most black households remained headed by men.

To offset unstable incomes, many households took in boarders, friends, and extended family to help care for children and provide resources for rent. Many families encouraged younger or older female relatives to join them. Single black women with children found it especially difficult to work and they often had limited access to private and public charity. Instead, they needed to work for wages, which necessitated help with childcare. Many families sent children north alone to take advantage of better education, necessitating some elaborate household arrangements. Families with older wage-earning children made calculated decisions to send younger children north to live with siblings or other relatives.

The higher rents and fewer housing options imposed great hardships on unskilled workers without families. Wartime wages increased many single black men's ability to rent rooms if they were available, but as wages decreased after the war, their options diminished. Employers found that more than any other group of male workers, black men had the most difficulty locating housing near their work. Most could not rent rooms in the boarding houses available to other groups of male workers. Few found a room or a bed in the crowded kitchenettes that black migrant families rented. In some cities, many men spent several hours each day walking to work; others devoted nearly as much time traveling on streetcars. The inability to find housing compelled many men to seek work elsewhere.

Black women without families found few options because of their race, but gender and their more limited wages added burdens to their searches. Most women of all races generally earned lower wages than men and most could not live on their own. As the urban population of women living in cities alone skyrocketed in the decades before the war, social welfare activists pushed for the construction of low-cost boarding houses. Few of these new boarding houses rented rooms to black women. In 1905, young and single Jane Edna Hunter arrived in Cleveland with little money and her first tentative inquiry led her "unknowingly [to] the door of a house of prostitution." After a protracted search, Hunter rented a room that consumed most of her weekly wages; she had to pay extra for laundry and gas privileges. Hunter concluded what other women soon discovered that "a girl alone in a large city must . . . know the dangers and pitfalls awaiting her."[10] She eventually found temporary accommodations when she received a job as a live-in nurse; when her patient got better, Hunter was once again without a respectable place to live.

Neighborhoods

In the early phase of the Great Migration, the rapidly expanding population of African Americans migrants from the Deep South moved into neighborhoods where longtime black residents and a diverse, large, and shifting population of immigrants from Europe and the Caribbean had previously settled. In Harlem the new migrants and immigrants from the Caribbean found rooms and apartments in the brownstones around 134th Street, then moved west and then along Lenox Avenue. In Cleveland, migrants settled along Woodland Avenue and East 55th Street, an area known as the Central Area.

The sounds and smells in these neighborhoods changed as migrants and immigrants settled in close proximity. On the street corners and streetcars of the east side of Cleveland, southern black voices mingled with those of immigrants from Russia, Poland, and Italy. In Harlem, street vendors and peddlers from the South vied with peddlers from the Caribbean for customers. They walked the streets and called out swinging rhymes to attract the attention of black women from North Carolina, Jamaica, and Trinidad shopping for their daily food.

In every neighborhood where the migrants congregated, new businesses provided familiar foods and services. Peddlers, small grocery, and dry goods stores coexisted with street vendors, storefront churches, and amusement arcades. In Harlem, migrants from Mississippi set up street stands, or wheeled carts from which they sold familiar meats and vegetables to other migrants from the Deep South. Immigrants from Haiti established clothing stores; West Indians created banks and grocery stores where they sold pepper sauce, yams, and West Indian pumpkins. By 1920, many of these neighborhoods acquired a distinctly southern milieu. In Cleveland, for example, longtime residents remarked that before 1917 "there were no barbecue joints and storefront churches or jook joints up here until all these Negroes came from down South."[11]

Work

African Americans moved north for a variety of reasons, but the majority of the tens of thousands of men and women arriving between the start of World War I and the Great Depression hoped to find more remunerative work. Newspaper advertisements in Birmingham and Atlanta, as well as those in newspapers like the *Pittsburgh Courier* and the *Chicago Defender* heralded plenty of jobs in steel, railroad, and service work. Letters and visits from family and friends, along with rumors, lent credence to the promises of higher wages and better work conditions touted in the newspapers.

Despite the encouraging advertisements and personal testimonies, the range of northern industries that hired black workers remained narrow and the pay levels they typically received stayed low. In the Midwestern industrial cities, black men were concentrated in particular industries: steel in Pittsburgh and Cleveland; the stockyards in Chicago; and auto in Detroit. These employers tended to hire many black workers or none at all. In Chicago, nearly half of black workers labored in the packinghouses and stock yards. And in these industries they were confined to a few positions, mostly unskilled and onerous. Others found some employment in the city's Pullman shops and yards. Black men did not find work in the higher paying metal fabricating or munitions works, although these industries scrambled for new workers and hired significant numbers of white women, a group employers previously considered undesirable. Black women rarely worked outside industrial laundries or domestic and service work.

By the spring of 1917, the limited availability of white workers for positions in the railroad yards, steel mills, and foundries forced many employers to reassess their restrictive labor policies. Reports from city and state employment offices, as well as from black organizations such as the Urban League, noted that after months of sporadic requests for black workers, employers now competed for them. Well into the summer months, employers of large companies demanded workers of all races and many readily accepted black workers. In Cleveland, thousands of black men found employment in railroad yards, the blast furnaces, rolling mills, foundries, cast and wrought iron pipe factories, and malleable iron works. In Chicago, meatpackers hired thousands of black men for common labor and rough work in meatpacking.

By late 1917, the wartime labor shortages and expansion of production across the North pulled black men into industrial work at a rapid pace. The new employment opportunities were most dramatic in Pittsburgh, Cleveland, Chicago, and Detroit. The 1920 census for Cleveland documented that the percentage of men employed in domestic service dropped by more than half from 29.6 percent to just over 12 percent; male employment in manufacturing increased dramatically from nearly 30 to 63 percent. More than 79 percent of black male workers in Detroit labored in manufacturing jobs, which was a threefold increase from the previous decade. Although left with far fewer options, African American women gained access to some industrial, clerical, and other nondomestic employment. Even those women who continued to labor in households found their wages double over what they had earned in the South. One Cleveland manufacturer voiced the growing consensus heard from other large employers in the Midwest when he declared that "colored labor is the only available class of labor at this time, and the manufacturers have made up their mind to employ them permanently."[12]

Until World War I, northern railroads excluded black men from skilled and semiskilled positions and typically hired them as baggage and freight handlers. The contrast in the hiring patterns between northern and southern-based railroads was sharp, including those companies that crossed regional lines. On some of the southern lines of the Illinois Central, black men predominated as firemen and brakemen, but in the North the railroad brotherhoods effectively kept them confined to yard work. In Chicago and Cleveland, the large immigrant population meant few blacks could challenge or breach these barriers. After 1915, these hiring patterns shifted markedly as thousands of white and immigrant men abandoned jobs in railroad yards for higher wages in war jobs. Unable to hire enough new workers, railroad labor recruiters trawled the southern lines of the Illinois Central Railroad looking for black men to labor in the northern yards. By May 1917, New York Central Railroad reportedly brought 5,000 to 10,000 black men from the South to work in Cleveland; thousands more were hired to work in Chicago. Investigators found that the Baltimore and Ohio Railroad recruited similar numbers of black men in the South for jobs in Philadelphia and Pittsburgh.

Black women found new access to work as common laborers in railroad yards. Before the war, white women cleaned railroad officials' offices, worked in the cafeteria, and cleaned coaches and few black women held such positions. When better-paying industrial jobs lured men of all races and white women away from the yards, railroad managers hired hundreds of black women to labor in the roundhouses, scrap yards, and docks for the New York Central, Baltimore and Ohio, and Pennsylvania Railroads. Some of these women had experience from working for railroads in the South; many others came to the yards out of domestic service. By the summer of 1918, numbers of black women had jobs as truckers, shearers, and yard workers sorting and hauling scrap and freight. Most employers restricted white women from many jobs that required heavy labor, but they nonetheless hired black women, believing that they were stronger than white women. Black women found the work arduous, but steadier than either common labor in factories or daywork in households. Married women with children noted that the early hours allowed them time to care for households and children.

In this period of competition for labor, increasing numbers of black workers received better wages overall. As steel and railroad employers competed for male labor, black men's wages increased to match those of white men in similar positions. A 1918 study revealed little discrimination among black and white men working in the same positions in northern industries, where overall they earned an average pay of about $20 per week. Still, black men remained

A woman subway porter with her cleaning gear
in 1917. (Library of Congress)

concentrated in the occupations with the lowest wages; their job
classification, and not their race, determined the lower wages they
received. Their lower wages in Pittsburgh were associated with their
assignment to the lowest job categories and their lack of seniority
that would allow them to move into better paid work. In Cleveland, the differences in black men's hours and wages from those of
white men in similar positions reflected not only their low-level occupations but also their status as a majority of the work force in
some plants and shops. In Cleveland, some companies hired black
men on piecework, though white workers received weekly wages.
Others confined blacks to particular departments where wage rates
were the lowest even when white workers performed similar tasks
elsewhere. And some hired black men, or women, to work at night
where they typically received lower wages and worked in the least
desirable and most dangerous jobs.

With a greater number of African Americans in workplaces, employers created segregated shops and sections, which they viewed as necessary and desirable. They claimed segregation allowed for better supervision of black workers; and they claimed that white and immigrant workers did not tolerate mixed shops. The shop floor segregation, employers insisted, demonstrated that blacks' jobs differed essentially from those of whites. Typically, blacks' job assignments closely resembled those performed by immigrant workers. By creating differences through job classifications and assignments, employers maintained racial divisions in a work force that had increasingly similar tasks. Such segregation allowed employers to replace whole groups of workers from one race with a group from another when labor was abundant, or when attempts at work place organization occurred.

African American women found most of their new employment opportunities in the industrial laundries, jobs that black women had traditionally performed in white households. The majority of these mechanical laundries in northern cities had typically excluded black women as workers until the war, but after 1917 employers hired them in increasing numbers. By the end of the decade, mechanized laundries became the largest single employer of black women in the North. In Chicago, black women accounted for at least half of the female industrial laundry laborers. Excluded from other industries, black women steadily sought these jobs and rejected the more undesirable conditions of the household laundry service. Yet, with the proliferation of larger mechanized laundries, the wages decreased. Laundry workers' daily tasks were varied and strenuous as they moved from sorting the dirty linen to handling the manglers. They labored in unhygienic conditions and in poorly ventilated rooms; and they stood at steaming machines in hot, low-ceilinged rooms.

Beginning in the first decade of the century, Detroit auto manufacturers sought scores of new workers to fill the ever-expanding jobs. By the war, employers had implemented mass production continuously moving assembly lines throughout the industry. Between 1910 and 1920, industrial engineers had reduced auto manufacturers' need for skilled workers and reduced this population from 75 percent to 10 percent. As machine tenders became the most numerous group of workers, employers preferred eastern and southern European immigrants as new recruits. When immigration waned, employers actively recruited migrants from the South, including black migrants, to fill these positions. By 1920, more than two-thirds of black male workers in Detroit labored in manufacturing jobs. By 1930, the majority of these workers worked in the city's auto industry and nearly 14 percent of all autoworkers were black.

Most auto work, while highly desired, was also distinguished by its high mechanization where monotony, noise, and filth characterized workers' daily experiences. With mechanization, the majority of positions in auto became largely unskilled and repetitive. These jobs had the lowest pay scales, but they also required considerable physical stamina and the highest tolerance to noise than other jobs in the factory. Charles Denby, who found his first job in a foundry in one of the few auto plants that hired blacks, described the job as "very rugged." He faced constant heat from the furnaces. Within minutes of exposure to the heat, grease and grime adhered to his skin. Many of the workers "passed out from the heat" and others suffered severe burns as they poured iron. "The iron would drop on a wet spot and hit the men like a bullet" and then "pierced the skin."[13]

Only a few of the auto manufacturers employed African Americans before 1940, with Ford employing the most in numbers. The Ford Motor Company and in particular the Ford River Rouge plant in Dearborn, hired more black workers and placed them in the most desirable jobs than any of the other auto employers. The company had hired a few blacks prior to 1915, but by the mid-1920s, black workers were 10 percent of the plants' workforce, and this percentage comprised near three-quarters of the city's black autoworkers. Several thousand more black workers found employment there by the end of the decade. While nearly 70 percent of black workers at Ford labored in the foundry at River Rouge, some blacks worked in skilled and supervisory positions. The company's trade school trained some blacks in skilled positions and then placed them in better-paid skilled work. When Packard and Dodge employed some black workers after World War I, manufacturers that supplied parts for the companies hired them, too.

Ford did not replicate these hiring patterns in its plants outside of Michigan, and its hiring patterns within the state arose from the company's antiunion philosophy. Henry Ford was paternalistic in his understanding of workers' characteristics and habits. Like other employers in Detroit, he advocated thrift and punctuality as twinned habits for industrial discipline. He intended his rhetoric of paying workers "five dollars a day" to instill their loyalty to the company and as a preventative against their desire to form unions.

Despite Ford's use of a standardized pay rate, he believed workers labored best in segregated shops. Thus, every job category in the plants was organized around the race and gender of workers.

Across the Midwest, large numbers of black men found work in steel mills and yards, but despite employers' need for skilled and semiskilled workers, few black men found work in the higher paid and skilled work. In the blast furnaces, for example, the majority of blacks remained concentrated in the lowest skilled positions or labored as casual laborers. In the rolling mills, employers acknowledged they all defined rollers' jobs as jobs for white workers, and usually native-born whites. And few employers reportedly inquired whether black workers had the experience for more skilled positions.

Steel work was also dangerous work. In 1917, approximately one of every eight steelworkers in the United States had an injury on the job. Yard laborers and night workers, positions that black men held in disproportionate numbers, had high rates of injuries. Workers regularly encountered objects falling off of overhead cranes, explosions of hot metals, and the overturning of molds or ladles of hot metal. The heat from the blast furnaces left scars and burned workers' clothes. Langston Hughes described both the physical and psychological toll of these work conditions on his stepfather, who worked in a steel mill in Cleveland during the war years, earning "lots of money. But it was hard work, and he never looked the same afterwards." Despite higher wages, the incessant noise, extreme heat, and long hours drove Hughes's stepfather out of the mills for less remunerative and more irregular employment. "He couldn't stand the heat of the furnace and he never looked the same after that."[14]

MIGRANTS' STRUGGLES: RIOTS AND STRIKES

The wartime labor and housing pressures on migrants created tensions in the homes and crowded neighborhoods where their homes frequently abutted equally dense neighborhoods of immigrants and white southern migrants. Each group competed for housing and access to affordable recreation. During the war, numerous riots erupted between blacks, whites, and immigrants. Many of these riots had their origins in the street scuffles taking place between young working-class black, white, and immigrant men. Verbal and physical scuffles erupted daily over control of public space, access to jobs, and renting of kitchenettes and apartments. Along with the everyday experiences of material deprivation, these frequent skirmishes sparked more prolonged street and workplace battle riots. On July 2, 1917, a horrific riot occurred in East St. Louis, Illinois. Steel employers sought to quash union organizing by white aluminum ore workers; they transported black workers from the South and elsewhere. As rumors swirled about the arrival of more migrants, white workers gathered and made plans to march into black neighborhoods. Over the next five days, the rioters killed 200 blacks and burned another 6,000 out of their homes and businesses.

The summer following the war was particularly deadly, with more than 26 riots occurring in 1919 alone. During the wartime struggles over jobs and housing in Chicago's Southside and Black Belt neighborhoods in 1918, blacks' homes were bombed. Over the next months, white street toughs and gangs taunted and attacked young black men, who frequently fought back. These daily street skirmishes continued on the city's crowded beaches along Lake Michigan. In late July1919 a young white man—someone no one could later identify—threw rocks at five black boys as they jumped off of a raft into the lake. One of the rocks struck eight-year old Eugene Williams on the head, who then drowned. His death and the skirmishes on the beach set off immediate reprisals. The riot began on the beach and continued over the next five days in the streets of the Southside stockyard neighborhoods. The Governor of Illinois called in the state militia, but by then, 15 whites and 23 blacks had died; more than 520 were injured and twice this number lost their homes. In all of these battles, black Americans readily defended themselves and their neighborhoods. This assertiveness, especially prominent among young, working-class men, did little to relieve the postwar struggles over scarce jobs and affordable housing.

After World War I, recent and long-time migrants found that industrial employment became scarce and over the next decade blacks struggled to find and keep work. As industries curtailed production after 1919 and the economy slid into recession between 1920 and 1923, many black workers lost jobs in war manufacturing and were forced to find work in the service and transportation sectors. Throughout the decade, most manufacturers hired black workers more sporadically, or not at all. In Pittsburgh, few black men held on to skilled jobs. In most northern cities, black men worked as unskilled laborers in greater proportions than before the war. Many moved between a number of workplaces, and they experienced periodic bouts of unemployment. By the mid-1920s, 72 percent of black male workers in New York City labored in unskilled or service positions. Data gathered by the National Urban League showed similar trends in Chicago and Cleveland.

As war manufacturing ceased, black women also found their labor opportunities greatly constricted, including in domestic work. Throughout the next decade, black women remained confined to domestic work in proportions greater than prewar levels. Even in domestic work they remained at the bottom of the job structure. Their narrower wage opportunities contrasted sharply with white women's shifts into nondomestic employment generally. In the postwar decade, white women found more jobs in retail, secretarial, and light manufacturing, while black women rarely found employment in these occupations.

With the cessation of war production and the increased use of mechanization generally, many northern employers hoped that black migrants would disappear as quickly and easily as they had appeared. At a meeting of the Committee on Unemployment for the Cleveland Chamber of Commerce, a member expressed the common hope that blacks would willingly return to the South. As in the prewar years, many employment ads included "no colored help wanted." Langston Hughes found plenty of advertisements for help in the early 1920s, but "unless a job was definitely marked COLORED, there was no use applying." He left Cleveland and found it very hard to get work in New York City; instead, he found work on a small farm on Staten Island. Along with immigrants from southern Europe, Hughes picked and prepared vegetables for the New York City markets. The next fall, he delivered flowers, but found the hours too long and his employer too harsh. Unable to find another job, he went to work on a ship.[15]

Blacks' occupational status became increasingly unstable over the course of the decade. Between 1910 and 1920, black men had made gains in manufacturing employment and though they maintained a presence in these occupations in the decade after the war, more than 90 percent of these workers labored in industries that were vulnerable to the vicissitudes of the economy. These workers experienced seasonal fluctuations in steel, automobile, and related industries characterized by frequent layoffs and long bouts of unemployment and underemployment. They competed with new migrants and other groups of workers for an increasingly limited number of jobs. And as primarily unskilled workers, blacks experienced longer bouts of unemployment and underemployment than other groups of workers. Along with the contraction of jobs, wages in many industries plummeted. In steel, wages fell from the wartime high of $.71 per hour in 1920 to $.50 per hour in 1922. Wages rose to $.63 per hour in the mid-1920s, but they never again approached the wartime highs. Stagnation in wages and the decline in the rates of reemployment demonstrated black workers' diminished opportunities in industrial experiences generally.

In some cities, including Pittsburgh and Detroit, black men typically left to look for work elsewhere, while in other cities increasing numbers moved between unskilled jobs in steel mills to casual labor in transportation and services. During the war, Daniel Jerome and Vincent Easter, two migrants from Alabama, quickly found work as laborers in Cleveland's steel mills, but by the early 1920s the steady work evaporated. For the rest of the decade, both men cobbled together a variety of jobs as common laborers. They worked as garbage collectors but found the work sifting and hoisting waste arduous and Easter thought that the stinking garbage made him constantly nauseous. By mid-decade, both joined gangs of black men who cut and lifted 50-pound blocks of ice from Lake Erie, which were sold for home iceboxes. Icy winds and sudden thaws during the late winter made the work intermittent and dangerous.

The employment data for black women in these years reveals few lasting gains in occupational mobility made as a result of the war. Black women remained confined to domestic service, and in many cities, their representation in household service returned to pre-war levels. The combined impact of fluctuations in black men and women's employment meant that black migrant households' everyday economic stability faltered. William Davenport, a migrant from Alabama, labored in a Cleveland foundry during the war, but by the early 1920s he found only intermittent work; by mid-decade, he was unemployed for months at a time. He eventually found work sorting and packing laundry, but his low pay forced his wife, Ocelie Johnson Davenport, to find daywork whenever possible.

A WHOLE NEW WORLD: MAKING NEW COMMUNITIES

Migrants hoped to relieve the vicissitudes of work by shaping their daily lives at home and in their communities. Bertha Cowan watched the high wages of the wartime period evaporate in the 1920s, but the expanding presence of family and friends anchored her to the city despite the vagaries of the postwar economy. "This is when the South all came up here and it turned into a whole new world."[16] For Cowan and other southern migrants, making "a whole new world" mattered as much as finding and keeping jobs with higher wages. As they looked for more remunerative labor and better homes, migrants worked to establish familiar institutions and organizations. While some migrants intended to reestablish the familiar features of a black community with deep roots in the South, others considered the creation of new communities, churches, and organizations as an opportunity to make themselves "new Negroes."

After finding homes, many migrants considered finding a "church home" to be the next important step in creating new communities. Many first joined the established and predominantly mainline churches in their neighborhoods. These churches scrambled to accommodate the much larger membership. Some congregations expanded older structures; other congregations purchased or built new ones. Some of the memberships in the older denominations in Harlem, Cleveland, and Chicago had grown large enough to buy larger churches from white congregations moving to the suburbs. Adam Clayton Powell Sr. moved Abyssinian Baptist Church from Manhattan to Harlem in 1908. The influx of migrants made the church the largest and wealthiest of African American Baptist churches in the United States. St. Philip's Episcopal Church had a similar history, becoming the wealthiest and largest black church in the denomination. By 1935, it owned most of the property on 135th St. in Harlem.

At the height of migration, these larger black churches provided resources to meet not only members' spiritual expectations but their many social and economic needs as well. Most of the large churches held a variety of evening and weekend classes to provide migrants with instructions on how to live in the city. They offered advice about marriage, childcare, and finances. Occasionally, churches offered health care for pregnant and nursing women; some provided inoculations for children and visits with dentists. Abyssinian Baptist Church in Harlem established a home for the elderly and a social center. Migrants with little money for such services eagerly stood in long lines to get them. Anxious about the mounting criticism of the new migrants and efforts to segregate blacks generally, some established churches sponsored lectures that emphasized thrift, cleanliness, and public decorum. Fearful that the riots signaled a protracted backlash against black participation in urban social life, ministers encouraged social welfare agencies to help migrants adapt to what many considered more modern and re-spectable behavior.

For many migrants, activities in these mainline churches offered an immediate introduction to their new communities. Many women sent children off to Sunday schools and received a much needed reprieve from childcare. On any Sunday afternoon throughout the decade, the large churches held concert and lecture series. Long established churches in Harlem, Cleveland, and Chicago offered weekly literary forums and debates. Well-known speakers, including W. E. B. Du Bois, George C. Schuyler, Walter White, Mary McLeod Bethune, and Carter G. Woodson delivered lectures in Chicago, Cleveland, Philadelphia, and Harlem. These social activities appealed to some of the new migrants and retained longtime members. Such programs proved so popular that regardless of size or resources, churches established speaker series, showed films, and organized concerts.

Many migrants attended these activities because custom, not law, barred or restricted their regular access to urban commercial entertainment. Blacks' clubs and organizations had limited access to spaces owned or frequented by whites; the few amusement parks and dance halls that did admit blacks did so in a segregated manner. Though urban social welfare agencies expanded their activities to accommodate the growing black population, these organizations soon replicated the patterns of segregation as they created separate times and clubs for each race. Faced with such restrictions in the public realm, blacks turned to their own churches, which increasingly provided space for secular activities, ranging from gatherings for music and drama clubs, to meeting places for fraternal organizations and the ladies auxiliaries, and political clubs. In the North, then, black churches continued their historic and familiar roles as spiritual, social, and political spaces to support the variety of black organizational life.

Even as the older churches expanded their activities to accommodate the interests of new members, many migrants found it difficult to continue and assert the religious activities and spiritual lives they had crafted in the South. As newcomers, many migrants found themselves marginal to the well-established social networks and worship habits of the established churches. Longtime congregants typically held the most prominent positions, and new migrants found it especially difficult to become leaders of deacons,' trustees,' and mothers' boards, the most prominent organizations. Migrants from small towns and churches felt relegated to the periphery of church activity. Many had practiced more demonstrative and expressive worship styles. Migrants learned quickly that the established congregations downplayed the expressive worship more prevalent in the rural and smaller urban churches in the South. Some congregations experienced tensions over these roles and differences in worship styles and migrants tended to leave and create their own churches.

These new urban dwellers intended to make these community institutions their own and they wanted to participate fully in their churches. When migrants did not feel comfortable in the congregations they joined, they left and met in homes. Soon, they rented storefronts, or older, smaller churches. They soon built or purchased their own churches. Bertha Cowan articulated what many other migrants believed when they arrived in the North: finding a church home where she would be comfortable was as important as finding work. Indeed, as music historian Viv Broughton has reminded us, migrants "didn't just build churches, they built homes where they and their God could dwell together."[17]

Many new migrants first joined mainline churches, but then they drifted toward new nondenominational congregations. This membership grew most in the Pentecostal, Holiness, Apostolic (originally Ethiopian), and Sanctified churches. By the late 1920s these churches predominated in North, Midwest, and West Coast cities. Located in former stores, taverns, and theaters, these churches settled in the heart of migrant populations. Between 1920 and 1930, the number of black churches in Cleveland nearly tripled from 54 to 132. Independent storefronts had been only a fraction of the churches, but by 1930, 56 percent of the churches were storefronts organized by recent migrants. Observers of Chicago's churches noted that three-quarters of the black churches were small churches that formed as migrants arrived. While membership in Chicago's older black churches grew steadily and the number of denominational churches grew slightly, the number of nondenominational churches more than doubled from 73 in 1928 to 158 a decade later. Overall, more than one-third of blacks in Chicago belonged to one of these churches while the proportion of congregants in traditional churches declined from 64.4 percent to 59.8 percent. In Harlem new storefront churches appeared and flourished in the wake of migrants' arrivals, rather than through the conversion of longtime residents. By 1930, storefronts predominated, with 42 of the 75 churches in the Central Area of Harlem. Working-class migrants formed the majority of these new congregations. Some of these new churches formed as a result of disputes with older churches; others emerged out of the numerous revivals held by itinerant ministers from the South.

Migrants' affiliation with a particular church continued associations developed in the South where, especially in rural areas, churches provided spiritual sustenance, social contact, and most of the entertainment. For young women in particular, churches provided one of the few opportunities where they could meet young men while under the watchful gaze of parents. Churches helped migrants adjust to the city, and they provided contact with other migrants. Going to church, which occurred most frequently on Sundays, was an important event in migrant communities. In Harlem, congregants went to church "in the latest and newest creations of the tailor's and dressmaker's art." St. Clair Drake and Horace Cayton observed that "Sunday morning in Bronzeville is a colorful occasion." The congregants arrived by foot, cab, streetcars, buses, or in freshly polished automobiles. The church mothers wore "little gray caps perched on their heads and secured by chin straps." Children wore "their stylish Sunday best." By 11 A.M. the churches were filled.[18]

For many migrants, the proliferation of new churches represented their struggles to recalibrate their worship practices forged in the South with northern ideals and aspirations. This struggle was most evident in the debates about worship styles. Some migrants, who had joined newer churches that practiced more expressive worship styles more common in the South, occasionally left for older churches as they sought to identify as northerners. This pattern was most evident among the children of migrants who were either too young to remember the South or had been born in the North. And many older churches incorporated these worship styles. More typically, many migrants joined churches that retained southern-style ecstatic worship. Overall, the influx of migrants into mainline churches and new churches meant that most adopted diverse styles of worship. While many of the new denominations made ecstatic worship integral to their preaching and worship practices, even congregations in mainline churches boasted rousing sermons and lively music. Sanctified and Holiness churches used dance and song as part of their worship. Langston Hughes visited a Holiness church in Chicago and he "was entranced by their stepped-up rhythms, tambourines, hand-clapping, and uninhibited dynamics. The music of these less formal Negro churches early took hold of me, moved me, and thrilled me."[19]

In northern cities, black women found more opportunities to serve as ministers and church leaders in the smaller churches and storefronts. Within the Holiness and Pentecostal churches, women formed the majority of the membership and often controlled the finances. But just as the African Methodist Episcopal (AME) and Baptist churches prohibited women from ministering, these new denominations limited women's roles as ministers to specific tasks, such as leading the women's auxiliaries. Nonetheless, some women rejected these boundaries and formed their own independent churches. In Cleveland, Addie M. Battle, also known as Madam A.M. Johnson, organized the Mt. Zion Holy Trinity Spiritual Church after a vision instructed her to leave her church and become a "prophet for the Lord." In Chicago, migrants Lucy Smith and Mary Evans each established large and influential churches that reshaped the black religious practices in the city. Smith established the All Nations Pentecostal Church in the 1920s and later broadcasted her services on the radio. Unable to be ordained as a minister in the AME church, Evans left in the 1930s and pastored the Cosmopolitan Community Church. As the congregation's minister, she launched building projects and participated in the struggles for civil rights. Other migrant women created small storefront churches in the interwar years and they provided particular guidance for women concerned about their roles as mothers and wives, offering what was commonly called *motherwit*, a mixture of secular and spiritual wisdom. Battle also demonstrated that ecstatic worship was more than emotional outbursts and otherworldly exhortations. Services like hers enabled women and men to testify openly and collectively about their daily experiences as workers, migrants, and spiritual people.

Despite the formal choirs and music practices, the dramatic influx of migrants into congregations altered the music in old and new churches. Before migrants' arrival in significant numbers, worshippers in the older churches sang classical Protestant hymns and anthems. Many mainline congregations organized jubilee choirs that sang European-influenced spirituals. Churches with more resources created choirs, hired music directors, and used standard hymnals. These formal institutions and practices meant congregations downplayed improvisation and congregational participation common in smaller churches. As migrant congregants became more prominent, churches tolerated more ecstatic sacred music. In the smaller, nondenominational churches, the new gospel music flourished. While some churches allowed only a cappella performances,

A service at a Pentecostal church in Chicago, Illinois.
(Library of Congress)

others embraced tambourines, handclaps, and ecstatic singing and
vocalizations. Migrants from the Deep South states and Tidewater
Virginia created this new music before they migrated and they continued to refine it in northern churches. After Thomas Dorsey migrated from a secular blues performer in Georgia to Pilgrim Baptist
Church in Chicago, he translated southern blues into blues gospel.
This new music had roots in shape-note singing, Watts' hymns, folk
music, minstrel quartets, and college jubilee singing. Gospel quartet music arrived with migrants from Virginia and the Deep South
states.

ORGANIZATIONS: CLUBS

Out of their personal desires and as responses to their exclusion
from whites' clubs, longtime residents and the new migrants created their own clubs and organizations. African Americans' partic-

ipation in fraternal and mutual benefit associations, much in evidence before 1915, continued in the postwar decade. Men continued, or joined, the Masons, Odd Fellows, Knights of Pythias, and Knights of Tabor, which instilled middle-class ideals of sobriety, thrift, and respectability. Male member's occupations varied from professionals and small-business owners to Pullman porters, but these jobs conveyed respectability and steadiness of character. Most held these jobs for some years; most owned their own homes; and only a few had wives with full-time wage work. The lodges generally considered unskilled migrants from the Deep South as less desirable members. Many of the fraternal organizations included ladies auxiliaries, where women held distinct and supportive roles. Members displayed the quasi-military and quasi-religious characteristics of these organizations in the numerous balls and parades they sponsored.

Along with membership in fraternal societies, new migrants joined or created a variety of other secular clubs. Black newspapers, especially the *Chicago Defender* and the *Cleveland Gazette*, documented the numerous clubs, fraternities, sororities, garden clubs, reading clubs, bridge clubs, and singing groups. Many of these clubs had rigorous requirements for induction, while others were more casual and open. Each city boasted a list of clubs named after states and cities in the South. Each of these clubs and organizations filled critical needs for leisure and conviviality. Others provided financial support, or guidance for employment. By the mid-1920s, high school clubs reflected the impulse for support and congregation.

Single and young migrants joined the clubs and churches, but they also turned to the new commercial leisure. The young congregated in saloons or dance halls. Jane Edna Hunter, a social worker in Cleveland, viewed the new commercial entertainment with great alarm. She described these dance halls as little more than brothels. "Here to the tune of St. Louis voodoo blues, half-naked Negro girls dance shameless dances with men in Spanish costumes, while daughters from highly respectable families, attended by escorts, clap their dainty hands and shout their approval. The whole atmosphere is one of unrestrained animality, the jungle faintly veneered with civilized trappings." Langston Hughes's description of this leisure in Chicago was far more generous: "South Street was in its glory then, a teeming Negro street with crowded theaters, restaurants, and cabarets. And excitement from noon to noon. Midnight was like day. The street was full of workers and gamblers, prostitutes and pimps, church folks and sinners."[20]

Most African Americans had limited time and resources for leisure activities outside churches, and since many clubs excluded African Americans, the majority attended inexpensive entertainment at home parties and in private clubs. Richard Wright attended these house-rent parties in Chicago, "parties given by working-class families to raise money to pay the landlord, the admission to which was a quarter or a half dollar."[21] Harlem rent parties acquired a ubiquitous flair as they began after midnight and lasted until dawn. Guests paid their quarters and were treated to southern food and the latest music. At these gatherings, Pullman porters, well-dressed society ladies, and working people danced and laughed and hoped to make the rent.

Others spent their few extra dollars on the movies, which became one of the most popular, yet controversial forms of leisure in migrant communities. First the nickelodeons, and then the shorts and feature films, typically portrayed blacks in racially stereotyped and derogatory ways. Critics derided blacks for paying to see these derogatory images. In most films, black characters were simply absent, an omission that drew considerable additional critiques from black critics. In response, a small black film industry emerged, but this early black film culture took place in settings and locations many critics considered vice ridden and dangerous. Movie going also became increasingly segregated, a process that drew much debate. Although absent from or derided on the screen, and increasingly relegated to segregated spaces in theaters, by World War I, black migrants formed a conspicuous portion of cinema's new urban audiences. They also became a critical audience, who confronted their exclusions on the screen and in the theater.

From the inception of the movie theater, black Americans grappled with the collision between commercial culture and the practices of Jim Crow. In the South, blacks were relegated to the balconies, or to separate showings; in the North, blacks increasingly attended theaters in black neighborhoods. By the end of the new century's first decade, blacks owned some of the theaters and other blacks made the films. The Pekin Theater, the first black-owned theater, opened in Chicago in 1906. Located on State Street, the Pekin showed films and staged vaudeville shows. Saloons were nearby, which invited controversy. Still, the theater thrived because it showed the newest films and most affordable entertainment. The theater advertised itself as black owned, high class, and moral. It also appealed to prevailing ideas of race pride by emphasizing the theater as a modern space filled with the latest, and most comfortable (and plush), amenities. The Pekin spawned similar arrangements in other cities with growing black populations (and many of these new theaters took Pekin as the name).

By the Great Migration, white-owned and increasingly national companies owned large theaters in black neighborhoods, but they continued to emphasize morality and accessibility to working people. These theaters attracted large audiences as they typically included live theater along with the showing of feature films, serials, and comedies. They also hired musicians to perform the new jazz and blues. Theaters featured adult films with sensational topics, including films about "murder, suicide, birth control, unwed pregnancy, and sexual affairs."[22] Some theaters featured "race films," such as William Foster's *The Railroad Porter* (1913), and Oscar Micheaux's *The Homesteader* (1919). Micheaux advertised his films as "race spectacles" where the horror of lynching and southern violence kept the audience spellbound and writhing in indignation. Micheaux's films were part of a small black film industry that attempted to depict blacks' perspectives, concerns, and experiences, and to impart blacks' complex constructions of the modern world. Theater owners and moviemakers made appeals to new audiences who saw these commercial movies and shows as sensational and modern.

Along with going to the movies, migrants found affordable leisure in the new Negro Baseball Leagues. Teams like the American Giants played games in nearly every major city. They traveled in a private railroad car and spent winters playing in Florida or California. Few teams in these years lasted beyond a season and the segregated teams meant few teams found nearby opponents of all-black teams. Instead, most teams barnstormed around the United States, Canada, and the Caribbean. Some teams overcame the dearth of opponents by playing amateur, semiprofessional, and professional teams; others compensated by playing mixed-race teams, including teams that boasted players from the white league teams. These frequent games allowed fans to become acquainted with teams and individual players. In these games showmanship and skill, not longstanding rivalries, lured audiences. Teams offered fans daring base running and base stealing, feats that waned in the white leagues. Years later, these skills were described as "clowning," but contemporary descriptions emphasized the skill and daring of players during these games. Despite the thrills such games displayed, few teams made significant profits, or had the means to pay players steady salaries. While some owners sold tickets at the gates of stadiums in large cities, most did not and teams passed buckets, or "passed the hat," to collect donations to cover their expenses.

Playing conditions varied. When teams barnstormed—games played outside regular league play—they played wherever they found a field. Black teams in cities with major white teams, such as Chicago and New York City, frequently played home games on the fields, or in stadiums owned by the major leagues. The Pittsburgh Homestead Grays played their games at either Greenlee Field or at Forbes Field, where the Pirates played. In contrast, black teams in Philadelphia played on a field with a wooden grandstand that held 5,000 fans. In Kansas City, Missouri, crowds of 8,000 to 10,000 watched the Monarchs in a stadium with a modern lighting system. In Chicago, the American Giants owned their grandstand, but not the park. Teams in St. Louis and Detroit had leases with white teams. The Cincinnati Cuban Stars also had a lease with fairly reasonable terms that allowed them access to gate receipts, an arrangement few teams had managed. Most teams played on fields only when white teams were out of town, thus making for fewer home games and more frequent barnstorming on fields under less desirable conditions. Such arrangements meant these teams had erratic schedules and many found it difficult to build home audiences, stable finances, and equitable schedules across the leagues. The early years of the Depression decimated the league, but new teams emerged later in the decade, marking the emergence of fairly stable teams, including the Pittsburgh Homestead Grays, who briefly hired Satchel Paige and Cool Papa Bell.

Black businesses that provided services, from barbering to shoe repair, were quite visible in large cities like New Orleans, Atlanta, and Birmingham. Smaller cities in the South, too, had black commercial districts that rivaled those in the North. While many of the larger cities had a few black-owned banks and insurance companies, the smaller service-oriented businesses were more numerous. These small service business required less capital and limited in-

Panorama of the first Negro League World Series, Kansas City, Missouri, 1924. (Library of Congress)

vestment, but segregation required African Americans to provide these services for themselves, thus barbershops, beauty shops, grocery stores, bars, and cafes were essential to the daily life of their neighborhoods. Still, some of these businesses catered to whites, too. Historian Julia Kirk Blackwelder observes that though African Americans were just "ten percent of the population in 1935, they operated one-third of the shoe repair shops in the country and one-fifth of the dry cleaning establishments."[23] Whites in many of these cities also used these services, especially black barbershops and shoe repair shops. Of the 369 barbershops in North Carolina in 1916, African Americans owned half.

These sorts of businesses migrated with African Americans. Harlem, Chicago, and Cleveland soon had black commercial areas where small shops, photography studios, cafes, bars, and funeral parlors appeared. Allan Cole migrated from West Virginia and established a photography studio in Cleveland. Some thrived, but most stayed solvent only because family members worked for little or no wages. While black barbershops were numerous, black women began to establish beauty salons that met the needs of women. The advertising and beauty culture of the 20th century typically excluded black women and other women of color, but the entrepreneurial tradition provided alternatives. Just as black midwives were trained by other women and worked in the homes of their clients, beauticians "learned about braiding, wrapping, straightening, and conditioning hair" from the "women in their communities."[24] This homework soon changed as Annie Turnbo Malone's Poro Company, Sara Breedlove Walker's Madam Walker, and Sara Spencer Washington's Apex beauty company catered to the hair and skin needs of black women. These companies trained thousands of women in techniques to care for black women's hair and skin. Many of these saleswomen opened beauty salons in their homes or neighborhoods. On the 1920 census, for example, more than 800 women in Harlem identified themselves as beauticians.

All of these women were exceptional, but they were part of communities of women who refused to accept the exclusion from the beauty industry, which was the fastest growing industry in the United States. Born in the South, Sara Walker first worked for Annie Malone, but she moved to Indianapolis in 1910 where she developed and marketed Madam C.J. Walker's Wonderful Hair Grower. She perfected the use of agents, sold products through mail order catalogs, and developed advertising techniques for the black press. By World War I, Walker had an estate valued at more than one million dollars. Her agents did more than selling hair products and styling women's hair: they also advocated that being well groomed ensured a woman's spiritual beauty and instilled her with race pride. Their business model and philosophy reached beyond black communities. Avon Company, for example, adopted the use of agents to demonstrate and sell cosmetics.

ENTER THE "NEW NEGRO"

As they grappled with the spread of segregation into northern cities, African Americans used new scientific, philosophical, and sociological studies to challenge and upend popular ideas that portrayed blacks as inherently and racially inferior. These ideas, which were disseminated in scientific theories, popular culture, and political discussions justified racial discrimination and segregation. In the early 20th century, few blacks had access to positions in universities; blacks did not hold positions in Congress; and the dominant entertainment industries did not hire blacks to produce popular culture for the mass entertainment industries of film, amusement parks, and music. But since the early 19th century, African Americans had created music, literature, and art for their own entertainment and as a challenge to racialism in the dominant culture. During the antebellum period, former slaves wrote narratives that denounced slavery and presented new black literary traditions. In the late 19th century, a generation of black writers, which included Frances Ellen Watkins Harper, Charles Chestnut, and T. Thomas Fortune, wrote popular literature that attracted an international audience.

These artistic endeavors flourished in the context of migration. Popular and high art, literature, and music provided particularly potent forums to create complex and more dignified representations of blacks' experiences, ideas, and aspirations. This diverse self-representation contradicted the popular and scientific racialism. Most of this new interest in black life and thought turned to the cultural practices of black migrants from the South and immigrants from the Caribbean. Howard University scholar Alain Locke defined this new movement as a "Negro Renaissance" that represented a "new mentality," a "new psychology," and a "new spirit." These men and women, he stressed, represented the New Negro. After a half decade of anti-black violence, the retrenchment in civil rights, and the rise of barriers in their access to social and economic opportunity, black intellectuals, writers, and artists presented the

New Negro as "a new vision of opportunity" to use art and literature to challenge discrimination and "mold a new American attitude."[25]

Black cultural production in the two decades after World War I not only flourished, but musicians, writers, and artists introduced new genres that fundamentally transformed American cultural life. New genres of music, which included jazz, blues, and gospel, had their genesis in southern music traditions, but as performers moved north, they transformed the music as they found new audiences among migrants. Black American and Caribbean immigrant writers, artists, and musicians introduced new formal practices that merged southern folk and African aesthetic traditions with European Modernism. Harlem attracted many black writers, including James Weldon Johnson, Langston Hughes, Jessie Fauset, Nella Larsen, and Claude McKay, an immigrant from Jamaica who wrote one of the first volumes of poetry published in the Renaissance. Chicago, too, became a Mecca for writers, artists, and musicians.

Other frameworks for understanding and organizing black cultural and political aspirations included radical associations that linked black southerners, immigrants, migrants, and longtime urban

Alain Locke, editor of the *New Negro,*
1926. (National Archives)

dwellers. In Harlem, Hubert Harrison created the Liberty League in 1917 and Cyril Briggs, a writer for the New York *Amsterdam News* and an immigrant from Nevis, organized the African Blood Brotherhood (ABB) for African Liberation and Redemption, which was an anticapitalist, anticolonial, and antilynching organization. Modeled on black fraternal organizations, the ABB attracted a diverse membership of migrants and immigrants in Harlem and other cities in the North and Upper South, but it nurtured a group consciousness that favored socialism (and eventually communism) and black nationalism through its journal, *The Crusader.* Other African American advocated radical trade unionism; and others, including Hubert Harrison and A. Philip Randolph, joined the Socialist Party. Randolph also advocated a separate black socialist organization and in 1920 he formed Friends of Negro Freedom, which advocated black-owned businesses and black trade unionism.

An important expression of such consciousness appeared in the rise of Garveyism. Marcus Garvey, who was born in Jamaica, migrated to London in 1914, and then immigrated to Harlem in 1916. Before he left for England, he founded the Jamaica Improvement Association. As he traveled, he met Africans, African Americans, and Caribbean immigrants mobilized against colonialism and the new racial hierarchies in the Western Hemisphere and his ideas about what his organization could be evolved from a hemispheric to a global organization. An admirer of Booker T. Washington's philosophy of self-improvement, Garvey also admired W.E.B. Du Bois's public protests and Pan-Africanism.

By the time he sailed for New York, Garvey's vision had become the Universal Negro Improvement Association (UNIA). Everywhere he went, Garvey spoke about this new organization, and he immediately attracted interest from activists in London, New York, and the Caribbean. U.S. divisions rapidly appeared in Boston, Philadelphia, Cleveland, Pittsburgh, and Chicago. By the mid-1920s, large divisions appeared in Detroit and Los Angeles. While more than three-quarters of its following came from migrants, African immigrants, and Caribbean immigrants in northern cities, divisions appeared throughout the South, particularly in New Orleans, Miami, and Norfolk, Virginia. By 1919 the UNIA had more than 30 branches throughout the United States, the Caribbean, Latin America, and Africa. By the middle of the following decade, Garvey claimed that more than one million people had joined his organization. Wherever black migrants and immigrants lived, UNIA divisions appeared.

A member of the UNIA in Harlem. (Library of Congress)

Even as black migrants and immigrants considered the North as opportunity, Garvey considered these cities as inhospitable to the aspirations of dignity and freedom for people of African descent. As an antidote, he espoused a black nationalism that privileged black economic and political independence and cultural separatism. He argued that Africa was the ancestral home and spiritual base for all people of African descent. While in London, his vision had been informed by the nationalist and anticolonial movements unloosed by World War I, including Irish nationalism, Zionism, and the Russian Revolution. Influenced by African and Asian immigrants organizing independence movements against British and other European colonialism, he urged blacks to take back Africa from European domination and build a free and United Black Africa. In the United States he advocated a "Back-to-Africa" movement and sought to unite people of African descent around the world to return to Africa and establish a government of their own. Garvey considered the UNIA an African government in exile.

Garvey linked blacks' control of their own finances and businesses to his goal of creating a black nation. To facilitate this effort, he bought several ships and organized a shipping company called the Black Star Line and invested members' monies in factories and other businesses, all part of his program to conduct international trade between black Africans and the rest of the world. Owning a shipping line would allow blacks to transport raw and finished goods between black nations, thus establishing a black global economy owned and managed for themselves. The UNIA wrote a constitution with a "declaration of rights." It established a newspaper, *The Negro World,* which was published in French and Spanish as well as English and reached a diverse audience around the world.

As Garvey stoked entrepreneurial, institutional, and anticolonial sensibilities of the UNIA, he also created a visible and formal organizational life that included regular meetings, parades, forums, and military displays. These rituals drew on institutional practices found elsewhere in black southern and black immigrant life, particularly in the fraternal, political, and labor organizations. The local UNIA divisions were self-run and provided new migrants and immigrants opportunities for self-governance and freedom. As Garvey and the other leaders of the UNIA visited, they appeared in elaborate military uniforms, emphasizing the desire for independence. In his speeches and writings, Garvey urged members to be "mighty black men and women." At a time when government policies and popular culture denigrated black people and described them as little better than animals, Garvey's call for race pride, black self-organization, and an end to black subservience resonated among people seeking dignity and self-determination.

By the end of the decade, the UNIA emerged as the largest mass movement of people of African descent. Its size and goals elicited the derision of mainstream black political and religious leaders, particularly the ire of W. E. B. Du Bois, and the scrutiny of the new FBI. Unable to arrest him on charges of sedition, the U.S. government convicted Garvey on mail fraud and deported him. Working-class migrants and immigrants continued the UNIA despite Garvey's departure. From its inception, the UNIA quickly pulled in African Americans frustrated by the limited activism of other protest organizations and their exclusion from labor organizations. Those men and women who joined—and remained members long after Garvey's deportation in 1925 and death in 1940—appreciated the structured organization and opportunity for leadership roles. Blacks in divisions in the United States, Latin America, and Africa learned from its militant resistance to racial hierarchies, and these efforts became the springboard for participation in other militant organizations. In Montgomery, Alabama, E. D. Nixon turned from the UNIA and helped organize the Montgomery Improvement Association, which launched the 1955–1956 Montgomery Bus Boycott after Rosa Parks's refusal to obey the bus segregation laws.

THE BLACK MODERN METROPOLIS
ON THE EVE OF THE DEPRESSION

Richard Wright described this post-World War I period of black cultural activism as dynamic, but his bouts of unemployment unnerved him. By late 1929 he found no work whatsoever. "Stocks Crash" the headlines blared. Now a young adult, Wright "had grown up in complete ignorance of what created jobs." He noticed others agitating for change. Some protested with the growing ranks of the unemployed, while others pushed for unions, or agitated with the Communists. Wright admired these activists, but he maintained an "emotional distance" and refused "to follow them." Without work and food, he became emaciated. He felt "bleak" as he felt he "had not done what [he] had come to the city to do."[26]

Other migrants shared Wright's apprehensions and desire for change. Throughout the 1920s, many had been relegated to low-wage jobs, substandard housing, and increased social and physical segregation, and the economic collapse at the decade's end exacerbated their already precarious lives. As the Depression continued and its impact reached across all social classes, African Americans found the usual aid from churches and community organizations quickly depleted. Migrants learned that adjusting to the urban North necessitated new personal and community strategies, such as new churches, art, and the UNIA. Surviving the Great Depression demanded new approaches to address their immediate needs of protracted joblessness and poverty. As the economic collapse of late 1929 continued into the next decade, the local and state responses to unemployed black workers and their impoverished families frequently excluded them or offered them only limited relief. As African Americans launched bolder efforts to address their daily needs in the urban North, they also created new efforts to advance their long pursuit of full citizenship.

NOTES

1. Aaron Siskind, *Harlem Photographs 1932–1940* (Washington, D.C.: Smithsonian, 1992), 15.

2. Emmet J. Scott, "More Letters of Negro Migrants of 1916–1918," *The Journal of Negro History* 4 (October 1919): 457–58.

3. Quoted in William Howland Kenney, *Chicago Jazz: A Cultural History, 1904–1930* (New York: Oxford University Press, 1993), 13.

4. Arnold Rampersad, *The Life of Langston Hughes,* Vol. I (New York: Oxford University Press, 1986), 25.

5. Scott, "More Letters of Negro Migrants of 1916–1918," 460.

6. Richard Wright, *Black Boy* (New York: Harper and Brothers, 1945; reprint, New York: Harper Perennial, 2006), 261.

7. Charles Denby, *Indignant Heart: A Black Worker's Journal* (Detroit, MI: Wayne State University Press, 1989), 28; Wright, 263.

8. Quoted in Kimberley L. Phillips, *AlabamaNorth: African-American Migrants, Community, and Working Class Activism in Cleveland, 1915–1945* (Urbana: University of Illinois Press, 1999), 130.

9. E. Franklin Frazier, "Negro Harlem: An Ecological Study," *American Journal of Sociology* 43 (July, 1937): 73; Langston Hughes, *The Big Sea: An Autobiography by Langston Hughes* (New York: Alfred A. Knopf, 1940), 27.

10. Jane Edna Hunter, *A Nickel and a Prayer* (Cleveland, OH: Elli Kani, 1940), first quote 70; second quote 77.

11. Quoted in Katrina Hazzard-Gordon, *Jookin': The Rise of Social Dance Formation in African-American Culture* (Philadelphia, PA: Temple University Press, 1990), 79.

12. Quoted in Raymond Boryczka and Lorin Lee Cary, *No Strength Without Union: An Illustrated History of Ohio Workers, 1803–1989* (Columbus: Ohio Historical Society, 1982), 141–42.

13. Denby, *Indignant Heart,* 30–31.

14. Hughes, *The Big Sea,* 26–27.

15. Ibid., 87–92.

16. Quoted in Phillips, *AlabamaNorth,* 130.

17. Viv Broughton, *Black Gospel: An Illustrated History of the Gospel Sound* (Poole, England: Blanford Press, 1985), 45.

18. Shane White and Graham White, *Stylin': African American Expressive Culture from its Beginnings to the Zoot Suit* (Ithaca, NY: Cornell University Press, 1998), 234; St. Clair Drake and Horace Cayton, *Black Metropolis* (Chicago, IL: University of Chicago Press, 1945, reprint, 1993), 416.

19. Quoted in Lawrence W. Levine, *Black Culture and Black Consciousness: Afro-American Folk Thought from Slavery to Freedom* (New York: Oxford University Press, 1977), 180.

20. Hunter, *A Nickel and a Prayer,* 132–33; Hughes, *The Big Sea,* 33.

21. Wright, *Black Boy,* 278.

22. Jacqueline Najuma Stewart, *Migrating to the Movies: Cinema and Black Urban Modernity* (Berkeley: University of California Press, 2005), 161.

23. Julia Kirk Blackwelder, *Styling Jim Crow: African American Beauty Training during Segregation* (College Station: Texas A&M University Press, 2003), 10.

24. Ibid., 16.

25. Alain Locke, ed., *The New Negro* (New York: Atheneum, 1980), 10–11.

26. Wright, *Black Boy,* 286–99.

4

Migrants and Migration during the Great Depression and World War II

12 MILLION BLACK VOICES

A decade into the Great Depression, writer Richard Wright described the nearly 1.6 million black migrants living outside the South as "children of the black sharecroppers, the first-born of the tenements." While other observers of recent migrants might have disputed Wright's efforts to describe them as beleaguered sharecroppers from the South, many also agreed with his observation that black America had been forever altered by "cataclysmic social changes"[1] brought about by the mass movements during the first four decades of the 20th century. At the same time, hundreds of thousands of blacks moved from the Caribbean to eastern cities. This large migration described then and since as the Great Migration occurred within the context of a world war and a global economic depression. Millions of black southerners and immigrants from the Caribbean brought new aspirations for freedom into northern cities where many found that prosperity often eluded them. From Seattle to New York City, migrants discovered how racial barriers confined them to low-wage jobs, substandard housing, and increased social and physical segregation.

The collapse of the economy in 1929 had a deleterious impact on working- and middle-class people, but migrants, especially,

Richard Wright, author of *12 Million Black Voices*. (Library of Congress)

experienced chronic unemployment through the end of the next decade. Journalist Roi Ottley noted that migrants' terrible "situation in one city varied only in degree from another."[2] As African Americans found only limited local and federal help during the depression and the war that followed, many organized new strategies in their household and communities to address their daily economic deprivations; they also developed new political actions, including store boycotts, and turned to organizations, such as unions, to address their needs.

* * * *

Many African Americans who left the South in the first decades of the 20th century viewed the North as their future. "Harlem for blacks," historian Nathan Huggins notes, became "synonymous with opportunity" during the World War I epoch.[3] Over the course of the 1920s, the black population in Manhattan rose from 5 to 12 percent. Harlem boasted large populations of immigrants from the West Indies—55 percent of these immigrants resided in the city and the majority settled in Harlem. By 1940, nearly one million African

Americans lived in close contact in less than two square miles. Other cities evinced a similar appeal. "To Negro migrants fresh from the South," St. Clair Drake and Horace Cayton observed, Chicago "presents a novel experience—a substantial measure of equality before the law. There are no lynchings."[4] Richard Wright, one of these new migrants, noted how migration "sets up a war in our emotions: one part of feeling tells us that it is good to be in the city, that we have a chance at life here, that we need not turn a corner to become a stranger. Another part of our feelings tells us that in terms of worry and strain, the cost of [housing] is too high, that the city heaps too much responsibility upon us and gives too little security in return."[5]

Beginning in 1927, African American migration out of the South slowed as if in anticipation of the economic downturn, but while the following decade of privation may have staunched their heavy departure for the North, it did not diminish their desire to move, or

Residents protesting against high rents during the Great Depression. (Library of Congress)

to make it a viable place of freedom dreams. In the early 1930s, blues singer Robert Johnson performed across the South, but he rarely received much money for his efforts. He lacked resources to move north and he spoke longingly about going to Chicago. He only once traveled as far as St. Louis, but he had no money to stay. His blues songs included a wider geography, and like other blues performers, his references to the North animated some of his best performances and recordings. Johnson's wistful plea, *Sweet Home Chicago,* which was a remake of Kokomo Arnold's "Old Original Kokomo Blues," reminded southern audiences that the North was the promised land, "From the land of California/to my sweet home, Chicago." Such songs documented blacks' odysseys in the previous decade and they kept alive the continued aspiration to leave the South for something better. By the 1930s, blues music announced blacks' intentions to bide their time and wait for better circumstances.

MIGRANTS AND THE COLLAPSE OF THE ECONOMY, 1929–1932

In every large city migrants felt the economy shake after the stock market crashed in October 1929. The aftershocks continued over the next months, impacting real estate and industry. Employers responded by shutting down production, which fell 50 percent by 1933. Nearly 17 million Americans had no work. Nearly 6,000 banks failed. The value of agricultural products fell from $8.5 billion to $4 billion. As the financial institutions collapsed and prices tumbled, every social group encountered economic upheaval. For African Americans, many of whom had not experienced steady employment in the previous decade, the rapid deterioration of jobs proved particularly devastating. Between 1920 and 1930, blacks returned to, or became concentrated in, unskilled occupations. More than any other group of workers, African Americans experienced the deepest and most prolonged losses of jobs, wages, and savings. Many employers chose to keep white workers and lay off black workers. Even in jobs considered appropriate only for blacks, some employers hired white workers, instead. In the rural South, more than two-thirds of blacks laboring in cotton production drew no profit, or experienced greater debt. Unable to obtain relief, many migrated to nearby southern towns and cities already overwhelmed with unemployed black and white workers. By 1931, one-third of African Americans in southern cities had no employment.

Outside the South, the economic turbulence rolled from city to city. Black Harlem felt the Depression almost immediately. Blacks' declining job rates in the city skyrocketed as the economy contracted overall and by 1930 more than 25 percent of Harlem workers had no jobs, compared to one in six whites in New York. Black median annual incomes dropped nearly in half from $1,955 in 1929 to $1,003 two years later. As these workers had incomes decline and others lost jobs, many faced eviction from their homes and apartments. More children went hungry. Early each morning, National Association for the Advancement of Colored People (NAACP) field organizer Ella Baker watched black domestic workers gather and wait for employers to look them over and hire one for daywork. These gathering spots became known as slave markets because these workers earned wages that did not provide for their needs.

Black unemployment in Midwest cities had similar and sharp declines. In Pittsburgh, blacks were 38 percent of the unemployed in early 1931, although they were only 8 percent of the population. Cleveland's Central Area, where 90 percent of the 84,000 African Americans in the city lived, many of them migrants, had one of the highest concentrations of jobless. By 1931, one-third of the 100,000 black workers in Cleveland had no work of any sort. Male job displacement was particularly evident in unskilled and semiskilled industrial employment and the building trades. As early as 1929, the Urban League documented widespread unemployment in construction and foundry employment, the two sectors where black men found employment as unskilled workers. Overall black male unemployment rates dramatically increased, and many of the remaining men who had jobs were constantly subject to layoffs or underemployment. Social workers noted that at the onset of the Depression many of these men went each day in search of work, but by 1932 most had become discouraged and had ceased to look any longer. Many men hitchhiked to other cities in search of work, but they, too, appeared to have given up the search for permanent employment.

Signs of the Depression appeared in Chicago's South Side immediately after the economic upheaval in October 1929. Nearly every bank closed, and people lost jobs in droves. As in other nearby cities, African Americans had a similar and disproportionate share in the ranks of the unemployed, which topped 16 percent of the jobless workers while they were only 4 percent of the population. Those with jobs had significantly reduced hours. U.S. Steel laid off more than half of its workers and not one of the company's remaining

employees worked full time. African American workers were especially vulnerable. Urban League investigators reported that the
"combination of low-skilled jobs, lack of seniority resulting from frequent lay-offs, and employers' attitudes about race generally" meant
black workers had higher rates of joblessness and underemployment. By 1932, more than 40 percent of black men and 55 percent
of black women in Chicago had no employment, more than double
that of white unemployment. As the Depression worsened, Richard
Wright observed the rapid evaporation of his own and other blacks'
job prospects in Chicago. He "haunted the city for jobs. Unemployed
men loitered in doorways with blank looks in their eyes, sat deject-
edly on front steps in shabby clothing, congregated in sullen groups
on street corners, and filled all the empty benches in the parks of the
city's South side."[6]

African American women, regardless of marital status, found it
difficult to secure and retain employment because of their location
in the labor market. Confined to low-waged household and laundry work in the 1920s, black women competed with white women
for these jobs in the 1930s. Employers in every sector preferred to
hire white workers, including in domestic work. Numerous reports
from the Urban Leagues in every city confirmed that the downward
occupational mobility of white women displaced black women
from jobs as stockroom attendants, bundle wrappers, and elevator
operators.

As blacks lost jobs, their resources to pay for housing evaporated.
Each month, hundreds of black families in northern cities faced
evictions. For the more than 236,000 African Americans living in
Chicago's Bronzeville, the Great Depression made the crowded
and impoverished conditions worse. By 1930, nearly 90,000 lived in
one square mile as compared with 20,000 for other Chicagoans. The
majority lived in kitchenettes, a term duplicitous landlords used to
describe single rooms let to whole families. Three to four families
shared a kitchen; dozens shared a toilet. Relief workers described
the living conditions as "tightpacked," a term that dated back to the
slave ships. Wright described how "the kitchenette is our prison."
Dempsey Travis watched neighbors drift to sleep in "pool halls,
police stations and doorways." His relatives boarded freight cars,
which became their only hope for lodging as they illegally "road the
rails." Many others settled into makeshift camps called "Hoover-
villes."[7]

Conditions in Harlem were little better. African American social
worker Anna Arnold Hedgman described people crowded into

"cellars and basements, which had been converted into makeshift flats. Packed in damp, rat-ridden dungeons, they existed in squalor not too different from that of Arkansas sharecroppers."[8] Some had tin cans for toilets; others lacked heat. Most had terrible leaks in ceilings and walls, while drafts of cold air poured through broken windows. As living conditions deteriorated, blacks' mortality rates rose. They died from tuberculosis, typhoid, and other infectious diseases. Malnutrition and poor medical care also claimed more victims. In Detroit, blacks' death rate from tuberculosis was 373 people per 1,000—nearly seven times as high as that for whites. In Pittsburgh in 1933, 17.7 percent of all the city's African Americans died from tuberculosis.

Applications for relief increased precipitously as unemployment continued. Nearly 15 percent of Americans—almost 18.6 million people—received some form of relief, with millions more in need. In New York, applications to relief agencies rose by 75 percent and blacks' applications tripled. The very forces that drove thousands to seek aid from private welfare agencies also made it difficult for these sources to provide applicants with much help. Many private agencies lost their funds in the bank closures; many of the private agencies did not extend services beyond their segregated neighborhoods and clientele. The limited public relief did not have any greater resources, but in most northern cities these agencies extended some aid to African Americans. Still, these agencies had more limited resources and few met the increasing needs precipitated by the prolonged and high unemployment in black neighborhoods. In New York, for example, relief agencies allotted African Americans only $.08 a meal. The very attributes that many Americans, including African Americans, valued as solid citizens also made them ineligible for relief. Owning a home, or having multiple wage earners in the same household, prevented applicants from receiving aid. Early in the Depression, some large employers did extend some aid to destitute workers, but as the economic downturn deepened and extended, these employers reduced or ended their support. As private agencies faced strained resources, they closed their offices the majority of the week, reduced their services, and limited their allotments.

When public and private relief agencies no longer had the resources to meet the demands of the unemployed, destitute workers searched for every available resource. Women and children foraged for food in garbage cans and scrounged for fuel along railroad tracks. Some parents pulled children from school and sent them out to work. James Baldwin and his brother shined shoes in Harlem to supplement their mother's meager wages that she earned from day work. But children lost jobs. Dempsey Travis delivered newspapers for the *Chicago Defender,* but soon after the stock market crash he was let go. Older children fared little better. Ralph Ellison discovered that having a high-school diploma did not aid his search for work. Jobs once considered for African Americans now went to whites. Ellison worked intermittently serving meals at a club, tending an elevator, assisting a window dresser, and as a chauffeur.

MIGRATION AND DEPRESSION, 1932–1937

African Americans continued to migrate during the Depression, but at a substantially slower pace than the previous decade. Some migrants returned to the South and to former homes where some family remained. Charles Denby, who migrated to Detroit in 1924, returned to Lowndes County, Alabama, in 1930 after he lost his job the previous year in the foundry of an auto plant. He had no desire to return to Alabama, but after months searching for work and with his savings gone, he no longer had any resources to live in the North. He found the South in distress, as well. While more whites returned to the South than blacks, Denby's return was not unusual.

Black migration resumed in mid-decade as some northern cities showed glimmers of recovery, but the much smaller population of travelers differed from those leaving in the previous decades. Since blacks' unemployment rates remained alarmingly high in Northeast and Midwest cities, more migrants went to cities in the West, choosing to settle in San Antonio, Los Angeles, and Seattle. These new migrants tended to be better educated and from the urban South. Less than one-quarter had lived on farms. Only those migrants with strong connections in the other cities dared travel to Detroit, Cleveland, and other industrial cities. At the urging of relatives in Detroit, James Boggs left Alabama hoping to find work in an auto plant. He managed to do so, but it took several years after his arrival. Until then, he washed cars, cleaned summer cabins, and built roads outside the city. Many potential migrants found husbanding resources for travel nearly impossible and they made selective and highly calculated moves. Desperate to attend college in the North and unable to save money for travel, Ralph Ellison learned how to hobo from a friend. It was dangerous and physically demanding work. Ultimately, he went to Alabama via Illinois, where he attended Tuskegee. Four years later, he arrived in New York simultaneously disoriented by the possibilities the city presented and the poverty wrought by the Depression. Despite his unease, Ellison had learned about Harlem from what he had read in black newspapers and heard from others.

BLACK UNEMPLOYED

Unable to find work or much aid from relief agencies, the black unemployed turned to resources within their own communities, particularly churches. In Chicago, black storefront churches organized by migrants in the 1920s provided social outreach to members and others in the community who experienced economic distress. On her weekly radio program, "The Glorious Church of the Air," Elder Lucy Smith, who pastored All Nations Pentecostal, called for contributions and advertised her church's outreach efforts. Father Divine, a New York City minister, launched a religious effort on Long Island, where he appealed to domestics and unskilled laborers. He watched his membership jump in 1927 as black migrants and immigrants experienced a protracted joblessness and economic deprivation. In response, he provided the unemployed a range of support, including food, clothing, and housing. Along with meeting their everyday material needs, Father Divine promised a better life to anyone, including the jobless and poor. Along with economic relief, Father Divine practiced a dynamic and participatory church, from its worship, to its literary and music traditions. He preached self-help, thrift, and study to a racially and economically integrated following that included professionals, laborers, former Garveyites, and ex-convicts. This combination of spiritual and material aid appealed especially to single women and mothers, two groups with the lowest wages. By 1932, his followers established businesses of their own and organized free employment agencies where they also offered job training. Over the next year, these efforts appeared in other cities and reportedly attracted two million followers. By 1935, Father Divine claimed the Peace Mission movement had 10 million members. While this number was inflated, many African Americans joined in large numbers in cities across the United States.

Mostly the unemployed cobbled together the meager aid they received from churches and other social agencies with resources they gathered from families and friends, or from their own ingenuity. Women regularly visited markets to retrieve rotten food; husbands and children peddled rags and paper; children ran errands and sold newspapers for pennies and scavenged for coal and food at freight yards. Others turned to prostitution, gambling, rent parties, and playing the numbers—anything to provide additional income. But for those families whose economic position had been precarious before the Depression, these makeshift efforts and intermittent relief did little to provide steady sustenance needed for daily life.

As workers found few jobs, faced evictions, and received little relief, their frustration grew. While Richard Wright took any work he found, no matter how short term or undesirable—including selling insurance policies—he observed the shift in some unemployed migrants' perspectives from quiet desperation about the economic collapse to a belligerent restiveness. As he "went from house to house collecting money" from people who could ill afford to pay, he saw black men "mounted upon soapboxes at street corners, bellowing about bread, rights, and revolution." Wright "liked their courage," but he wondered how these "agitators" might appeal to the "masses." Soon, he lost his job and he headed for a relief station. There, he witnessed something remarkable: the unemployed and hungry talked to one another and as they talked, "they sensed the collectivity of their lives, and some of the fear was passing. I sat looking at the beginning of anarchy." He witnessed thousands of unemployed workers "surge through the streets" as they followed political agitators, some Communists, others labor organizers.[9]

Tens of thousands of black Americans joined in these frequent protests. Along with the organizing at Relief Stations, the genesis for these protests began in black neighborhoods. On Chicago's South Side, black families organized rent strikes and protested evictions. Many then joined the new Unemployed Councils; others joined the Communist Party USA (CPUSA), which called for an equitable distribution of income, the end to racial discrimination, and unemployment relief. The Unemployed Councils, established by the Communist Party, encouraged blacks to mobilize around evictions and too little aid from relief agencies. Beginning in December 1929, and through the first bitterly cold months of 1930, these newly formed Unemployed Councils organized interracial marches of the jobless. Throughout the Midwest, unemployed workers protested in mammoth marches. Gigantic interracial crowds of the unemployed claimed the streets. In late 1931, 3,000 unemployed women and men in Chicago called for tax relief and the end of child labor. They also demanded the end of Jim Crow lynchings that plagued the South. As economic conditions worsened, 50,000 protested the mass evictions. As scores of police stormed the crowds and fired bullets, the people chanted: "Not bullets, bread!" Similar marches erupted in

Cleveland and Detroit, with large interracial crowds of unemployed gathering to protest the lack of jobs and relief. City officials typically called the unemployed hunger mobs and described them as protests organized by Communists. While the Trade Union Unity League helped to organize the marches, other groups of unemployed workers participated as well. Nearly every day thousands took to the streets and roared their demands for work and food. Cleveland employers and local officials dismissed the marchers as a disorganized throng influenced by Communists. The black press chastised the unemployed for storming, stampeding, and heckling.

"DON'T BUY WHERE YOU CAN'T WORK" MOVEMENTS

As the Depression continued, blacks' efforts to find jobs acquired new urgency and they soon appealed to owners of neighborhood stores and theaters for work. Gaining access to these jobs remained elusive. Beginning in the late 1920s, African Americans in large cities mounted boycotts to challenge exclusion from employment in stores where they were the majority of the customers. By the end of the next decade, these efforts had expanded to 35 cities, ranging from boycotts in Chicago and Cleveland, to pickets in St. Louis and Harlem. Each of these boycotts extended from new community organizations of unemployed workers who hoped to end job discrimination in stores that depended on black consumers. In New York City, for instance, the Negro Industrial and Clerical Alliance picketed stores whose owners refused to hire black workers but had majority black customers. Although it had little initial success, the Alliance affiliated with the Greater New York Coordinating Committee for Employment, another organization of unemployed workers. This alliance eventually negotiated an agreement with the merchants of Harlem to hire blacks when jobs became available.

The majority of these boycotts emerged in the midst of a range of black consumers' responses to their increased housing and shopping segregation that characterized their neighborhoods. While the post-World War I chain stores increased in number, many stores in the black neighborhoods of Cleveland, Chicago, and Detroit were small family-operated grocery and dry goods stores, pharmacies, dress shops, shore stores, and movie theaters. Regardless of size, small merchants and chain stores and theaters depended on black consumers, but these stores rarely hired black workers. Added to these exclusions, black- and immigrant-owned businesses found it difficult to compete with the new chain stores, and they, too, hired few black workers. Yet, the chain stores and theaters in these neighborhoods typically refused to hire black workers.

In late 1929, editors of the *Chicago Whip,* Joseph A. Bibb and Arthur Clement MacNeal, who later became head of the Chicago NAACP, urged readers: "Don't Spend Your Money Where You Can't Work." Others involved in the campaign included Jamie Hale Porter and former heavyweight boxer "Big Bill" Tate, who later organized the Butchers Union. Over the next months, the organizers concentrated on the chain stores, particularly Woolworth and Walgreens. Bibb denounced storeowners whose businesses thrived on black consumers and who also—sometimes vehemently so—refused to hire black workers. He urged readers to understand their collective purchasing power to leverage jobs. The first wave of picketing continued through July, drawing together an eclectic group of advocates: the Chicago Urban League, the UNIA, ministers, middle-class journalists, and attorneys. The participants drew sharp criticism for its use of pickets, and participants were accused of racketeering and extortion.

News of and reports about the *Whip*'s support for store boycotts received instant attention from editors of other black weeklies in Detroit, Pittsburgh, and Cleveland. The Pittsburgh editors agreed of that picketing stores was a radical response, but the dismal employment prospects the unemployed faced made the actions imperative. Numerous editorials concluded that merchants who solicited African Americans' business must be taught that they needed to hire them as workers, too. If these merchants refused to hire them, African Americans had the right, even the duty, to shop in stores that did employ blacks. These sorts of editorials repeated the slogans on the streets: DO NOT SPEND YOUR MONEY WHERE YOU CANNOT WORK.

The boycotts in Chicago sparked similar efforts in Pittsburgh, though with very different organizational ties and tone. In mid-April 1930, the newly created Opportunity Campaign pushed for investigations of stores and the creation of a citizens' committee to form a coalition with any other group in the city interested in black employment in stores. Their efforts, they announced, would extend to regular broadcasts of programs and activities on radio station WCAE. Women canvassed neighborhoods, and the Housewives' League visited neighborhood stores who reportedly relied on black customers but failed to employ them. Women made numerous visits to these stores, documented blacks' buying patterns, and arranged meetings with managers of independent and chain stores. Despite their efforts, few of these stores hired black employees. As the campaign struggled to gain momentum and support from consumers, women increasingly turned to the women who shopped in these stores and persuade them to shop elsewhere.

Throughout the spring and into the fall of 1930, editorials in the *Pittsburgh Courier*, the *Cleveland Gazette*, and the *Chicago Defender* encouraged African Americans to use their collective power to accumulate capital, wealth, and property. More than providing an individual with a job and steady income, supporters insisted these efforts would provide the basis for a new national black political power. Readers and editors of the black press praised every announcement of a boycott. The protests in northern cities spread to the South. Blacks in Atlanta organized a boycott against a dairy in Atlanta that refused to rent them an empty building for a school, yet claimed them as their customers. After cheering the boycott, northern editors goaded readers with the observation that black southerners faced the prospect of violent retaliation and they wondered why the boycotts in the North did not gain more support.

In contrast to this approach of appealing to women to stop shopping in stores that did not have black workers, organizers of the boycotts in Cleveland used more aggressive tactics to acquire jobs for black men and women. Organizers harangued readers in the weekly newspaper aimed at blacks who shopped in the boycotted stores: "WAKE UP! Don't Trade Where You Cannot Work." This confrontational tone extended to tactics used on picket lines to intimidate and prevent black consumers, particularly black women, from entering stores. Through these highly organized picket lines, black workers confronted both consumers who refused to honor store boycotts and employers who refused to hire them. Sometimes these struggles became violent and resulted in the arrests of organizers. By the late 1930s, organizations in Chicago, Detroit, and Youngstown used similar tactics. While the Pittsburgh boycott suggested a disciplined, but not confrontational approach, the job campaigns in interwar Cleveland, Detroit, and Chicago used more aggressive and direct action, illuminating sharp differences in ideology and tactics within black political and economic struggles. These debates foreshadowed the debates over philosophy and tactics in the post-World War II civil rights movement.

The majority of these boycotts, popularly known as "Spend Your Money Where You Can Work," "Buy Where You Can Work," or "Don't Buy Where You Can't Work," used dramatic tactics to sustain the participation of black consumers. The numerous direct-action boycotts that swept through black communities between 1935 and 1941 exhibited an urgent and militant tone and most used confrontational tactics not typically seen in earlier boycott efforts launched before 1929 and after World War II. The boycotts in Harlem, Baltimore, Cleveland, and Detroit used noisy and aggressive street protests that drew people into the organizations. The movement in Cleveland organized by the Future Outlook League in 1935 continued into the next decade and transformed into a union movement that challenged the racial barriers of the American Federation of Labor (AFL) and the Committee for Industrial Organization (CIO)—later known as the Congress of Industrial Organizations (CIO). Participants in the store boycotts in Detroit soon joined the struggles over the integration of neighborhoods and public housing. Store boycotts in Detroit were part of a multipronged assault on racial discrimination that established the foundation and tactics for the post–World War II civil rights and labor struggles.

RIOTS

> I am the people, humble, hungry, mean—
> —Langston Hughes, *Let America
> Be America Again*

While many of the boycotts succeeded and some African Americans found new employment opportunities, the majority of these struggles did not end overall job discrimination. Cuts in public relief during 1935 and the continued economic distress reinvigorated unemployed workers' street protests and calls for expanded relief. These demonstrations against unemployment, evictions, and cuts in relief and wages attracted thousands of protestors almost daily. As the policies of the New Deal Works Progress Administration replicated local patterns of job discrimination, blacks' frustrations exploded into open rebellion in Cleveland, Chicago, and Harlem.

When a store clerk in a Harlem store on West 125th Street accused Lino Rivera, a teenager, of shoplifting a cheap knife, a riot ensued. Other observers of the midday conflagration on March 19, 1935, insisted the uprising differed little from the other struggles between the poor and the police. Several clerks chased and caught Rivera, and then moved him into the store manager's office for questioning. First the chase, and then a young woman's shouts, agitated the hundreds of shoppers in the store. Reports about the accusation and chase spread like a wildfire to spectators outside the store. The store manager caught and beat the teenager, they murmured. When no one saw the teenager leave the store with police, rumors that he had been killed reverberated through the growing crowd. After a hearse passed by the store, rumors circulated that a young boy, not a teenager, had been accused of stealing candy, and then the storeowner shot him. These conflicting reports further inflamed the crowd. By late afternoon, picketers arrived and the crowd expanded to several thousand. Meanwhile, workers in the store reported that the "customers had gone on a rampage" and sent for the police. More than 500 police arrived, nearly one-fifth on horses and all of them carrying short-barreled riot guns. Groups of young men began to throw rocks at the police; others smashed windows. The crowds grew and so, too, did the police presence. Sometime late in the evening, the police shot and killed a man. Hundreds were injured, and nearly equal numbers were arrested, most unemployed young men.

Days after the uprising, officials described it as a race riot, but they soon characterized it as the Harlem riots to indicate both its racial geography and class dynamics. But the trials that followed the uprising revealed a diverse group of protesters charged with rioting: recently arrived black migrants, native-born whites, West Indian immigrants, and Puerto Ricans. Many of the arrested young men were unemployed, and they typically attacked shops, and not shopkeepers or owners. Many were charged with tossing rocks into windows, or at police. Similar confrontations between police, unemployed young men, and shop owners occurred in other cities.

MIGRANTS AND THE NEW DEAL

In an effort to combat the Depression, the Franklin D. Roosevelt administration launched a massive government intervention into the United States economy, but many of its initial policies did little to ameliorate blacks' poverty and they did not fundamentally challenge the nation's racial ideas and practices that shaped employers' discriminatory hiring practices, or public aid. Congress established the Agricultural Adjustment Administration (AAA), the Civilian Conservation Corps (CCC), and Public Works Administration (PWA) in 1933, but it did not begin to pass major relief legislation until 1935 (called the Second New Deal). Even this legislation, which produced the Social Security Act and the Agricultural Adjustment Act, offered blacks little relief. Administered at the local and state level,

New Deal policies, as practiced in the segregated South and in the context of racialized job structures in northern cities, provided too little help for many African Americans. In many instances, these policies reaffirmed, not challenged, existing ideas about the need for racial segregation. The PWA and the CCC created separate units for blacks and allotted only 10 percent of overall funding to blacks, though they comprised 20 percent of the poor. Ensuring black family solvency or increasing blacks' participation in skilled work did not concern many policy makers. The vast majority of black workers were domestic, agricultural, and casual workers, categories that did not figure into New Deal relief and recovery policy, thereby ensuring that two-thirds of wage-earning African Americans did not have access to Social Security or Unemployment benefits.

Launched in May 1935 through Executive Order 7046, the Works Project (later Progress) Administration (WPA) provided limited relief to unemployed African Americans. The mandate for the new agency eschewed discrimination in job training and assignments on public employment, such as road building, construction of municipal buildings, or public housing. Additional administrative orders, including a 1939 amendment to the Emergency Relief Act, made it unlawful to "discriminate on account of race, creed, or color." While these policies for the WPA and the ERA made important inroads in challenging historic exclusion of blacks from federal jobs and relief, local practices tended to exclude or limit their hires. In most northern cities, black men received short-term and unskilled labor. In the South, officials refused to register them for relief; blacks in WPA jobs received little work and lower wages. New federal mandates did not eradicate previous practices of excluding blacks from public work and racial segmentation of jobs generally. In late 1939, black men's assignment to skilled and semiskilled work would be based on their proportion of such positions in the 1930 census. Given that less than 4 percent of African American men held skilled positions at this time, the majority of men who received WPA employment labored in unskilled positions.

Compared to barriers in private employment, federal jobs and relief programs provided some African Americans important economic stability. By 1939, one million African American families received some form of relief, whether through the WPA or the ERA. Although African Americans held only 10 percent of the WPA jobs in the years between 1936 and 1940, outside the South blacks in these jobs gained new job skills and access to jobs where they then earned wages equal to whites. Through other federal programs, including the Writers' Project Administration, the Federal Theater Program, and the Federal Art Project, black writers, including Zora Neale Hurston, Margaret Walker, Richard Wright, Ralph Ellison, Charles Alston, Elizabeth Catlett, and Langston Hughes, found work. These writers and artists then trained scores of other African Americans. Charles Alston, for example, taught art classes at the Harlem Art Center where he trained Jacob Lawrence. At the same time, these men and women left a remarkable record of plays, literature, music, and art. Many more African Americans heard in the rhetoric of the New Deal the possibility of fundamental social and economic change. The New Deal's aspirations to provide for working people and redistribute the nation's wealth more equitably resonated across diverse groups of people, including African Americans. Although the New Deal agencies operated in a segregated manner, some in the Roosevelt administration expressed deep commitments to civil rights and the expansion of government programs to all Americans, regardless of race.

LABOR UNIONS

Many black workers hoped the Roosevelt administration's support for workers' right to organize would end barriers to their participation in unions. At the start of the Depression African Americans found that labor unions did not admit them, or they were relegated to segregated auxiliaries. Yet, many African Americans insisted that labor unions might provide them with more jobs and better wages. Labor officials, however, needed to take seriously how blacks' exclusions from many jobs and unions impeded workers' organizations. President of the Brotherhood of Sleeping Car Porters A. Philip Randolph boldly confronted the AFL on its racial exclusions and he encouraged black workers to organize themselves. But the AFL refused to charter the Brotherhood of Sleeping Car Porters. Frustrated by the exclusions and lack of recognition from organized labor, Randolph and other trade unionists, including John P. Davis, organized the National Negro Congress (NNC) to focus on the particular economic needs and concerns of black workers, such as the right to vote and equal access to employment. The NNC then worked to mobilize African American workers around broader concerns of the working class through community-based organizations. Nearly a year after its establishment, 5,000 members of the new NNC met in

Chicago for the first annual meeting. By the next year, the NNC had 585 affiliated organizations. The NNC advocated collective action around work and community needs. Local councils nurtured these alliances and many of them evolved in local black labor organizations, the Unemployment Councils, and women's clubs. The NNC linked its interests in the needs of workers to form connections with organizations that held similar concerns in neighborhoods and workplaces. Wherever possible, the NNC worked with labor unions open to a multiracial union movement; in other instances, the NNC brought information about union drives to black organizations. The NNC organized new workers, and it served as an important mediator for interracial labor efforts. In Chicago, the NNC was integral to organizing black steel workers in the Steel Workers Organizing Committee (SWOC), the Packinghouse Workers.

As the NNC and increasing numbers of African Americans agitated for access to unions and better-paid industrial work, other black organizations and civil rights leaders ended, or softened, their resistance to unions. During World War I, the National Urban League (NUL) had been indifferent or opposed to unions. A decade later, it pressured the AFL to lift its discriminatory rules. When the 1934 National Industrial Recovery Act (NIRA) recognized workers' right to bargain collectively for fair wages, better hours, and safety, the Urban League continued its pressure on unions to end their racial exclusions. The NUL created Workers Councils in every city where it had a local office. These programs informed black workers about the benefits of unions.

The new Committee for Industrial Organization (CIO) emerged within the AFL in late 1935 and launched a separate effort to organize mass-production workers, especially unskilled workers in steel, auto, and mining industries. From the start, the CIO included African Americans, who then quickly endorsed it and the subsequent independent Congress of Industrial Organizations (CIO), which appeared in 1938. Spearheaded by John L. Lewis, president of the United Mine Workers (UMW), the CIO intended to organize mass-production workers, regardless of skills, and it professed to organize "the working men and women of America regardless of race, creed, color, or nationality." African Americans occupied the lower ranks of industrial jobs, and the new CIO promised to change the relationship between unions and black workers. But the CIO's initial platforms focused on establishing unions and organizing workers already in jobs, not on pressuring employers who refused to hire black workers.

Despite the CIO's focus on organizing within industries to the exclusion of a challenge to discrimination in hiring, African Americans across a wide organizational base and political spectrum embraced the new union. Ella Baker, a key field organizer for the NAACP, immediately supported the CIO because of its plans to include blacks in the organization of mass-production workers. She especially appreciated the CIO's support for black civil rights. This willingness to organize black workers and endorse blacks' civil rights signaled a challenge to the AFL's long exclusion of black workers and some locals began to end racial exclusion. Baker and others pressed black workers to join both organizations. As the interracial organizing drives continued, both the NUL and NAACP offered varying degrees of support for the CIO platform of interracial unionism. And as some AFL locals ended racial barriers, the NUL and NAACP encouraged black workers to join these unions.

More radical locals provided the forum where workers planned challenges to employers' refusal to hire black workers. In these forums, organizers worked to close the "chasms" that "separated workers of different races and ethnicities." Employers, not workers, these organizers argued, benefited from these divisions. Forget the color of skin, or the religion and ethnicity, one steelworker insisted: "You work together,—FIGHT TOGETHER!!!!"[10] These more radical organizers and locals sought to bridge the divide between workplace and community concerns. For many workers, the CIO's broad focus on economic issues became a social movement that spilled into their everyday lives and they spent the second half of the 1930s trying to build a united, strong, and interracial industrial union. In Chicago, old and new labor activists emerged and organized for the CIO. In the Chicago packinghouses, radicals—some Communists—and older workers committed to industrial unionism joined black activists. Among steelworkers, organizers now included black union and community activists. They all sought to overcome workers' suspicions of unions. They addressed concerns about hiring, promotions, and segregation on the shop floor; they addressed discrimination outside the workplace. And black workers responded. They were the first to rally to the union campaigns, the most militant in the workplace, and the most loyal to the union. They appreciated the presence of black organizers in the CIO and the sincere effort by workers of different races, nationalities, and religions to create a workplace where all could work in dignity. The union, not employers, spoke to their interests and aspirations for decent pay, job stability, and promotions.

MIGRANTS AND WAR

World War II simultaneously accelerated and stymied these struggles. As U.S. manufacturers strove to meet Great Britain's military needs and as the War Department established a segregated draft in 1940, shortages of workers immediately appeared in mines, steel plants, converted auto factories, and shipyards. By early 1941, these shortages extended to industries producing food and textiles. Black workers and their allies pressed for training and jobs, but most employers remained resistant to hiring black workers. In contrast, when civil rights organizations pressed for greater black workers' greater participation in the CIO, the new union agreed. The United Auto Workers, one of the largest new unions in the CIO, openly supported civil rights, and they pressured auto employers converting plants to war production to hire more black workers. In doing so, the CIO leadership confronted great hostility toward blacks' participation *within* its ranks. Union leaders and many in the rank and file denounced the anti-black hate strikes initiated by some white workers within the affiliated unions. The resistance by some white workers and many employers portended responses across war industries.

As newspapers reported a demand for workers in war jobs, black migration out of the South began again and surged through the years of World War II. Just as the location of war industries during World War I shaped the direction of migration, the rapid appearance of airplane and shipbuilding along the Atlantic and Pacific coasts and war industries in Midwest cities informed black migrants' moves. Nearly 1.5 million black migrants left the South hoping to work in the aircraft plants and other war industries in Detroit, Chicago, Cleveland, and Buffalo; they also moved to East Coast cities, especially Philadelphia and Baltimore, seeking jobs in the large shipbuilding plants. The concentration of war industries in California and Washington especially attracted migrants, where they sought work in the shipyards of Los Angeles and Seattle. While the military pulled black men and women back to the South for training, the military's need for civilian workers to build instillations everywhere drew black workers.

The established industries of steel and railroads became the first location for black migrants seeking war work. Archie Nelson, who weathered the Depression in Montgomery, Alabama, headed for Youngstown, Ohio. He first repaired tracks for the Pennsylvania Railroads, and then he sought work in a steel mill. He noticed how only the white workers held "every decent job" in the mills and black workers had "all the greasy, nasty, cheap jobs" in the coke plants, blast furnaces, and plate mills.[11] Black men were concentrated in shops where they labored in low-skilled and poorly paid positions. These companies, like other companies across the Midwest, refused to hire black men in the better-paying, decent, and skilled positions. White workers' resistance to union efforts to hire or promote black workers already in the plants exacerbated the already tense climate in factories.

When more progressive white workers pressed for integrated shops, or when labor shortages forced employers to integrate the shops, white workers stopped work and went out on strike. Even as unions vowed to cease strikes for the duration of the war, white workers staged numerous sit-down strikes, work stoppages, and hate strikes when blacks—and women of any race—took positions considered a white man's job. Surveys repeatedly revealed that the majority of whites believed blacks had "to be kept in their place." Many insisted that segregation in America was necessary for victory against fascism in Europe. Even as the new interracial unions struggled to advance shop floor equality, black workers found themselves stymied by resistance from employers and other groups of workers. First, many could not *get* a job as employers refused to hire them for better paid war work. Second, black workers in plants retooling for war work found themselves confined, still, to the most onerous, poorly paid jobs with no mobility. Their employers refused to train or assign them to the new positions needed for war work. Outside the plants, black workers, especially black women, encountered few opportunities to train for war jobs.

With the prospect of war work limited and subjected to the segregated draft and military, African Americans' growing restiveness coalesced into organized protests. Unable to persuade employers to hire and promote them, and limited by unions' acquiescence to the "no strike pledge," black workers sought help from civil rights organizations. Local branches of the NAACP organized protests against employers' hiring and training practices in the defense plants of Detroit, Chicago, Los Angeles, and other cities. Almost daily in each of these cities, picketers carried signs demanding: "Let's Blitzkrieg the Color Line," "Down with Jim-Crow National Defense," "If We Can Fight for Democracy, We Can Work for Democracy," "A Bullet Draws No Color Line But Bullet Makers Do," and "Not Hitlerism But Americanism, Jobs for All." Arguing that the hire and promotion of black workers angered white workers and stalled war production, employers resisted these appeals and refused to yield.[12]

African Americans upped the pressure on the federal government. At an early spring meeting in Chicago, a black woman frustrated by the barriers to war work called for a mass demonstration in Washington: "We ought to throw 50,000 Negroes around the White House, bring them from all over the country, in jalopies, in trains and any way they can get there, and throw them around the White House and keep them there until we can get some action." Her call resonated among African Americans experienced with both their restricted access to jobs and the military during the World War I epoch and the organizing drives of the 1930s. Labor organizer A. Philip Randolph called for a march on Washington to protest discrimination in the military and war industries. He and others launched the March on Washington Movement (MOWM). Using the tactics of nonviolent mass protest, he believed in the power of the people engaged in mass and peaceful action to bring about change. "Negroes have a stake in the National Defense," he argued. "It is a big stake. The stake involves jobs. It involves equal employment opportunities." He demanded an end to discrimination in defense industries and in the military. The United States had not yet entered the war, but it had inaugurated a segregated draft with a quota system limiting black enlistment to 9 percent. He urged blacks to mobilize in a mass demonstration. Doing so, he argued, would pressure President Roosevelt to issue an Executive Order "abolishing discrimination in all government departments, Army, Navy, Air Corps and national defense jobs." His call for a "thundering march" on July 1, 1941 elicited an enthusiastic response across black America.[13]

The widespread endorsement sent shock waves through the Roosevelt administration. The threat of tens of thousands of black people protesting racial discrimination in the streets just as the nation announced its support of a war against Nazism pushed President Roosevelt to issue Executive Order (EO) 8802 in late June, which created the Fair Employment Practices Committee (FEPC) in June, 1941. Little changed: The military remained segregated and job and training discrimination persisted in defense industries. Several months after Roosevelt's order, employers refused to hire blacks even as they faced labor shortages. Two years later, Lawrence W. Cramer, executive secretary of the FEPC, acknowledged war needs did not vanquish discriminatory hiring practices.

Through the end of the war, black workers faced discrimination in many sectors of defense employment. Employers used an array of tactics to limit black men's access to skilled industrial work and bar black women entirely from defense work. Even as white workers abandoned nonindustrial employment in droves, African Americans found that these jobs remained closed to them. Ironically, the threat of mass black protest that had sparked the president to issue an executive order did not bring about a diligent effort by the federal agency to investigate complaints of discrimination. The FEPC lacked an adequate budget and enough investigators to enforce EO 8802. Federal officials viewed community-based protest as an impediment to the war effort. The MOWM may have shaken the Roosevelt administration, but federal officials accepted employers' claims that African Americans' protests against employment discrimination instigated a backlash from white workers and slowed down wartime production. Repeatedly local employers insisted that blacks confine their grievances to FEPC forms, wait for various agencies to investigate, and rely on mediators to plead their cause, if at all.

In city after city, employers vigorously recruited white workers, but refused to hire blacks. The majority of employers claimed that they intended to hire blacks "only when the supply of white workers had been exhausted."[14] Even in plants where blacks worked personnel managers refused to hire more, claiming they had filled their color quota. Unions committed to interracial unions and job mobility in the workplace could not keep pace with recruitment of new workers and counter their demands for segregated shops. In 1943, thousands of white workers rioted and protested the upgrading of black workers in defense plants. When federal agencies intervened, they typically allowed segregation to continue.

Blacks found some access to jobs only when pressure for more labor exceeded the availability of white workers. With the continued labor shortages in shipbuilding and airplane manufacturing in 1943, blacks made some gains. Although they held just 3 percent of defense jobs in 1942, by late 1944 this increased to 8.3 percent. Black men held onto jobs in foundries, and together with black women, they comprised 12 percent of the labor force in the shipyards and steel mills. Nearly an equal percentage of black workers labored in the 450,000 United Autoworkers. Blacks' wages increased, but on average they made 60 percent—up from 40 percent—of what white workers earned.

As more black men entered the military after 1943, many of the defense jobs went to black women and they claimed 600,000 of the one million defense jobs filled by African Americans. Black women's participation in industrial work overall climbed from 6.5 to 18 percent of the female workforce. These women, like the majority of white women, worked before the war and the demand for women to enter defense jobs allowed many women to leave domestic work and seek better paid and more skilled work that had typically gone to men. In industries and plants, such as ship-building and airplane manufacturing, where they had made little or no gains in employment in the previous two decades, black women tripled and quadrupled their numbers. At the same time, the percentage of black women employed in domestic work plummeted from 60 to 45 percent.

Although they made these inroads into jobs previously closed to them, black women did not find the path easy. Despite the new FEPC, many defense employers refused to hire black women, or confined them to the lower paid, less skilled, and more monotonous jobs. In response, many black women joined unions like the United Autoworkers where they helped gather evidence to file lawsuits against employers who discriminated against them. Other groups of women turned to the FEPC for investigation of employers' hiring practices. When the agency proved too slow or ineffective, women and their communities pursued investigations of their own. In Cleveland, black women turned to the Future Outlook League (FOL), a local organization that had successfully agitated for jobs during the Depression. When the FEPC refused to hold hearings in the city, the FOL filed lawsuits on behalf of women and then took Cleveland defense employers to court. They staged boycotts against other companies that refused to hire black women, including the telephone company. These efforts garnered significant publicity, which pressured employers to abandon practices of job discrimination based on race and gender.

MIGRANTS AND THE DRAFT

Unlike the previous war, the new draft laws required African Americans to participate in a segregated military. The draft had a quota system, which limited blacks' participation to 9 percent. Whether they enlisted, or were drafted, blacks entered segregated units. The navy confined blacks to positions as messmen or stewards, all labor positions. The army placed blacks in labor units and trained most men in the South. Some blacks criticized the program as limiting black participation. Others experienced it as a system that sent black men draft notices, then notified them the quota had been met, yet required they stand ready for enlistment. Despite the segregation and confinement to labor units, black men enlisted or responded to their draft notices. Thousands of black women volunteered for the WACs and WAVES as nurses, clerks, and other support positions. Nearly two million African Americans eventually served, and three-quarters of them were sent to Europe, Africa, and the South Pacific. Many men served in combat, though few Americans would read or see evidence of their efforts. The Tuskegee Airmen flew in combat squadrons and black Marines fought in the South Pacific. Southern congressional representatives and senators successfully pressured the military and the Office of War Information (OWI) to refrain from printing news, photographs, and newsreels about blacks in combat positions. Few Americans knew the extent of blacks' military participation; and most Americans did not reflect on the irony of the nation "fighting to save democracy" with a segregated military.

Some black men ignored their draft notices, or used subterfuge to avoid induction. After Malcolm Little, who later renamed himself Malcolm X and became one the most prominent leaders in the Nation of Islam, received his induction notice in early 1943, he determined to avoid the army. He arrived for his physical examination "costumed like an actor in a wild zoot suit, yellow knob-toe shoes, his hair frizzed into a reddish bush of a conk." As he greeted the army clerk, he used a jive patter certain to suggest a drug-induced hipster: "Crazy-o, daddy-o get me moving. I can't wait to get in that brown." By then, he caught the attention of a nurse and she ushered him into the psychiatrist's office. There he claimed he looked forward to organizing other black soldiers into a rebellion and stealing "some guns to kill up crackers!"[15] As he intended, his erratic behavior and inflammatory talk induced alarm among the army officials. He was declared mentally unfit for service and given a 4-F card. Others used less dramatic, but equally effective tactics to be classified as unfit for service. Howard University professor Sterling Brown learned that many men ate soap before their physical exams, a practice that made them so ill they failed.

MIGRANTS AND WAR: HOUSING

Along with struggles over jobs and the military, migrants battled anew over access to limited housing. During the Depression the federal government built public housing and the availability of some housing expanded during the war. With rare exceptions, these federal housing projects were segregated. In Detroit, the massive in-migration of white, black, and Mexican American war workers strained the capacity of the city to meet the migrants' need for housing. The federal government built public housing in an area where whites dominated, but with nearby interracial and all-black neighborhoods. The Sojourner Truth Housing Project, named after the famed black antislavery activist, was designed especially for black workers who had been excluded from other housing projects. The plan received strong support from the UAW, but leaders hoped for interracial housing. As a committee began to select tenants, protesters, including Polish Catholics, newly arrived southern white migrants, and supporters, including middle-class blacks, UAW workers, and NAACP members gathered. Federal officials reversed their occupancy plans and designated the housing project as all-white. Confrontations between protesters and supporters continued and the officials reverted the project to all-black occupancy. This time, the protests were organized by the local Ku Klux Klan, which burned a cross and picketed the night before the arrival of tenants. Early the next morning, a mob attacked the new tenants. By then, hundreds of African Americans arrived and fought the mob and the police. The battle lasted for hours; hundreds of blacks and whites were arrested. Despite more pressure to prevent blacks' from moving into the units, officials kept to their final decision. Throughout the war, the Detroit NAACP and the local UAW unsuccessfully pressed for interracial housing.

Added to the tumult, officials pushed unions and African Americans to cease many protest tactics used against segregated labor and housing during the 1930s. In the context of the war, many union, civil rights, and government officials argued that strikes, walkouts, and protest marches stalled war production and aided the enemy. Labor pledged to cease strikes. Prominent intellectuals asked African Americans to quit their calls for equal rights. Labor complied and African Americans confined their protests to the newspapers and journals. But the cessation of criticism allowed for racial oppression: internment of Japanese Americans; surveillance of radicals; and a paltry enforcement of EO 8802. Black workers everywhere staged work stoppages to protest employers' and unions' resistance to war production jobs.

In Detroit, white and black workers battled over too little housing and employers refused the UAW requests to assign blacks and women to better-paid war production work. Some employers purposely sparked and fanned white workers' fears of integrated work places. Frustrations festered, particularly on the assembly line. Interracial and intraracial clashes flared nearly every day on buses and streetcars and in theaters and factories. The city smoldered at the start of the new year. Nearly a dozen hate strikes in half as many months erupted at the Packard plant and another one exploded in early June after blacks were placed on the assembly line. More than 25,000 workers walked out, although some union members, including African Americans, remained. UAW leaders pleaded for the workers to return. Instead, they lingered outside the gates and listened to inflammatory speeches about the union and black workers. Strong UAW leadership helped end the strike, but the local also pushed members to accept interracial assembly lines.

In this charged atmosphere of unions and organizations determined to advance blacks' labor rights and many workers' resistance to change, a riot erupted. On June 20, 1943, a Sunday, crowds of blacks and whites jostled one another in the Belle Isle amusement park. Rumors spread that a race war had started. Gangs of whites attacked and beat black pedestrians; they pulled passengers from streetcars; they roamed through and shot up black neighborhoods. Black gangs tossed rocks and bottles at police patrolling their neighborhoods; they pulled white passengers from the streetcars. By the third day, white and black stores were looted, and fires burned throughout the city. Federal troops finally arrived, but by then, nearly 700 were injured and 34 were killed. The damage to the city surpassed two million dollars.

Reports of the extensive damage, injuries, and death did not quash Americans' propensity to riot, and over the next weeks, many more erupted. In July, prolonged skirmishes were reported in Boston and Brooklyn. Nearly simultaneous with the riot in Detroit, mob violence broke out in Los Angeles. Nearly 1,000 white sailors and soldiers grew enraged at the sight of working-class young black and Mexican American men engaged in flirtation and recreation with young women, many of them white women. They especially did not like the men's flamboyant suits, which critics claimed used "too much material" during the war. Soldiers and sailors roamed the streets chasing, attacking, and stripping the zoot-suited young men. These attacks were not confined to the West Coast. In Philadelphia, sailors attacked musicians wearing fashionable suits; in Baltimore, the police did the same. Some of the sailors and soldiers resented that the young men they attacked were not in the military, although some were recently drafted or had enlisted.[16]

The relocation of millions of Americans into the military and toward areas with war industries inexorably altered the nation.

African Americans' wartime migrations, which included their moves from the South to other regions, and their postings to the South or the North, and to Europe, Asia, and Africa for the war, invigorated and reoriented the civil rights struggles from the previous decades. Most critically, fighting in a segregated military while the nation claimed to battle fascism heightened blacks' critical consciousness as many became aware of the expansiveness of racial discrimination as a global phenomenon. The Roosevelt administration launched a "V for Victory" campaign to end Nazism and fascism. African Americans saw no difference between these two systems and the violence of segregation. Reluctantly, African Americans entered into the segregated military, but they also declared they intended to fight against segregation at home. Black communities called for a "Double V" campaign, victory against segregation in the United States, and victory against fascism. "We are fighting for democracy," Langston Hughes declared, "and democracy is what we intend to have."[17]

At the same time, many African Americans considered their war against fascism, Nazism, and segregation in the United States as part of the global struggle against colonial rule. France and Great Britain enlisted their colonized people into their militaries, which invigorated anticolonial struggles in South Africa, India, Algiers, Indonesia, and Syria. Colonized people furiously questioned and resisted going to war against Hitler when colonizers denied them rights and sovereignty. The tensions around mass migration of millions, the world at war, and the diminished rights at home threw Americans into daily rebellion as well.

RIOTS: FROM SEATTLE, TO HARLEM, TO PARIS

In 1943, officials documented at least 242 racial battles in 47 cities in the United States and black soldiers protested segregation on bases in the United States, Europe, and the South Pacific. The majority of riots in America erupted between early June and early August. Most began after weeks, even months, of skirmishes between blacks and police. Observers of these numerous rebellions typically characterized them as race riots, but most occurred within a wider context of anticolonial and nonviolent protests as in Calcutta, and uprisings against fascism, as in Paris. These urban clashes in the United States frequently coincided with antisegregation riots on, or near, military bases, and hundreds of anti-black sit-down and wildcat strikes in plants. Segregation persisted during the war and broadened with the military, including in areas outside the South and the United States. African Americans grew more restive and resentful as America's struggle against fascism failed to include its own destruction of segregation, especially in the South and areas near military bases.

African Americans' migration out of the rural and industrial areas of the South shifted from a spasmodic to a continuous pace during and after World War II. Their departure out of the South and their settlement in the North continued their century-long mobility, but it acquired a different character, direction, and pace in the second half of the 20th century. Many more African Americans migrated in the period between 1940 and 1965 than in the Great Migration. Tens of thousands migrated to the West Coast. This war, like the previous world war, initiated a dramatic departure of African Americans from the South. Their mass migration continued for more than two decades after World War II ended. For states in the Deep South, this migration would continue into the next century. As in the earlier migration, more whites left than blacks, but the latter group's proportion of this population redistribution continued to be more significant.

More than a move from one place to another, many blacks ascribed political aspirations to their post-World War II migration out of the South. Veteran Leroy Mosley considered his move to Los Angeles in 1945 as a response to the segregation he encountered in the military. Born and raised in the South, Mosley was drafted in 1943. He went to France during the invasion of 1944 where he used his mathematical acumen to tally the casualties of war. Usually he worked behind the lines and after battles, but one day his unit came under direct attack. With bullets "cutting through the air," Mosley "knew that the Germans were fighting the Americans." Mosley figured that since he could not vote and that whites in America did not see him as American, he would be safe in Germany. He quickly discovered that the "Germans wanted to kill me as much as they wanted to kill every other foreign soldier." And he had as much to lose as white soldiers. He "became an American in France, under fire, and afraid for his life." Reviled and attacked in the South because he had been in the military, Mosley determined to migrate. "I couldn't live among people who didn't know or couldn't accept [that] I had become in danger and under fire in war."[18] Mosley was not alone in casting this decision as a political response to the nation's demand that he fight in the military while the majority of Americans refused to end segregation.

When veterans returned to the South after the war and encountered segregationists determined to maintain the status quo, they promptly departed in search of the democracy they fought for overseas. Their families had struggled on the homefront, and they were equally determined to claim their rights as citizens. Oklahoman Lincoln Ragsdale, for example, joined the military to demonstrate his patriotism and refute popular notions of black inferiority, but the 1944 GI Bill provided him with the resources to attend Tuskegee, a black college in the South. Now well educated, Ragsdale found it impossible to vote in the South. Still in the segregated Army Air Corps, Ragsdale was assigned to Luke Air Field near Phoenix. Unwilling to return to the segregated South, he remained in Arizona after his discharge. Other black veterans settled in the area and Ragsdale, now married to local resident Eleanor Dickey, joined others in efforts to end racial discrimination in local hiring practices and public accommodations.

Black veterans everywhere discovered that prewar patterns of segregation undermined the benefits the new Servicemen's Readjustment Act of 1944 (the GI Bill) promised. Like the many migrants leaving the South during the war, veterans immediately experienced segregation practices that were a national, and not simply a southern, phenomenon. While serving in the Armed Forces, they witnessed how the military invigorated segregation as it imposed—frequently through violence—its policies in areas, including in Europe, Asia, and Africa. In letters to the NAACP, soldiers and sailors bitterly recounted how the military imposed segregation where such practices had not existed, or had been minimal. Informed by these experiences and determined to have the full democracy they had battled for at home and abroad, black veterans joined civil rights activists in rechanneling the wartime resistance to racial discrimination into older national organizations such as the NAACP and into new organizations, such as the Congress for Racial Equality (CORE). As veterans moved across the United States, they brought their aspirations, experiences, and discipline to the struggles for freedom and justice.

NOTES

1. Richard Wright, *12 Million Black Voices* (New York: Viking Press, 1941; reprint, New York: Thunder Mouth Press, 1988), 142.

2. Roi Ottley, *'New World A-Coming': Inside Black America* (New York: Houghton Mifflin Company, 1943), 154.

3. Nathan Huggins, *Harlem Renaissance* (New York: Oxford University Press, 1971), 25.

4. St. Clair Drake and Horace Cayton, *Black Metropolis* (Chicago, IL: University of Chicago Press, 1993, 1945), 108–9.

5. Wright, *12 Million Black* Voices, 105.

6. Wright, *Black Boy* (New York: Harper and Brothers, 1945; reprint, New York: Harper Perennial, 2006), 288–98.

7. Wright, *12 Million Black Voices*, 107; Dempsey J. Travis, *An Autobiography of Black Chicago* (Chicago, IL: Urban Research Institute, 1981), first quote, 35; second quote, 47.

8. Quoted in Ronald Takaki, *Double Victory: A Multicultural History of America in World War II* (Boston, MA: Back Bay Books, 2000), 38–39.

9. Wright, *Black Boy*, 294–301.

10. Quoted in Lizabeth Cohen, *Making a New Deal: Industrial Workers in Chicago, 1919–1939* (Cambridge: Cambridge University Press, 1990), 334.

11. Quoted in Bruce Nelson, *Divided We Stand: American Workers and the Struggle for Black Equality* (Princeton, NJ: Princeton University Press, 2001), 257–58.

12. Quoted in Takaki, *Double Victory*, 40.

13. Quoted in Takaki, 40–41.

14. Quoted in Kimberley L. Phillips, *AlabamaNorth: African-American Migrants, Community, and Working Class Activism in Cleveland, 1915–1945* (Urbana: University of Illinois Press, 1999), 229.

15. Malcolm X, *The Autobiography of Malcolm X,* with the assistance from Alex Haley (New York: Grove Press, 1965), 194, 196.

16. Pete Daniels, *Lost Revolutions: The South in the 1950s* (Chapel Hill: University of North Carolina Press for Smithsonian National Museum of American History, 2000), 100–103.

17. Christopher C. De Santis, *Langston Hughes and the Chicago Defender: Essays on Race, Politics, and Culture* (Urbana: University of Illinois Press, 1995), 121.

18. Walter Mosley, *What Next: A Memoir toward World Peace* (Baltimore, MD: Black Classic Press, 2003), 16.

5

"And the Migrants Kept Coming": The Second Migration, 1945–1965

Jacob Lawrence's 60th and final image in his 1941 "Migration" series echoes four previous images, including the first. Each of the five panels depicts crowds of black travelers waiting for a train north. Captioned "And the migrants kept coming," this last painting presents a perspective of the crowded station that is significantly different from the earlier paintings. At once repetitious and open ended because it captures the new surge in migration in medias res, the last panel links Lawrence's visual narrative of a migration already decades long and one that will continue decades more. Visual details in each of the panels set in or near the train station suggest how migration has changed over the three decades. In the first panel, titled "During the World War there was a great migration North by Southern Negroes," migrants crowd the train station. Lawrence rendered these figures in somber colors of dark green, black, and brown. The few women wear long dresses typical of rural workers; the men don old-fashioned tall hats. These are people from the fields and docks of the South, and the panel captures the confluence of their unease and hope. In contrast, the upright figures in the final panel wear stylish mid-century clothes and store-bought hats. Women and children are far more visually present in a scene that suggests more a parade than a crowd anxiously waiting for a train. These are modern and determined people on the move, and Lawrence portrays their hope and confidence with splashes of orange, yellow, and red.

Seven years after the 60-panel series appeared, Lawrence provided an ink drawing to accompany Langston Hughes's 1948 poem, "One-Way Ticket," which he wrote at the vortex of blacks' mass departure from the South. The taunt, uneasy poses of migrants in Lawrence's drawing, like the timbre in Hughes's postwar poem, convey a discernable ambivalence, even resignation, not present in either artist's earlier and more hopeful renderings of migration. Published in the context of post-World War II violence against black veterans and voters in the South, the third stanza of Hughes's poem begins with black Americans' collective abandonment of the South: "I am fed up/With Jim Crow Laws." Hughes's thinly veiled reference to the horror and secrecy behind lynching did not depict an earlier period of violence, but described, instead, the sharp rise in racial violence after World War II. Lawrence's image captures this distress in the huddled families clustered on their trunks in the crowded train station.

> Gone up North,
> Gone out West,
> Gone![1]

Journeying north after World War II arose from blacks' desires for safety and freedom from the constraints and violence of segregation, but blacks' desire for unfettered mobility and the full rights of citizens equally informed and sustained the mass migration. Arna Bontemps noted that "if efforts are made to restrict [a man's] freedom of movement, his determination to get away will become even stronger."[2] In the first half of the 20th century, many states imposed segregation as the means to bind African Americans to the land and end their political participation. The violence that flared after World War II frequently exploded on trains and buses as blacks challenged segregation laws. The violence continued as tens of thousands of African Americans, many veterans, attempted to register to vote. Along with the end to segregated buses and trains, black communities across the South demanded the right to vote and access to equal education.

As African Americans moved from Jim Crow cars to integrated cars on trains and from the back of buses in Cincinnati and other cities across the border, they hoped to assert their rights as citizens. In the literal movement from one seat to another on buses, or from a segregated car to an integrated car on trains, many migrants experienced for the first time the dignity and safety of travel. This ability to travel without restraint or danger and with a modicum of dignity was reaffirmed in northern train stations where they found integrated waiting rooms, drinking fountains, and restrooms. More than symbolic, the reclamation of dignity was also a hope for other claims to full citizenship, which included the right to vote, remunerative work, equal education for their children, and safe homes. Many blacks, particularly new migrants, found these desires difficult to achieve.

Hughes's poem captures the resolute march of black migrants out of Dixie, but the transforming qualities associated with the departure from the South and the arrival in the North, or West atrophied in the struggle to find a place to live and work. Other poems in his volume convey migrants' dwindling hope as they were confined to the lowest paid work and the most deteriorated neighborhoods in the urban North. They lived "Hemmed in/Can't breathe free." In Hughes's "Harlem [2]," which begins with a plaintive question, "What happens to a dream deferred?" migrants' hopes for better circumstances soon fester, explode, and then rot on the crowded streets of Harlem and Detroit. Lorraine Hansberry's 1959 play, *A Raisin in the Sun,* whose title drew from Hughes's poem, considers this petrified hope in the frustrations of the Younger family whose efforts to buy a home outside Bronzeville in Chicago meet with violence from white neighbors. Hansberry's play, which was based on her own family's lawsuit against restrictive housing covenants in Chicago in the 1930s, spoke not only of the real bombing of army veteran Henry Clark's home in Cicero in 1951 but also of the organized and persistent violence African Americans faced when they bought homes in areas designated as "white only." As northern newspapers gave only glancing attention to these racialized practices in jobs and housing, Hughes's poems and Hansberry's play documented the violence and physical limitations of blacks' daily experiences in the urban North.

The reorganization of the American economy during the war that fueled African Americans' moves north continued to provide incentives for their migration in the decade that followed. Along with the reconversion of northern industries to manufacturing cars and kitchen appliances, other industries promised higher paying jobs. Along with the appeal of northern jobs, the rapid mechanization of southern agriculture pushed black workers and the unemployed out of rural areas and into nearby towns and cities. More than five million African Americans left the South between 1940 and 1970, nearly three times the population that migrated between 1910 and 1940. By the 1960s, many states in the South had lost a quarter of their African American population, and Arkansas and Mississippi, both Delta states, lost greater proportions of black residents. By the 1960s, more blacks lived *outside* the South than in the region. This migration also reshaped the South, as more blacks resided in towns and cities than in rural areas and small towns. In 1940, 14 million southerners worked the land; by 1970, this number had plummeted to three million, meaning that only a fraction of black southerners lived on farms.

This later and larger migration after 1945, which has been variously described as "the Second Great Migration," the "postwar migration," and the "second diaspora," spanned three decades, and it occurred in the context of two wars, the Cold War, and the civil rights movement. Individuals, families, and communities responded to specific economic opportunities, political goals, and social impetuses, but the overall characteristics of the migrants and their contexts gave a political dimension to the migration. More families left the South as they sought better education for their children. After serving overseas, military veterans who were born and raised in the South constituted a significant portion of the migrants. And more migrants left southern cities than in the Great Migration.

WIDER GEOGRAPHY

Blacks' migration after the war was larger, with a wider and more distant geography than for migrants in the previous epoch. The newest migration continued blacks' moves into northern cities with mass industries, but the geography widened in this new movement. Deep South migrants continued to arrive in Chicago and Detroit daily, but many families moved in new directions, particularly toward the West. Cities with very small black populations, such as San Francisco, Portland, and Seattle had tremendous growth in black populations during and after the war. The demography of the migration differed, too. From its start, as many black women left the South as did men; in some cities, black women accounted for the majority of the recently arrived population.

Blacks left from every part of the South, but out-migration from the Mississippi Delta was especially large, where life after World War II remained structured around cotton production more so than in other parts of the Deep South. In Mississippi, the majority of black Americans worked as sharecroppers or renters on large plantations. During the war, planters no longer had access to workers with little alternative employment, but war industries drew migrants to Detroit and Los Angeles. Without cheap labor, planters rapidly mechanized cotton production. The cotton harvester replaced 40 or more cotton pickers. As agricultural production changed, cotton plantation owners faced competition from synthetics and cheaper cotton produced outside the United States. By the 1960s, these cotton plantations in the South needed one-fifth the labor used 20 years earlier.

The economics of cotton production changed, but landowners' labor practices remained draconic. Since the end of slavery, southern workers, especially black workers, rarely experienced the right to fair wages and treatment. Despite new agricultural policies put in place through the New Deal, landowners continued to short black workers their wages when cotton was weighed, or crops were settled at the end of the season. Most agricultural workers ended the year in debt, and state laws prevented them from moving to better work conditions, or arrangements before they reconciled their debt. After World War II, landowners continued to expect African Americans to yield to, and endure, harsh labor conditions.

Hoping to offset low wages from farm work, black women pursued low-wage field or domestic work. From popular ideas to state laws, black women were expected to pick cotton, or clean the homes of whites. Stereotypes portrayed black women who desired to work for their families and care for their children—roles considered appropriate for white women—as "shirking" work to "play the lady." Instead, black women were expected to work harder and for less pay than white women. Landowners and overseers rode through the fields, brandishing guns and intimidating women to work for them and not for their own families. Ruby Phillips Duncan picked cotton near Tallulah, Louisiana. She rarely saw whites and then only the in the fields "screaming at us while we was chopping cotton."[3] Southern states aided these practices by enacting and enforcing welfare and other policies that denied black women aid. Social Security policies excluded agricultural and domestic workers, and the majority of black women did not qualify for aid.

"WE PLOTTED OUR DEPARTURE"

Young African Americans, especially, dreamed about, and then plotted, their escape from this hardscrabble and draconian cotton culture. Stories they heard from those who left for nearby cities and towns stoked their desire to leave. Following routes established in the early part of the century, these men and women left rural areas and agricultural labor for nearby towns and cities in the South where they encountered and developed new ideas about, and expectations for, freedom and equality. Many blacks leaving rural areas, and especially young people, hoped towns and cities might provide safety, better schools, jobs, and entertainment. Migrants to Louisville and Memphis found more expansive opportunities and thriving communities, but others chafed under the continued strictures of urban segregation. They wanted the right to vote and an end to segregation that policed nearly every part of their lives and, frequently, exacted violent retribution against those who violated these laws and practices. Adding to the general air of expectations for full citizenship, black men and women returned from the military with similar hopes for fair treatment.

Violence against African Americans declined in the 1930s, but it rose again during and after the war. Between 1930 and 1950, 33 African Americans were lynched in Mississippi. Accused of a range of crimes, including economic prosperity, being "uppity," failure to pay a fine, or in possession of radical, or "biggity" ideas, blacks were raped, hanged, dragged, mutilated, burned (sometimes with a blow torch), and shot. In these years, local law officials frequently participated. The ferocity of these attacks and murders drew attention from the FBI in the 1940s, and federal agents began to investigate. Although the Department of Justice issued indictments, no individual or any organization was ever convicted for these murders. Along with the spike in rural violence, violence erupted in southern cities and towns, much of it directed toward black veterans and their families.

Despite the horrific terror, this generation of black people stood its ground, although to do so incited violent backlash and grave consequences. Throughout the South, African Americans, many returned veterans, organized to vote; and they joined the National Association for the Advancement of Colored People (NAACP) in droves. Hundreds marched for the right to vote in Alabama. Black and white veterans in Tennessee rioted as they pressed for the right to vote. But African Americans who resisted segregation laws were frequently ambushed and murdered. Mississippi senator Theodore Bilbo, for example, goaded whites to terrorize black veterans who dared register or who intended to vote. Mobs seized and flogged African Americans who attempted to vote. The mayor of Greenwood, Mississippi, gave J.D. Collins, a business owner, a list of black veterans and told him to warn them not to vote. A veteran who asked for the right to vote in Georgia was shot as he stood on his front porch. As news of these assaults on and mutilations of these veterans and soldiers reached the black newspapers, civil rights organizations, labor unions, and interracial veterans' organizations held demonstrations in northern cities.

As blacks' challenges to segregation increased, parents feared for their children's lives. Many worried that their children's audacity and restlessness, especially younger blacks' increasing willingness to question and challenge segregation on buses and other public accommodations might escalate whites' violent retaliation. The murders of African Americans in the South included the lynchings of black teenagers, most horrifically displayed in the murder of Emmett Till, a 14-year-old Chicagoan who had come to visit relatives in Mississippi. Despite the continued violence and vitriolic rhetoric of white supremacy, which intended to quash blacks' push for full citizenship, African Americans resisted segregation. From the voter registration drives after World War II and the Montgomery Bus Boycott in 1955, to the emerging nonviolent student movement young blacks launched to end segregated lunch counters in 1960 and segregated interstate buses in 1961, black southerners organized a formidable mass challenge to segregation.

But the widespread and persistent attacks against any challenge to segregation also fueled blacks' desire to leave the South. While African Americans developed a mass movement to challenge segregation in the South, especially the rural South, millions of others migrated to nearby cities, or to the North. Some African Americans settled in these large cities and bolstered the longtime efforts to end segregation in public accommodations. Others were only sojourners and quickly departed for cities in the North and Midwest. Thus, African Americans continued a collective departure out of the South through means that had been established decades earlier, but they also created new practices, furthering the prominence of migration in community consciousness as a political response to segregation and political repression.

As black southerners mourned the murders of civil right activists and mounted a resistance to segregation, news about opportunities and greater safety in the North circulated through the small towns and Delta plantations. Whenever family members returned south for funerals, or holidays, they informed southern kin and friends about life outside the South. Observers noted, too, a palpable "race consciousness" increasingly shaped by a national black press. As they read, or heard, about better schools and jobs in northern and West Coast cities, they also read about civil rights activism and black politicians elected by black voters. This news of opportunity when read against their daily experiences in the segregated South undermined blacks' willingness to participate in the "codes of ritual deference." Many southern towns and cities became platforms for their departures.

MIGRANTS, JIM CROW, BUSES, TRAINS, AND CARS

Having fought in the military or labored in war industries, many African Americans openly questioned the segregation they faced in the South, particularly as they traveled in Jim Crow buses and trains. Regular coach travel on trains, interstate and local, remained segregated in the South. During the war, black passengers were allotted limited space, and it took quite some time to find trains to take them from one place to another. The upkeep of cars assigned to blacks tended toward the shoddy, and train officials barred blacks from using the dining cars. Langston Hughes refused to subject himself to the dirty Jim Crow car that also lacked food. Fluent in Spanish, he affected an accent and asked for service in a whites-only dining car and confused a waiter prepared to remove him. Was he a foreign visitor, or black American? Unsure, the waiter left Hughes alone. As he traveled after the war, Hughes observed that southern rail companies regularly accommodated German and Italian prisoners of war, but subjected blacks to segregated cars.

How African Americans traveled changed significantly during and after the war. Jacob Lawrence's early 1940s migration sequence depicted iconic images of the train, which remained a key mode of travel for migrants leaving the South, but African Americans pursued other modes of travel. Blacks went north on buses beginning in the 1920s. Charles Cook, the father of singer Sam Cooke, hitchhiked and preached his way to Chicago in the early 1930s. Annie Mae Cook and their four children, including Sam, arrived by Greyhound bus at the Twelfth Street Station. Trains were used to move soldiers during the war and many migrants turned to interstate bus travel as the most accessible way to leave the South.

Despite traveling across state lines, buses followed local segregation laws when in the South and many practices were at the whim of drivers. What was expected or tolerated in one place frequently differed from expectations in another. These inconsistencies in expectations created confusion, strain, and confrontations between passengers, drivers, and law officials that frequently became violent. Bus officials possessed significant powers that went beyond taking tickets and locating seats. In the South, these individuals acquired a quasi-police power. They carried knives, clubs, and guns, which many used on black passengers. Some blacks in Virginia reported staying in their seats, regardless of the command to go to the rear of the bus, or to leave the bus. These were everyday acts of resistance, and challenges to Jim Crow escalated on buses, as interstate travel became part of blacks' strategy to leave the South. Little wonder that the post-World War II civil rights struggle to end segregation was invigorated by black travelers' confrontation with segregation on buses and trains.

One such challenge occurred in July 1944 when Irene Morgan hoped to travel in some comfort from her former home in Gloucester, Virginia, to Baltimore, Maryland, where she lived and worked in a war industry. She boarded the bus and found the segregated section crowded and hot. Still weak from a miscarriage, Morgan planned to return to Baltimore and her job. Until then, she needed to sit down, but she found that older women and children occupied the seats assigned to blacks. For part of the ride out of town, Morgan

A colored waiting room at a bus station in Durham, North Carolina. (Library of Congress)

sat on another woman's lap; she then sat near the front since no whites had boarded the bus. When whites boarded at a subsequent stop, the driver ordered Morgan and the other black passengers to stand. Morgan refused. At the next stop, the driver had the local police arrest her. As the deputy grabbed her and tried to remove her from the bus, Morgan resisted. The men dragged her off the bus, placed her in jail, and charged her with resisting arrest and violating segregation laws. She later admitted to the first charge, but she pleaded not guilty to violating the state's segregation laws. She then hired Virginia and NAACP attorney Spottswood William Robinson III to handle her case. She lost, but she refused to yield. Robinson appealed to Thurgood Marshall, one of the key lawyers in the NAACP legal office, who took the case to the Supreme Court. In 1946, a nearly unanimous Supreme Court ruled in *Morgan v. Virginia* that segregated interstate transportation was unlawful and unenforceable.

Despite the decision, bus and train companies continued to practice segregation. Some bus companies ordered the desegregation of interstate buses, while others ignored the decision. Without pressure from either the Interstate Commerce Commission (ICC) or the Justice Department, officials in nearly every southern state pressured bus companies to maintain segregation on interstate travel. Most companies got around the ruling by requiring bus travelers to purchase tickets in each state. This regulation meant that they boarded and reboarded buses to purchase tickets as they crossed state lines. The companies' refusal to abide by the *Morgan* decision galvanized blacks' resistance, especially from soldiers and veterans. Wilson Head, a World War II veteran, insisted on his right to travel unimpeded by segregation when he traveled from Atlanta to Washington, D.C., in July 1946 on the Greyhound line. Each time he encountered angry drivers, enraged passengers, and menacing police officers, Head insisted on his legal right to stay in his seat at the front of the bus. In Chapel Hill, North Carolina, one police officer threatened to shoot him, but he remained resolute and demonstrated how travelers might pressure buses to comply with the *Morgan* ruling.

After the *Morgan* decision, enforcement of segregation on train travel depended on the volume of passengers. When trains were crowded, railroad companies regularly carried mixed cars. First-class passengers and Pullman car passengers generally traveled in integrated cars. Companies strove to segregate passengers past the Mason Dixon line "as soon as possible." After the *Morgan* decision, train travel across the border states, and between Washington, D.C., and Richmond, sometimes operated in an integrated manner. These fluid policies both confused and emboldened black travelers. Some used the arbitrary and local logic of segregation to question its legitimacy. In 1948, William Chance, a schoolteacher in Rocky Mount, North Carolina, purchased a round-trip train ticket from Rocky Mount, North Carolina, to Philadelphia. On the return trip, Chance traveled on the Pennsylvania Railroad from Philadelphia to Washington, changed cars and proceeded by the Potomac Railroad to Richmond, where he changed to the Atlantic Coast Line. The first three coaches designated for black passengers were crowded, and a trainman directed Chance to go to a designated "white car" in the rear, where he found a seat in the last coach. From Washington to Richmond blacks and whites traveled together without comment or disturbance. When the train reached Richmond, the trainman segregated the passengers, directing whites to the rear and blacks forward. Chance refused and remained in his seat until the train reached Emporia, a small town on the border of North Carolina, where he was arrested. Charged and fined for disorderly conduct, Chance appealed to the United States Court of Appeals, where he prevailed. The Supreme Court declined to hear the case, and upheld the lower court's ruling that the train company's use of Virginia segregation laws violated interstate travel. After this case, integrated train travel became more typical in some areas of the Upper South, but in other areas, especially in the Deep South and on short local routes, companies practiced "local customs" of segregation. Railway stations remained segregated in the South and many did not have restroom facilities for black passengers. In many instances, ticket agents simply refused to sell tickets to blacks.

MIGRANTS AND CARS

In this context of confrontations between black passengers and company officials, increasing numbers of African Americans bought cars and they hoped driving themselves would also be a liberation from the humiliations of Jim Crow practices on trains and buses. In the early part of the century, only more affluent African Americans bought cars and "took to the road," though Jim Crow quickly shaped their experiences. Through the second half of the century, many roads in southern towns and counties remained unpaved, unmarked, and incomplete. Some areas forbade black travelers, or restricted the time that they could travel on roads. Navigating rough roads and segregation proved difficult, and blacks drove at their own peril. Finding gas stations that served black drivers created additional obstacles. Some gas stations provided service to black motorists, but if a car broke down on an unfamiliar road in an unfamiliar town, ignorance of the local racial customs added the potential of danger. Local vigilante groups pulled black drivers off the road, and local and state police regularly charged blacks with discourtesy—passing whites on unpaved roads and dirtying the cars or their clothes. Shiny, new cars frequently provoked whites, and the police frequently targeted black drivers, levying immediate and expensive fines. Sometimes black drivers and their cars simply disappeared only to be found later in a swamp or river.

Even after the World War II when the number of roads and businesses catering to drivers increased, black drivers rarely found rest stops, restaurants, and restrooms on main highways and back roads available for their use. Journalist Courtland Milloy recalled his 1958 drive through Louisiana as "too dangerous" for his parents to "let us pee."[4] The Milloys knew finding a place to stop for the night presented a special problem. Drivers relied on travel magazines and guides specifically created for African Americans, which provided addresses for hotels, motels, and gas stations that would accommodate them. Still, Milloy's mother spent the days before the family's car trips preparing fried chicken and boiled eggs. Milloy thought his mother worked so hard because she knew her children liked to eat while his father drove. Years later, he learned she could only imagine how nice it would be to stop for a cup of coffee and she especially wanted to stay in a hotel where her children might swim in a pool, but she knew such luxuries were not available. Singer Sam Cooke's family faced similar problems when they traveled back and forth from their former home in Mississippi to Chicago. Cooke's mother, Annie Mae Cook, spent days before a trip preparing food and carefully packing shoeboxes with chicken and pound cake. Born and raised in the South, Cook knew that stopping to buy a loaf of bread in a strange town could be dangerous.

Train and bus transportation to western cities were more infrequent and expensive, thus blacks migrating to these states more typically traveled by cars than did migrants leaving for other regions. In the 1940s, the military claimed the train routes and schedules and few trains reserved cars for black passengers. Buses provided little relief since most hotels and restaurants across the South refused service to blacks, but African Americans found that driving through the Southwest introduced still other obstacles. Cars

A gas station and juke joint in Melrose, Louisiana. (Library of Congress)

became the preferred mode of transportation, but travel to these western states required careful planning. Most blacks seeking to migrate did not own cars. Instead, they relied on already departed relatives and friends to return home and take them to their destinations. Others arranged to travel with friends and strangers who owned cars. Sometime these travelers camped along the roadside or they stopped to rest and eat with friends already out West, but more typically they drove nonstop from the Delta to Las Vegas or Los Angeles.

MIGRATION WEST

The West drew significant populations of black, white, and Hispanic workers during and after World War II. The black population grew exponentially in Tucson, Las Vegas, Los Angeles, San Francisco, and Seattle as war industries rapidly appeared. Overall, the black population in the region expanded by 443,000, or 33 percent, during the 1940s, with the majority settling in three cities: Los Angeles, San Francisco, and Seattle. Other cities in the southwestern states of Arizona and Nevada had significant increases in the black population, though more migrants arrived after World War II. During the war, the black population in Phoenix grew modestly and then more so in the next decade. The majority of these migrants came from four southern states—Oklahoma, Texas, Louisiana, and

Arkansas. Black women held a slight majority—53 percent—in this migrant population.

Migrants from southwest Texas and Louisiana moved first to Los Angeles, with more than 75,000 arriving during the war years. Some were recruited; others decided to migrate when they learned from family and friends about good jobs with solid wages. This large influx nearly doubled the city's black population, which was estimated to be more than 200,000 in 1944. Before World War II, the small black population in Los Angeles generally consisted of long-time residents, with a larger middle class than other northern cities. Reports circulated that this settled population resented the arrival of blacks from the rural areas of the South. The new black residents arrived into a city after the forced removal of Japanese Americans to internment camps. The city also had not easily accommodated the larger Mexican American population, and the police regularly stopped and harassed each group. The confiscation of Japanese Americans' property as they were forced into internment camps during the war further demonstrated the precarious experiences of nonwhites in the city. The 1943 riot, which became infamously known as the "zoot suit riots," indicated how violent the response could be toward African Americans, Mexican Americans, and Filipinos.

The U.S. entrance into World War II immediately altered the demographics of San Francisco. The interment of Japanese Americans led to closing of their shops and their removal from their homes. Within months of this forced departure, blacks from the South arrived to live and work. Maya Angelou, whose family migrated to San Francisco from Arkansas months before the war, watched how "the Yakamoto Seafood Market quietly became Sammy's Shoe Shine Parlor and Smoke Shop. Yashigira's Hardware metamorphosed into La Salon de Beaute' owned by Miss Clorinda Jackson." What had once been a Japanese American area in the city now looked like a Harlem neighborhood filled with southern migrants, who believed "themselves [to] have undergone concentration-camp living for centuries" under slavery and sharecropping. "Where the odors of tempura, raw fish and *cha* had dominated, the aroma of chitlings, raw fish, and ham hocks now prevailed." The constant dispersion of sailors in and out of ships added to the "never-ending" aura of change in the Fillmore district. These sailors "marched the streets in marauding gangs, approaching every girl as if she were at best a prostitute and at worst an Axis agent bent on making the U.S.A. lose the war."[5]

With its long coast open to the Pacific, southern California became the place to build the large military cargo ships, and black workers arrived in droves hoping to find work in the six new shipyards. Each of these shipyards employed tens of thousands of workers. One plant, located on Terminal Island in Long Beach, appeared almost overnight and employed nearly 90,000 workers. Hundreds of dry docks and smaller plants supplied the parts and employed thousands of workers. With an output of nearly 10 percent of the nation's wartime production, the Los Angeles area became a magnet for migrants in search of work. By 1944, more than 40 percent of African Americans who resided in the city listed shipyards as their place of work.

Despite the five new airplane plants and the high demand for workers, employers placed few African Americans in skilled or semiskilled jobs. Companies publically stated that they did not hire blacks for these positions, and they did not intend to alter their policies. Blacks could expect work as janitors and porters. Late in 1942, local officials noted the continuing shortage of workers and suggested that unskilled white workers be recruited for training. The black press reported these policies, and the federal government made the city's airplane factories its first investigation into discriminatory hiring practices. Employers argued that altering their policies would lead to white workers' protests and disruption of production. Since the FEPC lacked enforcement, many of the owners of plants refused to comply with requests to testify at the hearings. The newly opened War Manpower Commission alerted employers to its new policy: it would not make job referral for companies practicing discrimination. The inability to run factories solely with white labor led to African Americans getting jobs in substantial numbers after 1942.

The work was dangerous, which the crowded workplace conditions exacerbated. Thousands of workers labored in tight, noisy quarters. Workers battled each other, and supervisors were known to threaten, even shoot, workers. Workers regularly faced explosions and fires. African Americans created a shipyard rhyme that captured the danger: "This is iron, this is steel, and if they don't get you, the flying debris will." The International Brotherhood of Boilermakers, Iron Shipbuilders and Helpers controlled the hiring process, and it banned blacks from membership. During the war, the union's control over hiring continued and it created segregated auxiliary unions for blacks. Many white supervisors refused to upgrade black workers. As blacks pushed for seniority in these separate locals, white union officials typically charged them with loafing, which impeded job mobility. Company managers require that blacks work the swing shifts, or lose their jobs. Some white migrants from the South formed Ku Klux Klan cells in the plants. After a series of attacks from these workers, black workers organized themselves and demanded equal participation in the International union. They also asked the government to investigate the yards. Eventually 1,000 white workers supported this drive and called for a single, integrated local. Overall, the arrival of so many southerners, black and white, into a setting already embattled over unions made the yards more combustive and many officials considered these sites as prime for riots and labor clashes.

Writer Chester Himes, who came to Los Angeles and found work in the shipyards as a shipwright's helper, observed the tumult in the city's plants and streets. Expecting a city free from southern racial practices, Himes learned "Black people were treated much the same as they were in an industrial city of the South. They were Jim-Crowed in housing, in employment, in public accommodations." His father had trained as a mechanical engineer, and Himes knew how to read blueprints and he had the skills needed to for jobs in construction and building combustion engines. Himes had 23 jobs during the first three years of the war, "all in essential industries," but only 2 were skilled positions. In the first, he worked briefly building Liberty ships in Richmond, California; and in the other he installed ventilation systems for the navy. In his 1945 novel, *If He Hollers Let Him Go*, Himes captured the daily danger and discrimination in the shipyards. Bob Jones, the main character in the novel, is a newcomer and newcomers of every race made the city combustible. "Race," thought Jones, "as thick in the streets as gas fumes."[6]

SEATTLE

As a major port city, federal officials viewed Seattle as a critical location for the war effort. With a population of 342,000 in 1942, Seattle proved an equally important lure for migrants during the war. By then, nearly 16,000 African Americans lived in the city, a tremendous increase since the start of the century when the population numbered less than 500. Through their large in-migration and the simultaneous forced removal of tens of thousands of Japanese Americans into internment camps, blacks became the city's largest minority group after 1942. Before the war, some African Americans came to Seattle to work for the railroad, or they found low-wage jobs in hotels and bars that catered to longshoremen and loggers passing through the city. After World War I, blacks struggled to find and keep work as occupational segregation became more pronounced and rigid. Railroad and longshoreman locals barred blacks and other nonwhites from membership. Still, a visible population of black migrants arrived each year. Some found work on the docks during strikes. Most migrants remained in service positions, especially as domestic workers in private homes or as porters in hotels and for the railroad.

The migrants came to labor in defense plants during World War II. Many found work in shipbuilding plants where round-the-clock shifts cranked out navy vessels and B-17 bombers. Local unions sustained a closed shop, which barred blacks from membership. Desperate for skilled workers, war industrialists hired black migrants from Alabama and Michigan as temporary workers. By the war's end, Boeing and the shipyards employed nearly 4,000 black workers. As war industries decreased production, local unions scrambled to maintain their power and membership. Many locals voted to accept blacks, though American Federation of Labor (AFL) locals remained divided over the practice. After the war, blacks continued to labor in the city's factories, but generally in manual labor. Al Hendrix, guitar player Jimi Hendrix's father, returned to Seattle after time in the army and worked in a slaughterhouse; Jimi's aunt, Delores Jeter, found work at Boeing. Al Hendrix sought a merchant marine's license, but he was denied one for some time as the board considered his nonwhite friends who belonged to radical organizations a threat to the nation's security. The interracial Merchant Marines was one of the more radical unions during these years.

As in other West Coast cities, migrants to Seattle found few options for housing. The Central District remained an area where nonwhites, and especially black migrants, settled. In other areas of the city, migrants found segregation to be fluid, where small pockets of integration coincided with swaths of segregation. Some migrants moved into apartments and homes taken from Japanese Americans sent to the internment camps. Others found access to integrated units in the city's federal housing, a rarity in the region as other cities did not adopt similar policies. Like the earlier migrants, most were denied access to homes and rentals elsewhere because nearby townships and other districts in the city had laws "banning real estate sales to nonwhites." Instead, they crowded into the Central District and on Jackson Street. They lived in some of the city's oldest and most run-down buildings. Yet, the Central District was one of the most racially and ethnically diverse areas of the city. Blacks lived alongside Native Americans, Chinese Americans, Japanese Americans, Filipino Americans, and European immigrants. Although a relatively small population before the 1940s, African Americans established newspapers, businesses, and entertainment.

LAS VEGAS

Smaller cities in the Southwest attracted significant numbers of African American migrants, some leaving the South as early as the mid-1930s. Migrants left the Mississippi Delta states during the 1930s for Las Vegas where they hoped to find work building Boulder Dam. At first federal officials refused to hire them, but protests from the Nevada NAACP and the eventual need for workers changed the hiring restrictions. By World War II, recruiters went south looking for workers regardless of race to work in the magnesium plant in Henderson, Nevada, a war town about 350 miles from Las Vegas. Other defense plants in Arizona and Nevada hired African American men and so many left the Delta towns that plantation owners ordered bus companies to deny tickets to black travelers. Instead, migrants left by car and in the middle of the night. They continued to leave after the war and women migrated in significant numbers. Whenever migrants found someone with a car, they left the Delta for the West. They preferred drivers knowledgeable about the route, which was 1,500 miles most across a mountainous desert that was hot during the day and cold at night. During the three-day trip, drivers had to know where to stop for fuel, food, and water in the few segregated towns along the highway.

After the war, the defense jobs in Nevada became scarcer, but some blacks found jobs at the Las Vegas nuclear test site or the military bases that sprang up across the desert. African Americans considered this work "prize jobs" that offered better wages, respect, and decent work conditions. Jobs at the test site came with risks, however; years later these workers developed higher rates of cancer than those elsewhere in the region. Those that feared the health risks got other jobs because of the influx of so many workers and tourists into the state, especially for vacations and gambling in Las Vegas. Black men found work in construction building homes and hotels. As hotels appeared nearly daily along the strip, black women got jobs as maids, kitchen help, and laundresses. The work was generally service work as cooks and hotel maids, but it was steadier than in the Delta.

Despite steady work, blacks found daily life difficult. When they arrived in Las Vegas, most could not rent homes or apartments because of the scarcity of housing generally. Those with relatives already in the area made do as best they could. They moved into trailers and small apartments, some without running water or toilets. So many African Americans arrived in the early 1950s that some "camped outside the bus station [and] their suitcases became partitions." To new migrant Ruby Duncan Phillips, "the arrivals looked like refugees."[7] After the war, these migrants joined Mexican Americans on the edge of the city where they lived without paved streets, electricity, adequate sewage, and proper drainage. Most had outhouses and homes without running water. The mayor of the city soon ordered the clearance of blacks' homes failing to meet city codes. At the same time, the city refused to allow new homes to be built in the area; middle-class blacks were refused loans to buy homes in white neighborhoods. The irony that so many of these residents helped build new homes and hotels for whites in the city was not lost on the community. In the 1950s, African Americans continued to face restrictions, so they bought and rented homes near where nuclear bombs were being detonated. These were tracts that whites refused to purchase.

Women and families arrived with children and the ability to send children to school every day compensated for the other humiliations and inconveniences. Migrants returned home for visits and they told friends and relatives about better opportunities in these cities. The visitors traveled to Las Vegas and Phoenix with relatives and, over time, some families seemed to depart the Delta one by one. With this steady migration, similar to the "chain migration" of the World War I years, the black population increased by 40 percent over the next decade. By 1960, Nevada had the highest growth in its black population than any other state in the United States.

MIDWEST

Black migration to the Midwest continued as wartime industries ended and plants reconverted to making cars and appliances for the new suburban homes. Between 1950 and 1960, more than 183,000 black southerners rolled into Detroit from the Mississippi Delta, the Deep South, and the Carolinas. The number of white migrants arriving in the city, however, dwarfed this record number. Despite the difference, the concentration of blacks in older neighborhoods, not the dispersion of white southerners, challenged longstanding frustrations over unions and divisions in the city's neighborhoods. White southerners frequently encountered prejudice and hostility, but they did not face the sometimes insurmountable obstacles that blacks, regardless of regional origin, encountered as they searched for jobs and homes.

Defined as the "arsenal of democracy" during the war and the place to find a good job after its end, Detroit especially promised jobs in auto manufacturing. During the war, blacks constituted the majority of workers in some plants, though they held few positions in the majority of auto plants overall. After the war, even auto manufacturers favorable to hiring them for war jobs became more cautious about hiring "too many" after 1945. Instead, they specifically requested the U.S. Employment Service in Washington to send white workers, preferably from the South. They considered black workers and northern-born whites too favorable toward unions. Ironically, while some union leadership supported organizing black workers and championing civil rights, the white rank and file only endorsed some equality in wages; the majority resisted integrated job mobility and neighborhoods. For black workers, many of them migrants, access to better homes near good schools was as important as finding jobs with fair wages.

In Detroit, black migrants were largely confined to areas known as the Black Bottom and Paradise Valley—a 30-block district where Eastern European immigrants had settled earlier. All over the United States, returning veterans and migrants, especially, found a significant housing shortage. As migrants arrived in already overcrowded neighborhoods, the numerous churches, organizations, and social institutions scrambled to provide them with decent housing. All classes made Black Bottom home, which aided the rich cultural life in the area, but the dense population housed in deteriorated homes and apartments suffered from deadly diseases such as tuberculosis. Regardless of class background, or the availability of assets, including veterans' loans, African Americans found it impossible to move out of the unhealthy and impoverished neighborhoods. Real estate agents, sellers, and the Detroit Housing Commission adopted and practiced residential segregation. This practice of residential confinement dated from the early part of the century, and African Americans who attempted to move out of the area encountered deadly consequences. In 1925, Ossian Sweet, a physician, moved into an all-white neighborhood and faced a mob that assaulted him and attacked his home. Without police protection, Sweet barricaded himself in his home, with his family, brother, and friends. They defended themselves with rifles, and unknown participant fired into the crowd, killing one man and wounding another. Arrested and charged with murder, Sweet turned to the NAACP, who retained Clarence Darrow as counsel. Darrow successfully argued that Sweet defended himself.

As thousands of black migrants continued to arrive each year after the war, the need for housing in Detroit remained acute, but so, too, was the organized effort to prevent their moves into other neighborhoods. White neighborhoods on the borders of black neighborhoods organized to prevent real estate agents from selling property to blacks. In 1941, one enterprising real estate agent built a wall to separate black streets from whites. When a few agents resisted the practice of denying a sale to blacks, white homeowners used intimidation and brutal violence to prevent blacks from claiming occupancy. They also lobbied city officials to prevent the construction of new homes on land adjacent to black neighborhoods. In 1946, Mayor Edward Jeffries condemned 129 uninhabited acres near Black Bottom designated for public housing. In turn, the city removed thousands of black Detroiters from homes designated as "slums." Now "refugees," and with so few options in Black Bottom, African American veterans with access to the GI Bill, or those with higher incomes, increased their efforts to find housing elsewhere in the city. This meant they searched for homes in all-white neighborhoods, which quickly became segregated as whites sold their homes and fled the city. The number of census tracts in the city where blacks comprised more than 50 percent of the population increased from 24 in 1950 to 127 by 1960s. In contrast, few blacks found access to homes in the nearby suburbs.

NORTHEAST AND MID-ATLANTIC CITIES

East Coast cities, including Boston, New York, Philadelphia, Newark, and Baltimore, had similar growth patterns, and migrants there found similar residential restrictions. New York continued to see a "tremendous" growth in its black population, but reports indicated thousands left the city during the war for better jobs elsewhere. For all its fluctuations, the city remained a mecca during and after the war. The migrant population included a high ratio of well-educated African Americans, and the city had one of the highest concentrations of black professionals than in any other northern city. Still, black New Yorkers, migrants especially, had the highest proportion of residents earning low incomes. Those African Americans who sought homes outside the city, especially the new homes built on Long Island, quickly learned that real estate companies, builders, and homeowners refused to sell them homes. These restrictions were repeated in the nearby cities of Newark and Elizabeth, New Jersey.

Although not perceived as a northern city, many migrants to Baltimore considered their moves a departure from the South and a move "up North." The industrial development of the city before and after the war resembled the patterns of other mid-Atlantic and northeastern industrial cities. During World War I, the city had a much smaller in-migration of blacks than other mid-Atlantic cities. In the decade before and after World War II, however, the increase in the city's black population outpaced whites'. More than 33,000 migrants arrived between 1940 and 1942, and hundreds continued to arrive each week over the next years. By 1943, about 25,000 black workers, including nearly 3,000 women, labored in the city's 110 war industries. Employers insisted at the war's start that white workers would object to the hiring of blacks in semiskilled and skilled war production jobs, but such resistance rarely occurred. Instead, many of the shipbuilding and airplane plants employed thousands of black workers. While comprising close to 11 percent of workers in the city's war plants, the number did not come close to their presence as one-fifth of the city's population of workers. Despite need, some plants employed blacks in negligible numbers and others placed them in "homefront grunt jobs" where they loaded ships and cleaned plants. Some unions, including some steelworkers' CIO, and AFL locals, organized interracial locals, whereas others resisted blacks' inclusion. Despite the increase in access to defense jobs, the majority of blacks in Baltimore remained in service and transportation jobs abandoned by white workers leaving for defense plants. Overall, blacks made important gains into skilled positions; they served on key roles in unions and on Baltimore's Central Trade Union Council.

After the war, Baltimore's black population of migrants continued to outpace the arrival of white migrants. Between 1940 and 1960, the black population had a net increase of 100,000, with 55 percent arriving between 1940 and 1950 and another 45 percent migrating into the city between 1950 and 1960. These new residents measured their economic and social gains in increments and comparisons. Despite occupational gains during the war, they faced numerous restrictions in housing and where their children could attend school. These restrictions continued after the war, and increasing numbers experienced diminished access to industrial jobs. In 1940, black workers in the North earned half of what whites earned. By 1960, they earned three-quarters. Education did not help as a variable, however; and well-educated black men earned less than 66 percent of what similarly educated white men earned. Despite the barriers many migrants encountered in northern defense industries and workplaces during the war and after, they nonetheless informed their family and friends that the North had better jobs. Generally, those moving north found "more work options," which were also more secure, particularly in industrial jobs that were also unionized. By 1950, migrants on average earned 36 percent more than their cohorts in the South. Only well-educated black women earned more in the South than they did in the North. In the aggregate, the first generation of postwar black migrants fared better and they had slightly higher median incomes than they had earned in the South.

UP SOUTH

In the two decades after the war, migrants made the North and the West, anyplace but Dixie, home. As the previous generation of migrants had done, the new arrivals established institutions and a cultural life that continued their southern origins. The proliferation of nondenominational churches that first appeared in the South had greatly expanded populations in the North, competing with the older denominational churches for new members. Restaurants and grocery stores sold foods and brands that appealed to the migrants. During the 1930s, this pattern of southern influence was most pronounced in Midwest cities, particularly in Cleveland, Chicago, and Detroit, where the majority of the new migrants settled. After World War II, other cities and communities experienced this phenomenon as well. Southern accents, smells, and cultural life predominated. While the new migrants settled in to become permanent residents of a northern, or a western city, they also made the South part of their new communities. The new commercial and popular music, particularly gospel, jazz, and rhythm and blues, traced their origins to southern migrants.

These palpable references and affinities to a southern past, however, sparked an intense debate among writers, journalists, and sociologists, black and white. Perhaps, they argued, the rise in unemployment and the segregated neighborhoods could be attributed to so many black southerners migrating to the North. When Richard Wright visited Chicago in 1951, after a dozen years in New

York and Paris, he found a city remarkably similar to the city he described in his novel *Native Son.* While the South Side *had* changed and some of the most blighted neighborhoods had received some repair, the kitchenettes had all but disappeared, and there was a "flourishing" commercial district, these had not ended blacks' confinement to this area. Blacks, regardless of class or education remained "residentially contained and occupationally limited."[8]

After Wright's article appeared in *Ebony*, the premier mass-circulated monthly magazine that trumpeted black middle-class progress, readers sent letters of disagreement. In a later editorial, Jack Johnson, its publisher and owner, challenged Wright's assessment. Black life in Chicago, he insisted, had changed for the better even with signs of disproportionate black poverty and housing immobility. The rise in black homeownership—even in the older neighborhoods—voting, and education indicated progress, especially when compared to these possibilities in other cities, most notably the South.

Other observers found it difficult to make direct links between the dramatic increase in the number of black migrants and their apparent economic and physical limitations in northern and western cities. The housing and neighborhood conditions of black residents in many of these cities were substandard prior to the arrival of southern migrants and little was done to alleviate the problems after thousands of new residents arrived and settled in densely populated areas. Moreover, in city after city, and in every region of the United States, regardless of population size, African Americans faced restrictions where they could live. And they were not alone, especially in the West. Since the start of the 20th century, Mexican and Asian immigrants and their American-born children faced a variety of similar residential, school, and occupational restrictions. Native Americans, too, faced significant restrictions that limited their economic and social mobility. All of these groups tended to live in the most blighted neighborhoods with the fewest services.

This mixture of opportunity and restrictions made it difficult for many observers to see much progress. Working in the least desirable industries, living in the least desirable neighborhoods, and sending their children to dilapidated and under-resourced schools, migrants struggled to make economic gains in the North. Richard Wright's claim that Chicago in 1951 looked little different from the grim city that framed Bigger Thomas's decision to murder in *Native Son* was not lost on other writers. James Baldwin described Harlem in his 1957 short story, "Sonny's Blues," as a place of few options. Young black men, especially, grew "up in a rush," and "their heads bumped against the low ceiling of their actual possibilities." In his literary reconstructions of black neighborhoods, these young men lived in cramped cities with "killing streets" where the "housing projects jutted out like rocks in the middle of a boiling sea." Few, he noted, escaped. Instead, they came out of their homes and into "the streets for light and air and found themselves encircled by disaster."[9]

Migrants' optimism about finding work, which appeared in the post-World War II blues, gave way to a more tense tone that infused the electrified howl of rhythm and blues. These new songs, many written and performed by migrants, captured the dangers of the assembly line. John L. Carter's popular "Detroit, I Mind Dying" suggested the physical perils of daily work in the auto factories.

> Please Mr. Foreman, slow down your assembly line
> No, I don't mind workin', but I do mind dyin.'

Howlin' Wolf and Muddy Waters, both migrants, produced popular songs that blended their experiences of migration, too little work, and frustrations over the segregated spaces of northern cities.

The quickened pace of the line pushed many workers to seek other work, and some found an outlet through music. Berry Gordy Jr. was raised by two migrants in Detroit in a neighborhood filled with former southerners and their children. The son of migrants, Gordy served in the military and returned to the city to work as a chrome trimmer at the Fort Wayne, Indiana, assembly plant not far from Detroit. He aspired to write and produce records. Like other groups in the United States, African Americans' demands for music grew exponentially after the Korean War and Gordy wondered how he might produce the new 45s faster and cheaper, like the cars coming off of the Detroit assembly lines. He watched frames move along the line and emerge as "brand spanking new cars rolling off the line." He wondered how he might use the techniques and efficiencies of the auto factory to produce records for southern migrants streaming into the city. He wanted a "place where a kid off the street could walk in one door an unknown and come out another a recording artist—a star."[10] In 1958 Gordy launched Motown Records, a play on "Motor Town," blacks' popular name for Detroit and its auto industries. Within half a decade, Gordy's independent record label not only sold millions of records to diverse audiences, but also its recordings of popular music, religious sermons, and spoken records had become the "sound of America."

Yet, this successful company that celebrated black culture and challenged racial stereotypes developed in a city where African Americans increasingly struggled to find adequate housing and work. Despite numerous federal and local challenges to redlining and real estate agents' refusal to sell homes to black Americans, the city had some of the most segregated neighborhoods in the North. The city launched its 1946 "Detroit Plan" to purchase and then demolish housing deemed uninhabitable—slums—as a way to make inexpensive land available to real estate developers. Black neighborhoods were targeted, and by 1963 nearly 50,000 residents had been removed from their homes. Black businesses were targeted as well. These displaced residents and business owners did not have access to the new housing projects and commercial buildings the city constructed. And few African Americans had access to the new homes and commercial property in the suburbs outside the city. With nowhere else to go, the displaced people moved into already crowded and segregated neighborhoods.

Along with African Americans' removal from the homes and businesses in their neighborhoods and their exclusions from the new suburbs, Detroit's manufacturers moved many auto plants outside the city. They also introduced automation, which replaced the need for workers, especially unskilled workers. Recessions in 1957 and 1960–1961 meant that many of the city's workers experienced protracted layoffs, or underemployment. Some workers only had jobs for 7 to 10 months each year. The local black businesses were undercapitalized, and many blacks found few jobs in the chain stores and supermarkets as they, too, moved to the suburbs. Confined to urban homes with limited employment opportunities and faced with long commutes to jobs outside the city, many African Americans struggled to find and keep work.

When young black women and men organized sit-ins to desegregate lunch counters in 1958 in Wichita, Kansas, and Oklahoma City, many black Americans also wondered about finding work. That year, William "Smokey" Robinson's and the Miracles "Got a Job," responded to an earlier hit Coasters' hit, "Get a Job." In "Got a Job," Robinson's narration of a young man's search for work ended with long hours in a grocery store: "Walked all day till my feet were tired/I was low, I just couldn't get hired." In the economic downturn that coincided with John F. Kennedy's election as president in late 1960, African Americans were twice as likely to be unemployed. Nationally, white workers accounted for 7 percent of the unemployed and black workers 13.8 percent. In every major city, black workers had much higher rates of unemployment. Black workers faced the "harshest consequences" in the heavily industrial cities of the Midwest, the National Urban League reported. In Detroit, 39 percent of African Americans lacked jobs. In St. Louis, black workers accounted for more than half of the 72,700 reported unemployed. The majority of those without work had also exhausted their benefits. For many African Americans, Robinson's Motown songs captured the incessant search for work that plagued their lives in the urban North.

With too few jobs and limited access to homes, African Americans pondered how best to address the needs of their communities. In Montgomery, Alabama, in 1956 and in Greensboro, North Carolina in 1961, African Americans and their allies blended the economic boycotts northern blacks had used in the 1930s and 1940s with the nonviolent direct action efforts of Mahatmas Gandhi in India and the antiapartheid struggles in South Africa to call for political and educational rights. For many African Americans in northern cities, alliances and negotiations with labor unions, political parties, city officials, and church activists had been commonplace. Sometimes, these strategies had been very successful, as in the efforts of civil rights activists in Philadelphia in 1948 when they successfully persuaded the city's government to "enact one of the country's first municipal fair employment practices laws." By the late 1950s, however, many northern blacks began "to question the efficacy of government action in the struggle for racial equality." As northern cities became increasingly black and poor, with deplorable housing and limited economic opportunities, black Americans considered how best to achieve cultural pride, political influence, and economic power. Racial discrimination, these activists argued, was not confined to the South. Moreover, the troubles blacks faced in the North did not "migrate from the South."[11] The efforts for black freedom in the North, however, did not appear as ancillary to the protests and struggles in the South. Rather, each would influence the other in important ways.

NOTES

1. Langston Hughes, "One-Way Ticket," in *The Collected Poems of Langston Hughes*, ed. Arnold Rampersad (New York: Alfred A. Knopf, New York 1994), 361.

2. Arna Bontemps and Jack Conroy, *They Seek a City* (Garden City, NY: Doubleday, 1945), 249.

3. Quoted in Annelise Orleck, *Storming Caesar's Palace: How Black Women Fought Their Own War on Poverty* (New York: Beacon Press, 2005), 13.

4. Courtland Milloy, "Black Highways: Thirty Years Ago in the South, We Didn't Dare Stop," *The Washington Post,* June 11, 1987, B1.

5. Maya Angelou, *I Know Why the Caged Bird Sings* (New York: Random House, 1969; reprint, New York: Ballantine Books, 2009), 209.

6. Chester Himes, *If He Hollers Let Him Go: A Novel* (New York: De Capo Press, 2002), 7.

7. Orleck, *Storming Caesar's Palace,* 37.

8. James N. Gregory, *The Southern Diaspora: How the Great Migrations of Black and White Southerners Transformed America* (Chapel Hill: The University of North Carolina Press, 2005), 150.

9. James Baldwin, "Sonny's Blues," in *Going to Meet the Man: Stories* (New York: Vintage, 1995), first quote, 104; second quote, 113.

10. Quoted in Suzanne E. Smith, *Dancing in the Street: Motown and the Cultural Politics of Detroit* (Cambridge, MA: Harvard University Press, 1999), 14.

11. Matthew J. Countryman, *Up South: Civil Rights and Black Power in Philadelphia* (Philadelphia: University of Pennsylvania Press, 2005), 1–2.

6

Migrants and Civil Rights Cities

African Americans' largest and most sustained collective migration out of the South coincided with their organized mass and national effort to end the limitations segregation imposed on their aspirations for equality in the United States. As they searched for better work, schools, and freedom, the majority of these migrants gravitated toward the large industrial cities in every region outside the South. The 10 cities with more than 100,000 black residents continued to draw new migrants during and after the war, with Detroit, New York City, Cleveland, Philadelphia, and Chicago drawing the most. Smaller cities, including Flint, Michigan, and Youngstown, Ohio, saw a rapid growth in black residents. By 1950, 32 percent of black Americans lived outside the South and over the next two decades, this percentage climbed sharply to 47 percent.

Migrants who left the South after 1945 quickly discovered that their new homes resembled their old. Many migrants expected their new lives to differ from their daily lives in the segregated South, but as they arrived in northern cities in large numbers, they faced organized and spontaneous resistance to their aspirations for equal access to housing, schools, and jobs. Cities and towns in other regions may have lacked the elaborate legal structure of segregation, but they nonetheless practiced Jim Crow in myriad ways.

Migrants often described their new homes as "Up South" or "Ala-bamaNorth," as much for their similarities in racial hierarchies as for the familiarity of southern food, music, or nearby friends.

Across the United States blacks' efforts to expand their civil and economic rights had been in full swing since the early 20th century, but these movements for equality differed by region. Although struggles in the South erupted as African Americans and other civil rights activists pushed for the passage of civil rights laws, many of the northern struggles in this period focused on the *enforcement* of civil rights laws, particularly in public accommodations, housing, and jobs. From Boston, Massachusetts, to Seattle, Washington, these migrants organized and participated in boycotts, sit-ins, and protest marches. They demanded access to unions and union jobs. Migrants helped establish new organizations in these years between 1940 and 1951, including the Congress of Racial Equality (CORE), first organized in 1942, and they added to the membership and resources of others, such as the National Association for the Advancement of Colored People (NAACP) and March on Washington Movement (MOWM). These civil rights efforts that took place outside the South were multiracial, especially in unions and antiwar efforts.

While civil rights activists outside the South crafted strategies to address their specific local conditions and contexts, they also perceived their efforts as part of a national movement and integral to the civil rights struggles occurring in the South. Regardless of region, African Americans shared experiences of segregation, which was as rooted in the North as it was in the South. Because of the similarities of segregation, local civil rights activists often looked to national organizations and organizers, or other grassroots struggles for support and tactics. The Oklahoma City boycotts against segregated public accommodations, organized in 1958, and the bus boycotts that emerged in Tallahassee, Florida, and Montgomery, Alabama, in the 1950s, for example, drew from the experiences and resources of nonviolent boycotts that migrants staged in the North in the 1930s and 1940s. The legal challenges to segregated schools and housing had components drawn from a variety of efforts organized across the United States.

Migrants brought to the civil rights movement elsewhere their experiences and aspirations from the war and postwar civil rights struggles in the South. Their knowledge influenced the ideologies, resources, and tactics in the North. The convergence of their experiences with racial and economic inequality before and after

In Harlem, 15,000 marchers parade down the streets in support of voting rights efforts in Selma, 1965. (Library of Congress)

migration with their aspirations for a better life outside the South made migrants the adhesive between the different regions and tactics of the civil rights struggles. They funded the legal challenges to discrimination in housing, schools, and municipal services; they joined unions and pressed for inclusion in their processes. Black autoworkers in the United Auto Workers (UAW) successfully pressed their local and national leaders to provide financial support for the Montgomery Bus Boycott. Migrant communities raised money to support voting registration and school desegregation. At the same time, they organized boycotts and demonstrations. When jobs and other resources vanished, these activists challenged the older civil rights organizations. When these efforts stalled, they turned to new tactics organized in the Nation of Islam and the Black Power movement that focused on social and political change through grassroots organizations.

POST-1945 SEGREGATION OUTSIDE THE SOUTH

Migration north did not end segregation. Historian Thomas Sugrue notes that "racial inequality took different forms on each side of the Mason-Dixon line in the twentieth century."[1] As early as the

1880s, many northern cities and states passed antidiscrimination laws that banned discrimination because of race, religion, or nationality, but African Americans, Asian Americans, Mexican Americans, and Native Americans faced a variety of barriers to housing, schools, public accommodations, and transportation. Court cases proved ineffective since white juries evinced little sympathy for black plaintiffs. For the next half century, blacks launched numerous boycotts, including the two decades of protests between the wars.

These interwar efforts included activists who traveled across the United States on behalf of civil rights organizations. Field workers for the NAACP, the National Urban League (NUL), and the National Council of Negro Women (NCNW) traveled extensively through southern and northern towns and cities where they attracted others interested in building and linking local organizations into national efforts. While a field worker for the NAACP in the 1930s and 1940s, North Carolina migrant and Harlem resident Ella Baker helped forge the ties between southern and northern union and civil rights activists. In the 1950s, Baker worked with Reverend Martin Luther King Jr.'s Southern Christian Leadership Conference (SCLC), and she later nurtured the birth of the Student Non-Violent Coordinating Committee (SNCC). Baker's roles in national organizing efforts, while pivotal, were not unique. Migrants from the South arrived in Chicago during the 1930s and they joined longtime residents in reforming the city's moribund NAACP chapter into one of the most radical branches in the nation. In Cleveland, migrants from Alabama organized a mass boycott movement through the Future Outlook League (FOL) in the 1930s that later challenged unions to make equal access to jobs, especially for black women, integral to their organizing efforts. Melnea Cass, a migrant from Richmond, Virginia, led the Boston NAACP, worked with W. E. B. Du Bois, and was an active member of the NCNW.

Activists who flowed between the local struggles and national organizations raised money for the cause of civil rights. After her son, Emmett Till, was murdered in 1955 in Money, Mississippi, while visiting relatives, Chicago resident Mamie Till Bradley gave talks about lynching to raise money for civil rights struggles and press northern blacks to support the civil rights efforts in the South. Bradley's speeches, like others who spoke in these years, helped shape blacks' shared consciousness and understanding of racial and economic inequality as a national and international—and

Executive Secretary of the National Association for the Advancement of Colored People Roy Wilkins, 1963. (Library of Congress)

not simply as a southern—phenomenon. Longtime activists, such as A. Philip Randolph, Bayard Rustin, and Dorothy Height, all of whom had struggled for decades to end racial barriers in jobs, unions, housing, and schools, influenced new activists. As in the South, these struggles in the North were also social movements, changing the daily lives of participants. Many campaigns for better housing, schools, and services were led by women, many of them mothers, but veterans, pacifists, and Black Nationalists also participated.

Along with support for their local efforts, Africans Americans in the North nurtured and financed civil rights efforts in the South. Migrants raised money, especially for black activists in the South who faced reprisals for the open challenges to segregation and their demands for the right to vote. In New York City, migrant Ella Baker organized In Friendship, which raised money for activists in the South and then arranged for them to go on speaking tours to inform northern supporters about disenfranchisement and economic repression.

Pressing the U.S. claim that it was the model of democracy, blacks' protests against segregation in public accommodations accelerated as they regarded the barriers to restaurants, parks, and stores to be especially egregious. How could the nation promulgate such a declaration when its own citizens could not expect democracy at home? Similar to practices in the South, many northern department stores did not allow blacks to try on clothes before purchasing them; women could not try on hats or gloves. Many restaurants, especially family-owned diners and those that catered to the wealthy, refused to seat or serve blacks. When blacks defied these policies or when groups—some interracial—insisted on interracial dining, some of these restaurants retaliated by serving rotten and oversalted food. Finding a place to eat or sleep outside their neighborhoods proved daunting to African Americans, especially those traveling far from home. Many bars and clubs, particularly those that catered to workers as they left factories, did not admit black customers—a practice that greatly diminished the organization of interracial unions. Pools and parks established policies that denied blacks' access, or confined them to the day before managers scheduled the cleaning.

African American activists challenged segregation in public accommodations by demanding that cities and states enforce laws that banned discrimination. First in Fellowship of Reconciliation (FOR), and then when they organized CORE in 1942, civil rights activists James Farmer, Bayard Rustin, and George Houser targeted restaurants in Chicago with discriminatory practices. Using Gandhian practices of nonviolence, these men and other CORE members staged sit-ins at several restaurants in 1942 and 1943. Labor and civil rights activist A. Philip Randolph endorsed the efforts and called for "sit-down strikes" in restaurants and other public accommodations that practiced discrimination. CORE created a pamphlet that outlined how to challenge restaurant discrimination through "investigation, negotiation, public pressure and education, demonstration, and noncooperation." This process often took weeks, and each stage focused greater attention to these restaurants' policies. The NAACP, unions, and church groups launched similar campaigns and created how-to manuals that showed would-be protesters how to avoid violence. Few restaurants and pools capitulated easily, but these campaigns highlighted how widespread these practices were during the war.

Skirmishes and violence escalated after World War II. Police typically refused to protect black consumers, and many resorted to self-defense. This violence was brought to the nation's attention in early 1946 after three black veterans protested a proprietor who refused to serve them coffee and then a Long Island police officer shot and killed two. These deaths and other assaults and murders of veterans who demanded the right to ride buses, vote, and work forced President Harry Truman to create the President's Committee on Civil Rights, which produced the 1947 *To Secure These Rights*. This blueprint for civil rights did not stop either the discrimination or violence. International star Josephine Baker discovered in 1948 how these practices remained remarkably resistant to protests and committee recommendations when 36 hotels denied her and her husband a room.

The arriving migrants after the war demonstrated a considerable willingness to use their consumer power to end bias in public accommodations. Though the large chain stores, including Kresge and Woolworth, had resisted hiring blacks in the 1930s, the "Don't Buy Where You Can't Work Campaigns" had opened jobs and these stores readily served blacks. Smaller establishments did not yield. In Wichita, Kansas, Chicago, Detroit, and Newark, New Jersey, blacks held repeated sit-ins, stand-ins, and boycotts against restaurants, theaters, and pools. In Detroit, UAW member James Boggs and a white unionist organized migrants and they went restaurant to restaurant to test where they might be served. In New York City, the East Manhattan Committee on Civil Rights expanded this practice and sent groups of whites and blacks to test the policies of the city's restaurants. Black testers frequently received service, but more often restaurants served them cold food, inflated their bills, or seated them in separate areas. These investigation yielded immediate changes, including support from the waiter's union, but other campaigns lasted for years and produced a limited end to segregation. In other instances, businesses fought back, claiming that civil rights activists were Communists. In Kansas, business owners argued that though they had public restaurants, they had the private right to refuse service to blacks. Eventually, some restaurants, hotels, and public pools yielded, partly because blacks had become the majority populations. It took the 1964 Civil Rights Act to end the remaining discrimination.

But blacks' protests were more than an effort to participate equally in the new consumerism that emerged after World War II. Their protests against segregation in public accommodations were tied to protests for housing and jobs. In addition, they saw their challenges to discrimination in public accommodations as part of African Americans' national freedom struggles for full voting rights, equal public education and employment, and equal access to housing.

MIGRANTS AND HOUSING

The majority of the 1.5 million African American World War II veterans hoped their military service would translate into full citizenship, and the 1944 Serviceman's Readjustment Act, popularly known as the GI Bill, appeared to promise them equal access to its benefits. Black veterans planned to buy homes, attend schools, or open businesses. After the war, surveys revealed that more than 30 percent planned to migrate out of the South, 50 percent hoped to attend schools, and more than 65 percent hoped to find better jobs than they held before the war.

Black veterans quickly learned that the Veteran Administration's (VA) management of the GI Bill reinforced existing patterns of discrimination. The VA did not challenge local, state, or national discrimination in housing, lending, or education. Only one-fifth of the 100,000 black veterans eligible to attend college found access, and the majority attended the grossly overcrowded black colleges. Southern white universities and colleges did not admit blacks, and northern schools established quotas. Veterans with college educations who hoped to attend law or medical school found much narrower access. In 1946, more than 1,000 African Americans applied for 70 seats at Howard University. Few VA and United States Employment Service (USES) offices hired black personnel, and most offices directed black veterans, even those with much needed skills, to menial positions with low pay. One veteran noted in a letter to the *Washington Post* that he returned to the United States "to find myself what I was before—a second-class citizen. What is more, the fact that I was now a veteran, instead of buttressing my wartime hopes, actually was held against me. Now that I was a veteran, I was considered to be not merely a Negro, but a cocky one to boot."[2]

The GI Bill was meant to expand homeownership among ex-servicemen. It guaranteed mortgage insurance and expanded the

Fair Housing Administration (FHA), a New Deal agency established a decade earlier. Aided by government-backed mortgage assistance, access to credit to buy cars and homes, and federally funded highways that opened up outlying areas to development, home ownership increased overall by 43 percent between 1947 and 1953. Home construction entrepreneurs built tens of thousands of low-cost housing in communities close to city jobs. William Levitt was one of these new businessmen. During World War II, he shifted from building custom homes for wealthy buyers to building mass-produced homes for working-class and middle-class buyers. He demonstrated the dramatic access to land, financing, and advertising that emerged after World War II. Using techniques honed during the rapid construction of defense buildings, ships, and airplanes during World War II, Levitt perfected the mass construction of prefabricated homes.

From the start of his homebuilding, William Levitt intended to build segregated communities and he refused to sell to nonwhite buyers. He insisted white buyers did not want blacks living next door, so he especially resisted selling homes to African Americans and sought various ways to prevent resales to them. By 1953, the Long Island Levittown population had grown to 70,000 and it was all-white, making it the largest segregated planned community in the United States. Levitt's strategies to maintain this racial exclusivity, coupled with efforts to thwart black homeownership generally, had their effect. When a white owner in a Pennsylvania development sold his home to blacks in 1957, his neighbors gathered to throw rocks, burn crosses, and wave Confederate flags. After 1945, northern newspapers published numerous accounts of whites harassing prospective black buyers through bombs, arson, and graffiti. Most white homeowners who resisted selling their homes to blacks, or having them as neighbors, worked closely with realtors and home owners' associations to keep their neighborhoods segregated by pressuring their neighbors to withdraw offers, or not to make them in the first place.

The National Association of Realtors significantly aided this trend. Subsidized by government financing, from tax breaks to roads, realtors continued prewar patterns of excluding workers by race and class. After World War II, historian Lizabeth Cohen argues, real estate brokers "refus[ed] to help black customers, withheld listings, and distorted home appraisals." Most realtors simply refused to show blacks homes in white communities and steered them to all-black or majority-black neighborhoods. Until 1950, the association's ethics supported these practices since the bylaws stipulated that realtors were obligated not to introduce buyers of a different race into all-white neighborhoods. Contrary to much evidence, white homeowners, homeowners' associations, and realtors believed that property values plummeted when blacks bought homes in all-white neighborhoods.

The most frustrating failure of the GI Bill to serve black veterans was in the VAs almost nonexistent support for blacks' purchase of homes. Denied access to the new suburbs and federal housing projects, black veterans hoped to buy homes in increasingly black urban neighborhoods. VA and FHA lenders marked these areas red on government maps, which they defined as high risk because these homes were in urban areas with majority black populations. Mortgage lenders denied them loans or they provided smaller loans with higher interest rates. In a 1950 survey of mortgages, blacks received 1.7 percent of the nearly 500,000 mortgaged properties in New York and New Jersey. Even the VA succumbed to such patterns and black veterans could rarely count on the benefits they earned through military service to provide a buffer against discrimination from homeowners and lenders. Just 0.1 percent of these loans were VA mortgages. Advocates for open housing and anti-redlining legislation did not prevail until 1968, when Congress passed the Fair Housing Act. By then, many American suburbs had become racially and economically homogeneous.

By the early 1950s, some northern legislatures banned these practices outright, or significantly curtailed them. The New Jersey state legislature forced the National Association of Realtors to end its restrictions on selling homes to blacks. By then, agents created new strategies to maintain segregated neighborhoods *and* sell homes to blacks. Using a new technique called blockbusting, realtors colluded to alarm whites by claiming black homeowners would soon invade their neighborhoods. They pressured whites to sell their homes for less than their value, and they resold those homes to blacks for more than their value. Between 1950 and 1970, older suburbs near cities became increasingly black, while newer suburbs— many beyond the reach of reliable public transportation—were nearly all-white.

MIGRANTS AND *BROWN*

African Americans outside the South, including migrants, challenged the limited educational opportunities for their children.

Some states outside the South did not have de jure segregation and instead imposed segregation by confining blacks to specific schools. Other school boards passed legislation to ensure racial segregation. In Topeka, Kansas, a city with a visible black population that had arrived during the Exodus migration of the 1870s, the school board insisted on separate schools along racial lines. In the 19th century, the city's elementary schools were segregated, but the school board mandated an integrated high school. At the start of the new century, the state reversed this earlier policy and allowed the largest city in the state, Kansas City, to establish a separate high school for blacks. Other cities in the state soon followed this practice. African Americans in Topeka challenged the law in 1905, but the state successfully used *Plessy* as the legal precedent. While blacks in the city traveled on integrated buses, white owners of restaurants, pools, and movie theaters vigorously enforced segregation. The concentration of blacks in the low-wage and unskilled occupations aided the segregation in the city's public life. Few blacks had access to the social and political means to challenge the practices that pushed blacks in Kansas into the status as second-class citizens.

Some blacks dared challenge the laws, but with mixed results. In 1940, Ulysses and Beatrice Graham successfully sued the city to end its practice of segregation in the junior high and high school, but both institutions remained largely segregated. Black students entered the high school and promptly found segregation everywhere. Officials kept the sports teams, social clubs, and the cafeteria strictly segregated. And worse, they discouraged the black students from pursuing rigorous courses, or courses that might lead them to better paid work after graduation. Black girls could not take typing and stenography courses.

After World War II the individual challenges became a mass effort. Oliver Brown, a World War II veteran and longtime resident of Topeka, Kansas, decided to register his daughter in the nearby elementary school. His daughter, Linda Brown, later recalled:

We lived in an integrated neighborhood and I had all of these playmates of different nationalities. And so when I found out that day that I might be able to go to their school, I was thrilled. I remember walking over to Sumner School with my dad that day and going up the steps of the school and the school looked so big to a smaller child. My dad spoke with someone and then he went into the inner office with the principal and they left me outside with the secretary. While he was in the inner office, I could hear voices and hear his voice raised as the conversation went on. Then he immediately came out of the office, took me by the hand and we walked home from the school. I just couldn't understand what was happening because I was so sure that I was going to go to school with Mona and Guinevere, Wanda, and all of my playmates.[3]

The school denied Brown's request, and he took his case to the Topeka NAACP. He wanted his daughter to go to the school near their home. Before he attempted to register Linda, he carefully mapped her route. She had to walk along a busy road, and then cross train tracks. She would have to wait for the bus for 30 minutes, or more, and then ride for nearly an hour to the segregated school. Eventually, Brown and 12 other families requested the right to send their children to schools in their neighborhoods. Local lawyers worked with counsel from the national NAACP to represent Brown and the other families. By then, the national NAACP had started to shepherd a number of plaintiffs from southern states willing to challenge school segregation.

The school case in Topeka, Kansas, which was later combined with cases from South Carolina, Virginia and other states, laid the groundwork for what would be a landmark civil rights case that overturned the separate but equal doctrine articulated in *Plessy*. In Topeka, African American lawyer Elisha Scott and his sons, Charles and John Scott—both veterans—and also lawyers, challenged the state's segregation laws; McKinley Burnett, head of the local NAACP, Daniel Sawyer, another member, and Esther Brown, a white member of the branch outraged by the segregation, spent the years after the war organizing local support. Through the combination of this local effort and the legal resources of Thurgood Marshall and Robert Carter from the NAACP Legal Defense Fund (LDF), the 12 plaintiffs and their 20 children won. Bundled with cases from South Carolina, Delaware, and Virginia, the NAACP took the Brown case to the Supreme Court, where the justices unanimously ruled in 1954 that segregated education could not ever provide equal education. Black Americans readily agreed to the central claim in the *Brown* decision, both in Kansas and in the Supreme Court hearing, which insisted that segregated schools deprived them of education on equal terms to that available to whites. Writing for the unanimous opinion, Chief Justice Earl Warren noted "it is doubtful that any child may reasonably be expected to succeed in life if he is denied the opportunity of an education. Such an opportunity, where the state has undertaken to provide it, is a right which must be made available to all on equal terms."[4]

MIGRANTS AND SCHOOLS

Desegregation of the schools continued to hold activists' attention in the North. While nine high-school students attempted to integrate Little Rock High School in Little Rock, Arkansas, black mothers and their children called attention to the segregated and dilapidated schools in Harlem's Ocean-Brownsville School District. Mae Mallory, a migrant from Macon, Georgia, described the area's segregated schools in 1958 as no different from the Jim Crow system she encountered in the South. Mallory and eight other mothers kept their children out of Harlem junior high schools that fall as a way to protest the city's segregated education. The black press called the group "The Little Rock Nine of Harlem," a characterization that linked the parents' protest in the North with blacks' struggles against school segregation in Arkansas. The women were charged with illegally keeping their children out of school. Four women were fined; the judge who presided over the remaining five cases agreed with the women and ruled that New York City provided their children with an inferior education. Little changed, however, and over the next decade black parents staged additional boycotts and pressed for equal education.

These ongoing efforts to integrate northern schools exposed the similar struggles African Americans faced regardless of region. The patterns of segregation in the North emerged and operated differently from racial inequality the South. And while these patterns were not as visible and whites did not defend segregation as violently as in the South, "northern activists," historian Jeanne Theoharis noted, "had to prove that segregation actually existed, was harmful, and was enacted deliberately by the state."[5] To casual observers, school segregation in northern cities appeared unintentional and haphazard. Yet, Ruth Batson, the daughter of Caribbean immigrants, knew otherwise about the patterns in Boston. Along with white allies, Batson created the Parents' Federation to combat racial inequality. In the early 1950s, Batson's three daughters attended an all-black school in the Roxbury section of Boston where, she realized, they had far fewer opportunities than those available to whites across all social groups. Through her work with the Parents' Federation and the local chapter of the NAACP, Batson learned that black and white children who lived in the same area were placed in different middle and high schools, concentrating them by race. These and the other schools where black students predominated were overcrowded and in poor condition. Teachers used an outdated curriculum, and the city spent $100 less per student than in the all-white schools. After considerable study, the Parents' Federation determined that the 1954 *Brown* decision had as little impact on segregation in Boston as it had in Mississippi. Moreover, white parents in Boston supported segregated neighborhoods and aided the efforts to prevent change in the racial composition in schools. In another form of subtle, but effective resistance to ending the discrimination, the city school board allowed students to attend any school, yet denied these students access to busing. By 1966, five years after this decision, Boston public schools remained dramatically segregated.

MIGRANTS AND JOBS

In the decade after 1950, the number of blacks aged 16 to 54 grew from 5.8 million to 6.7 million. By 1960, a significant portion of this population sought work, with 83 percent of black men and 48 percent of black women claiming to have or need work. Fewer of these workers participated in agricultural work, with a sharp decline from 32 percent in 1940 to 8 percent by 1960. In this same period, the number of black blue-collar workers rose from 28 to 38 percent. Few of these workers labored in manufacturing, or construction— 7 and 9 percent, respectively—and the majority of black nonagricultural workers labored in service work, primarily domestic work.

The AFL-CIO gave tepid support to and enforcement of civil rights. Generally, the leadership refused to confront or expel unions that did not abide by civil rights policies, or practiced discrimination. Instead, unions aggressively denounced activists, especially black activists, who pushed for civil rights and charged them as communists or subversives. Then they expelled these activists. The accumulative impact of lax enforcement of civil rights policies at the national level and aggressive expulsion of civil rights activists at the local level meant unions remained overwhelmingly homogenous. Less than 2 percent of all apprentices in craft unions in Detroit were black. In Kansas City, Missouri, black workers found similar barriers to the steamfitters, plumbers, electricians, operating engineers, and sheet metal workers' unions. Black electrical workers faced similar union barriers in Cleveland, Ohio.

In other cities, especially the mid-Atlantic cities of Philadelphia and Baltimore, black migrants found better job opportunities than other cities in the mid-Atlantic. In 1950, just 2 percent of black workers in Philadelphia earned more than $4,000 a year; a decade later, 12 percent of black workers earned more than $4,000. Many black workers traced their rising incomes to access to public employment and unions. Philadelphia passed a fair employment practices ordinance in 1948, which made it illegal to discriminate by race in municipal jobs. Additional numbers found work when white workers left city, state, and federal jobs for higher paying jobs in the private sector. The city used color-blind merit exams, which allowed black workers to gain equal access to positions that had been previously denied to them. By 1963, African Americans held nearly 40 percent of the city's workforce and 30 percent of the public school teachers. Better employment opportunities and improved household incomes provided better access to homeownership, and black Philadelphians made rapid progress, with rates of home purchases outpacing the growth in their population overall. Over the first half of the 1950s, blacks' homeownership in the city grew by 84.7 percent from 30,000 to 554,111 and blacks' overall homeownership increased to 43.8 percent.

Even as some African Americans in Philadelphia found access to jobs in public-sector employment, others faced continued barriers, or limited access to private-sector jobs, a problem in the region generally. Added to these barriers, the overall occupational diversity declined in the city and region. Defense employers that employed blacks during World War II left the city, or closed plants almost immediately. Textile manufacturing for war work, first in World War II and again for the Korean War, ended. Some textile plants closed, others left for the South where employers found cheaper land and low-waged, nonunion workers (and these plants closed in the 1980s and departed for low-wage workers in other countries). Philadelphia lost 90,000 industrial jobs between 1950 and 1965, and the number of workers with manufacturing jobs declined from 50 percent in 1947 to 40 percent in 1970.

Throughout the decade between 1955 and 1965, cities in the Midwest showed similar declines in industrial jobs. Unable to find work in Arkansas, Ivory Perry, a Korean War veteran, joined thousands of other black southerners who left the Mississippi Delta and moved into St. Louis. He quickly discovered how segregation permeated his options for housing and employment. "[I]n St. Louis it said you could do it until you tried to do it, and when you tried to do it, they'd come up with another excuse to keep you from doing it."[6] Perry found the most immediate impact was in his efforts to find work. In 1950s St. Louis, black workers had a 50 percent higher rate of unemployment than other groups of workers and black workers made 42 percent less in wages. Perry and many other black men were chronically underemployed and frequently unemployed. The world of black men in St. Louis included random and frequent arrests, which pulled Perry out of work, claimed his limited resources, and challenged his dignity (and safety).

These workers were part of an urban working class whose employment options underwent episodic expansion and contraction in the decades between 1940 and 1960. As James Gregory has noted, "skin color mattered" in the postwar labor market. Black workers born in the South who migrated north earned far less than white workers. While poorly educated black men fared the worst, men with more education faced even greater wage gaps when compared with their white counterparts of similar age and education. "College experience earned a black male migrant on average only 63 percent of his white counterpart's income in 1949," Gregory observes.[7] A decade later, this gap only slightly diminished to 60 percent.

Black migrants, especially black male migrants, faced numerous obstacles to employment in northern, Midwestern, and western cities. After unprecedented access to industrial and public-sector jobs during the war, some of it precipitated by labor shortages and federal intervention through the FEPC, the racialized labor market emerged once again, though less visible than in the prewar years. While some blacks had access to white-collar jobs, the majority of black workers remained excluded from training programs, including those provided to veterans, and they received the least desirable jobs, regardless of experience. The deterioration of urban public schools added to the constraints on blacks' economic mobility. Both southern-born migrants and northern-born blacks found diminished access to industrial and service jobs that increasingly shifted from urban to suburban areas. As historian Manning Marable has concluded, black labor "became less essential than at any previous stage of its development."[8] The industrial black working class that formed between 1915 and 1945 began a slow contraction in the two decades that followed. Overall, fathers fared better than their sons, but both groups lagged behind white men with similar characteristics in wage and occupational mobility.

Despite the popular rhetoric of American affluence and rising household incomes, African Americans' occupational status and educational opportunities stagnated after 1960. In the period between 1950 and 1980, blacks' economic mobility and gains showed two consistent patterns: a small portion saw economic gains while a significant portion showed marked deterioration in economic status. Along with the larger historical context of racial discrimination in hiring and retaining black workers, the declines in employment in heavy industry, such as steel in Pittsburgh and Cleveland, and auto manufacturing in Detroit, prevented lasting gains in African Americans' economic stability. Between 1959 and 1965, the median income of African American men was half that of white men and the majority of black women earned one-third what white women earned—though the median income of this group was one-third of men's. On average, black households had fewer resources to transfer to their children.

Civil rights and some labor activists urged President John F. Kennedy "to insure the free exercise of civil and constitutional rights in and around the South," including access to employment in every region. Confidence in federal policies eroded further after he drafted a civil rights bill that failed to include a ban on private employment discrimination. This omission precipitated the 1963 March on Washington, which linked racial and economic justice.

A quarter of a million Americans participated in the Jobs and Justice March and urged President Kennedy to draft a civil rights bill that addressed the gross economic inequalities African Americans faced. Placards that demanded "Voting Rights Now!" shared space with signs that called for "Jobs and Freedom." Reverend Martin Luther King Jr.'s speech expressed black Americans' aspirations for the American dream of affluence that historically excluded them. Backed by the statue of President Abraham Lincoln who symbolized emancipation, black citizenship, and black enfranchisement, King drew on a century of African American political and theological critique that reached back to the Enlightenment's moral squeamishness with slavery, yet accepted ideas of blacks' racial inferiority. Nearly 100 years after the promise of full citizenship in 1865, King noted how "the Negro lives on a lonely island of poverty in the vast ocean of material prosperity." He honed in on concepts that had not only undergirded the nation's economic policies but also excluded African Americans. He demanded the expansion of policies as both moral and political obligations. "The

Bayard Rustin at the March on Washington,
August 1963. (Library of Congress)

architects of our republic," he insisted, signed "a promissory note
to which every American was to fall heir." This promise meant all
Americans "would be guaranteed the unalienable rights of life,
liberty, and the pursuit of happiness." For African Americans, he
argued, the nation "has defaulted on this promissory note." He
warned that black Americans no longer tolerated their exclusions
from their inheritance of racial and economic justice.[9]

MIGRANTS AND POVERTY

Along with underemployment, and chronic unemployment,
these significant wage gaps created a much higher African American poverty rate, especially for households headed by black women.
As a group, black women worked for wages earlier and longer than
other groups of women; more black women with young children
labored outside the home. Even as increasing numbers of black

children were born, or were raised by single women, the majority of children lived in households with both parents, and, more frequently, extended family. These differing responses to economic needs, particularly black women's greater labor force participation and their higher proportion of female-headed households, did not cohere with prevailing ideology of male breadwinners and female homemakers and came to be seen by experts as evidence that family breakdown led to urban poverty.

In the summer of 1964, black residents of Harlem protested after police shot and killed 15-year-old James Powell, a junior high-school student. Black residents had already organized demonstrations in response to the disappearance of three SNCC workers in Mississippi and the news of Powell's death spread quickly. Large crowds gathered and demanded an investigation into the shooting and police tactics, generally. But the primary recipients of police attention, young men of Powell's age, turned the protests into retaliation that began with rock throwing as police fired at the crowds. Very quickly the crowds of teenagers looted and burned stores; others clashed with police. This one-week conflagration escalated into the largest urban riot in the North since World War II. Other riots followed, first in Rochester, New York, on July 24, 1964, and in Philadelphia, on August 28, 1964. The Philadelphia riot began in the city's poorest section after crowds gathered to witness an altercation between a black motorist in a stalled car and police. A man in the crowd attacked one of the police, and he and the driver were taken into police custody. By then, dozens of police arrived. Angered by another encounter between blacks and the police, the crowd began to throw rocks and bottles at the police. Over the next hours, crowds looted stores and ignored pleas from NAACP leader Cecil Moore to desist.

After the riot in Harlem, critics described it as a city within a city where police served as "an army of occupation." An editorial in the *Amsterdam News* wondered: "Who will protect us from the police?" Investigations revealed that most of the injured were young African Americans or police accidentally shot by other police. Novelist and journalist John Oliver Killens determined that the United States was "fundamentally a Southern country from stem to stern, from Maine to California." Imagine, he asked, teenagers armed with pop bottles confronting helmeted police armed with guns, nightsticks, and tear gas. But the summer riots that followed the passage of the 1964 Civil Rights Act, he concluded, were not simply a response of unemployed youth to too few jobs and high

Crowds in Harlem during the 1964 riot. (Library of Congress)

rents for apartments crawling with rats, but a "Negro Revolt to save the country" from the expansion of segregation and poverty.[10]

President Lyndon Johnson's administration had a different perspective, which did not involve increased funding of the Great Society programs. Assistant Secretary of Labor Daniel Patrick Moynihan's 1965 report, *The Negro Family: A Case for National Action*, explained African Americans' poverty, specifically urban poverty, as a result of broken families headed by women. Though the study associated these ruptures in families with a history of oppression, it also described black households as pathological because sociologists perceived that women controlled them. Black sociologists and other scholars thought the study flawed and many critiqued Moynihan for his failure to consider the variety of personal responses to systemic barriers against economic and social mobility. What role did decades of inadequate housing, poorly funded schools, and too few jobs play in the endemic poverty that prevailed in increasing numbers of Americans' lives? The overwhelming majority of the poor were white, points made in other studies and documentaries produced between 1960 and 1965. Acknowledging their far greater numbers, Moynihan determined that welfare, not poverty, made black families fray.

The riots of 1964 and Moynihan's report caused the Johnson administration to consider a more comprehensive response to the nation's poor. The Kennedy administration had funded a variety of antipoverty programs, but a broad coalition of civil rights activists, labor activists, and antipoverty activists pressed for additional efforts. After the 1963 March on Washington for jobs and freedom, these activists continued the pressure on the administration for full and fair employment. By early 1964, Johnson inherited the unfinished effort and gave it his attention. Congress passed the Anti-Poverty Act to address poverty across many social groups, including children, single mothers, and the elderly; other programs were established to address unemployment through the establishment of the Job Corps. Though the act called for full employment, many of the job programs focused on providing unemployed men with training, but not jobs. And from the start, these programs were underfunded as the Johnson administration spent billions each month on the Vietnam War.

URBAN REBELLIONS, THE GREAT SOCIETY, AND VIETNAM, 1964–1966

Over the next two years, encounters between poor young black men and the police escalated into riots, but blacks of all ages participated. The Watts riot in Los Angeles erupted on August 11, 1965. Over the previous decade, more than 30,000 black southerners arrived in Los Angeles County each year, and by 1965, the city's black population numbered 650,000. Unable to afford housing in outlying areas, migrants lived in insufficient housing. Their children fared poorly in the overcrowded schools, and by 1964, two-thirds of high-school students in Watts dropped out, exacerbating household resources. With so many migrants from some of the most dysfunctional schools in the South, nearly as many black adults in the city lacked a high-school diploma. These trends differed from the national trend where, by 1960, more than half of America's teenagers completed high school. Over the next half decade, this proportion of teenagers continued to grow. Without diplomas and vocational training, blacks' unemployment rate in Watts was three times higher than that for whites. Forty percent of black residents had no car, a remarkable percentage in a city with little public transportation.

The effects of crowded and impoverished living conditions collided with the police's frequent stops of poor black men, causing the August 1965 riot in Watts. When a white police officer stopped a 21-year-old black man, the man's brother questioned the police and a crowd gathered to watch. Poor southern migrants lived in Watts, which was a section of Los Angeles. Blacks' rebellion against segregation in 1965 had a wide geography in South Los Angeles, which spread from Watts to over 46 square miles in the county. More than 1,000 were injured, 34 people were killed, and more than 4,000 were arrested. The property damage was estimated at $40 million.

Though Reverend Martin Luther King Jr. believed the next phase of the civil rights movement needed to focus on economic justice, the Johnson administration disagreed and instead increased combat troops for the Vietnam War by drafting more black men. In early 1966, Moynihan recommended the military as an antidote to male poverty just as President Johnson considered new antipoverty and jobs programs. More than 21 percent of young men between the ages of 14 and 19 who sought work were unemployed, the highest percentage of unemployed young men since World War II. Young black men had a higher rate of unemployment, nearly 25.5 percent (compared with 14% for whites). At the same time, more than one-third of young men failed the military's physical and military exams.

Fearing voters' backlash against higher draft calls and the cessation of deferrals for college students and married men, the Johnson administration proposed accepting thousands of volunteers and draftees who did not qualify for military service. The presumption was that the men "were not employable, or were only marginally employable in the civilian labor force."[11] Moynihan linked the need for combat troops with black poverty and proposed the military increase black men's presence in combat units. He argued that the military needed to serve as the surrogate family for black America, concluding: "Given the strains of disorganized and matrifocal family life in which so many Negro youth come of age, the armed forces are a dramatic and desperately needed change; a world away from women, a world run by strong men and unquestioned authority."[12]

After the riots in 1966, Secretary of Defense Robert McNamara announced Project 100,000. By late November, McNamara described the program as a way "to salvage the poverty scarred youth of our society at the rate of 100,000 men each year." This new policy, he announced, would take care of America's "subterranean poor" who had not had "the opportunity to earn their fair share of this nation's abundance." The armed forces, McNamara insisted, planned to "teach these youths skills, discipline, and self-confidence." Project 100,000 would provide these men "with the opportunity to serve in their country's defense and they can be given an opportunity to return to civilian life with skills and aptitudes which for them and their families will reverse the downward spiral of decay." Between 1966 and 1971, Project 100,000 filtered more than 400,000 men, 40 percent of them African American, into Army and Marine combat units sent to Vietnam.[13]

Many African Americans, especially younger men and women, looked beyond the older civil rights organizations, such as the NAACP and CORE, and embraced black nationalism through the Nation of Islam and the Black Panther Party. Both movements, and the Black Power movement more generally, emerged out of local struggles for jobs, housing, and participation in municipal politics. These organizations typically attracted younger African Americans, many the children of migrants from the South and immigrants from the Caribbean. Relegated to the worst housing and schools, frequently harassed by police and put in jail, pulled disproportionately into the Vietnam War and combat, and increasingly unable to find good-paying industrial jobs, these young men and women became disaffected by older civil rights leaders who appeared to capitulate to the power of union, state, and federal officials. Older civil rights leaders who operated at the national level became disconnected from local struggles. Young blacks looked to leaders and programs that espoused an alternative model through the ideologies of black separatism and self-determination that focused on grassroots efforts and the collective power of ordinary people.

THE NATION OF ISLAM

The Nation of Islam (NOI) became one of the most appealing of these northern efforts. In 1923, Elijah Poole had a confrontation with his employer and fearing for his life, he left Sandersville, Georgia, for Detroit. Like his father, Poole became a minister and worked in the sawmills in Georgia. Resettled in Detroit with his wife, Clara, Poole soon met Wallace D. Fard, a part-time cloth salesman and founder of the Temple of Allah. Fard's origins, age, and early life were mysterious, but he claimed he came from Mecca. Poole began to attend the meetings that Fard organized in the homes of Detroit's impoverished blacks. Fard told his audiences that they descended from Muslims and he planned to save them from the falsehoods of white Christianity and return them to their true religion of Islam. Poole and a cadre of other men became the NOI's first ministers. Poorly educated and ineloquent, Poole nonetheless inspired confidence through his quiet demeanor and ability to converse with other newly arrived migrants from the South. As Elijah Muhammad, he helped Fard establish Temple Number Two in Chicago. They had plans for a third in Milwaukee when Detroit police associated Fard with a follower who had committed a murder. He was then asked to leave Detroit, which left Elijah Muhammad to lead the NOI. Over the next eight years he led a peripatetic life as he attracted increasing numbers of African Americans to the NOI. Though too old to be drafted, he was charged with evading it in 1942 and put in prison. While there, he organized other black men imprisoned for draft evasion, drugs, and other convictions.

Elijah Muhammad left prison just as Malcolm Little arrived in 1946 after his arrest and conviction for burglary. Two years into his 10-year prison sentence, Little made his first connection to Elijah Muhammad and the NOI through the visits and letters from his brothers and sisters. They had joined the Temples in Detroit and Chicago and together they counseled their younger sibling to become a Muslim. Attracted to the NOI's daily discipline over the spirit and body, Malcolm Little slowly converted. Reading books from the prison library and copying and memorizing words and definitions from a dictionary, he created a "homemade education." Along with reading the histories of Asia and Africa, Little paid close attention to African American history written by W.E.B. Du Bois, Carter G. Woodson, and J. A. Roger, who also wrote for the *Pittsburgh Courier.*

Released from prison in 1952, Malcolm Little went to Detroit where he immediately became connected with the small Detroit Temple Number One. Not long afterwards, he sent Elijah Muhammad an application to become a Muslim in the Nation of Islam. Now Malcolm X—the X replaced the name Little, which the NOI associated with slavery—he began to recruit other members and in 1953 he was named the Assistant Minister of Detroit Temple Number One. But Malcolm's magnetic style attracted new members to the NOI and within a year he had reenergized older temples and launched several others. In 1954, he became minister of New York City Temple Number Seven. He perfected his technique of attracting new members by " 'fishing' fast and furiously" outside the "evangelical storefront churches" where southern migrants attended. He attracted them by promising "good preaching."[14] Under his ministry, the Nation of Islam had become sizeable and visible. In 1959, Louis Lomax, a journalist for the black press, made a documentary about the NOI titled "The Hate That Hate Produced," and C. Eric Lincoln, a sociologist at Clark College (later Clark University) in Atlanta, wrote *The Black Muslims in America.* Malcolm X wanted the NOI to have its own newspaper and he began *Muhammad Speaks.* The documentary, book, and newspaper made the NOI more widely known and criticized for its call for Black Separatism and its denunciation of integration.

What started as a fringe sect in Detroit began a remarkable ascendance across the urban Northeast and Midwest. In its early years, the NOI appealed to poor migrants in northern cities, but by 1960, its membership was strikingly diverse in class, education, and regional origin. Thousands now showed up to hear Elijah Muhammad, Malcolm X, and other NOI ministers speak about separation from an immoral society. They promised that African Americans could only achieve liberation "through the complete *separation* form the white man."

Followers attracted to the NOI especially responded to Malcolm X. Observers noted how "in his television appearances and at public meetings Malcolm X articulated the woes and the aspirations of the depressed Negro mass in a way it was unable to do for itself."[15] Gentle and quiet in private, his public persona was electric in his presentation of logic and facts. His militancy frightened some black middle-class intellectuals who considered his separatist views as too strident and he terrified white audiences when he claimed they were "devils" intent on destroying nonwhites. After a wider and prolonged contact with Muslims outside the United States, Malcolm X broke away from the Nation of Islam and decried Elijah Muhammad's inauthentic practices and theology. As he deepened his knowledge of Islam and visited Mecca, he organized the Muslim Mosque, Inc. and the nonreligious Organization of Afro-American Unity. His distance from the NOI escalated when in April 1964, he went to Mecca to make the obligatory pilgrimage called the hajj as a Black Muslim and there he became only a Muslim. Before he could realize a greater unity between black Americans and Africans, he was shot and killed two men from the NOI while giving a speech in New York on February 21, 1965.

Malcolm X's self-education that led him first to militancy and later to a broader understanding of blacks' struggles against their marginal economic and political status as a historical and global phenomena was replicated in the Black Power movement's self-education that began in Alabama in late 1966. Encouraged by SNCC organizers, which included Trinidadian Stokely Carmichael, to create an independent political party, rural black voters in Alabama formed the Lowndes County Freedom Organization (LCFO) and insisted they were "looking for power." They used the black panther as their new organization's symbol.[16] Already in a state of transition toward a more radical and black separatist approach to grassroots organizing, SNCC field workers in Alabama embraced the LCFO appeal for black political power. By 1967 the call for Black Power and the formation of the Black Panther Party (BPP) launched a national and radical movement through local grassroots social and political efforts.

Malcolm X waits at Martin Luther King Jr.'s press conference. (Library of Congress)

BLACK PANTHER PARTY

The Black Panther Party (BPP) was founded in Harlem in 1966. Modeled on the Lowndes County Freedom Organization (LCFO), the Harlem BPP considered itself an organization in a city where African Americans were in the minority. The Harlem Panthers insisted African Americans' needed to accumulate political power by strengthening local institutions and alliances with groups committed to grassroots organizing in cities where blacks formed the majority of the residents. From the outset, the Panthers had a political orientation and a high profile, partly because Stokely Carmichael, the new chairman of SNCC, used the media whenever possible to fuel fears of black separatism at a time when mainstream civil rights institutions pressed for integration of blacks into the political process.

Over the next months, dozens of other Panther chapters emerged, but few had the profile of the organizations in Harlem, Chicago, and Oakland, which was founded in October by Huey P. Newton and Bobby Seale. At the time, Seale and Newton worked in a federally funded antipoverty program, but they turned their attention to organizing young blacks marginalized by the nonviolent civil rights movement. Despite the Harlem BPP, Newton and Seale established the Oakland Black Panther Party as a national organization. While some new members may have been attracted to the Panther's aggressive display of militaristic and armed self-defense, many others, including intellectuals, veterans, and community activists, admired the local independence and activism in a national organization. The Oakland Panthers established control over older and newer chapters and rapidly formed chapters through its creation of a 10-point agenda, its focus on community service, and its newspaper. In addition, historian Yohuru Williams argues, programs like the Breakfast for School Children and its alternative jobs program provided a "blueprint for achieving power in a local setting."[17] In addition, the BPP issued a 10-point program that included demands for political representation, jobs, and freedom from police harassment. As SNCC splintered and mainstream civil rights organizations rejected the growing antiwar activism of Reverend Martin Luther King and CORE, the Panthers' program appeared clear and succinct. The 10-point program also addressed the needs of African Americans in the urban areas outside the South whose ability to vote had not brought about effective economic change, accelerated integration of schools and housing, or prevented brutal confrontations with police.

Young blacks, who felt disaffected from the mainstream civil rights leaders and organizations created their own study groups where they read and debated about African American history, black nationalism, radical political theory, and the writings of anticolonial leaders and intellectuals, such as Ho Chi Minh and Amilcar Cabral. Activists in Detroit and Omaha read about Huey Newton and Bobby Seale's creation of the Oakland Black Panther Party. Many of the northern blacks attracted to Black Power and the emerging BPP were children of migrants and between the ages of 18 and 22. Most had finished high school and some had attended college. Others were veterans from the Vietnam War and they used their combat tactics to instill discipline and camaraderie. Motivated by prominent women in the Oakland Panthers, such as Angela Davis and Kathleen Cleaver, young black women had prominent roles in these activist study groups and they determined to be equal to the men. The Detroit Panthers eventually made gender equality integral to its organization and purged men who practiced chauvinism.

By 1970, the Panthers claimed chapters from Boston to Seattle and the thousands of members primarily focused on local activism. Dozens of other organizations, including the National Committee to Combat Fascism (NCCF) in Omaha, Nebraska, and New Orleans, Louisiana, claimed unofficial affiliation. Women joined in increasing numbers and by 1973 they were half of the total membership. In 1974, Elaine Brown became the first woman to chair the Panthers. Most chapters focused on the day-to-day activities of shoe drives, employment activism, voter registration drives, and housing rights. As more women joined and ran these activities, the aggressive and masculine language changed. The party's newspaper, *The Black Panther*, made a conscious attempt to reject language that demonized and dehumanized others, especially women. Within many communities, the Panthers appeared to be local social activists providing much needed services.

Yet, the Panthers' armed encounters with police allowed critics to describe the organization and its members as armed thugs that needed federal intervention. In 1967, Huey P. Newton was in a shootout with Oakland police. One patrolman was dead by a bullet from his own gun, another injured, and Newton was seriously wounded. He stood trial and was convicted on manslaughter charges. Though not affiliated with the Panthers, the Omaha

NCCF was accused of planting a bomb in 1970 that killed one police officer and wounded several others. Other encounters with police that year led Congress and police to describe the organization as armed black guerilla units akin to the Viet Cong. Yet, evidence from investigations repeatedly demonstrated how the police instigated the confrontations with the Panthers and planted evidence. Moreover, polls demonstrated that the aggressive response from police against the Panthers generated sympathy for the organization. Though the majority of African Americans did not necessarily identify with the Panthers or the Black Power movement generally, they nonetheless believed they should stand together against police departments that used brutal tactics on a daily basis. Their sensibilities were verified during the many urban rebellions that began after 1964.

URBAN REBELLIONS, 1966–1968

For the next four years, hundreds of riots occurred. During the summer of 1966, urban rebellions occurred in 20 communities, including in the Hunter's Point neighborhood of San Francisco, Chicago, and the Hough neighborhood in Cleveland. While these uprisings did not result in the devastation seen in Watts, they signaled that the Johnson administration's War on Poverty was a failure. By 1967, the poverty rate in the United States declined to 12 percent—one in seven Americans—but African Americans had double this rate. That summer, more than 159 riots occurred, including rebellions in Atlanta, Boston, Newark, and Detroit. The latter two lasted for at least six days each. Newark and Detroit had the highest influx of migrants of the cities with large black populations, yet neither city provided adequate housing, education, or employment. Between 1960 and 1966, Newark shifted from a majority white population of 65 percent to a majority nonwhite population of 62 percent, a population largely of southern blacks and Puerto Ricans. Most of this population lived in decayed neighborhoods and dilapidated housing. The black unemployment rate edged more than 12 percent, three times the national rate. More than one-third of the students dropped out of school, and half of the teenagers over the age of 16 did not attend school. In Detroit, the black population increased by 40 percent between 1960 and 1966. The majority of this population crowded into the Twelfth Street area at twice the rate in other areas of the city. Here, they found 60 percent of the housing either condemned or below standards. The enrollment in the city's schools increased by 60,000, 57 percent black. The city needed thousands of new teachers and classrooms just to reach adequate standards. The dropout rate was 50 percent.

Just as in Watts, the Newark uprising, which began on July 12, 1967, occurred after the police stopped taxi driver John Smith and claimed he illegally passed them. Smith, who was a migrant from the South, had his license revoked weeks earlier and the police arrested him. The police then took Smith to the station, where a crowd watched them drag him inside. The crowd grew, and reports of the arrest circulated through the neighborhoods by other taxi drivers who observed the arrest. More police arrived, which angered the crowd. Smith was just one of many recent arrests by police, who regularly stopped blacks, provoked or not. Two black mediators attempted to break up the crowd, but then someone threw a Molotov cocktail and someone else set a car on fire. The crowd later dispersed, but the anger and frustration from the crowd continued. Despite the mayor's announcement of an investigation, protesters gathered the next day and rumors spread that the taxi driver had died in police custody. Some young men in the crowd began to roam the nearby streets, breaking car and store windows as they walked. Over the next week, 24 African Americans and two whites died in encounters with the Newark police. This number included bystanders, many women and children. Some died from stray bullets, others in car chases; most died in some sort of deadly confrontation, either on the streets or near police stations. More than 1,000 people were injured and 1,400 were arrested, the majority migrants and most for disorderly conduct. Millions of dollars of damage occurred in the Central Ward where the riots took place. Much of the looting and damage were directed at businesses perceived as discriminatory. A cascade of riots in other cities followed: Detroit, Milwaukee, Atlanta, and Cincinnati. And again, the majority began after the police stopped, detained, or arrested young black men. Many of these young men were beaten and the charges brought against them in the arrests appeared unwarranted. In every instance, military troops arrived and the riots became protracted and violent.

The most deadly riot in U.S. history began in Detroit a week later on July 23, 1967, after police raided a blind pig, an after-hours club on the city's west side, and arrested 85 patrons celebrating the return of two men from combat in Vietnam. A crowd gathered and watched the police become increasingly rough as they fill four paddy wagons. This was the 10th effort to raid the after-hours club, which had been masquerading as a meeting place for the United Community League for Civic Action. In reality, the club was a key social hub for working-class blacks in the neighborhood and the arrests exacerbated already tense police and community relations. Several men in the crowd threw bottles and bricks; others broke nearby store windows. More police arrived, but they were too few in number to subdue the large crowd. Some observers described the crowd as festive, and the police believed it would soon disperse. Instead, it grew and crowds of blacks and whites across the city began to loot stores. While black community leaders saw it as a rebellion against police tactics, the media and public officials called it a riot fueled by looters and arsonists.

Over the next four days mayhem appeared to reign, from residents and local officials alike. Local police firebombed activists' businesses, using tactics similar to those the FBI organized against black radicals and nationalists. Blacks and whites in the city looted stores, set fires, and attacked police and firefighters. Many black storeowners, including Joe Von Battle who owned and operated a record store, posted a "Soul Brother" sign and hoped it would deter looters. His store and other black-owned stores were also damaged, including Hardy's Pharmacy, well-known restaurants, and a popular clothing store. Little seemed to deter the looters. Detroit Tigers left-fielder Willie Horton, U.S. Representative John Conyers, and local NAACP officials pleaded with the crowds to stop. Nearly 2,500 handguns and rifles were stolen and close to 500 fires set.

By late Monday, July 24, the state's National Guard provided additional support to local and state police, but conditions in the city deteriorated. The overwhelmingly white National Guard taunted blacks as they moved through the streets, exacerbating an already dire situation. Mayor Jerome P. Cavanagh had reluctantly sought aid from Governor George Romney. Meanwhile, President Johnson considered deploying federal troops, but he hesitated since he did not want to appear supportive of Romney, who hoped to seek the Republican presidential nomination. By early morning on Tuesday, July 25, Johnson sent in the 82nd Airborne, a unit with a significant population of African Americans. Within 24 hours of the brigade's arrival, the riot diminished. Images of federal tanks and troops with fixed bayonets aimed at American citizens appeared in the news around the world. Overall, the destruction of the city was tremendous: 43 Detroiters died, the majority African American; 467 were injured; 7,231 were arrested, including 703 children. Half of the arrested had no previous criminal record.

Reverend King despaired after Johnson's decision to send federal troops to occupy Detroit, and he sent the White House a long telegram. The riots were a "revolt against the revolting conditions," and he warned: "There cannot be social peace when a people have awakened to their rights and dignity and to the wretchedness of their lives simultaneously." Grave poverty and affluence, he noted, could not coexist. A nation that could launch a space program, rebuild other nations, wage expensive wars, yet deny its own citizens' adequate health care, jobs, and education was a nation that "refused to be a just civilized society." Congress, he observed, had repeatedly abdicated responsibility and leadership. Now, he concluded, "the life of our nation is at stake."[18]

The Johnson administration pledged to restore law and order and moved quickly to uncover the causes for the riots. With the Vietnam War entering into a stalemate, President Johnson believed the riots threatened domestic stability. Privately he worried about the sharp decline in black support for the war and the news that King's denunciation of his war policy had gained favor. Some in his administration suspected deep wells of black anger; others believed that blacks had instigated a revolution to bring down the government. Behind the backdrop of a Detroit under military occupation, President Lyndon Johnson announced his creation of the President's National Advisory Commission on Civil Disorders, soon known as the Kerner Commission, which was headed by federal district judge and former Illinois Governor Otto Kerner. Popular depictions in the dominant U.S. press presented the rioters as criminals who engaged in unprovoked attacks on police. The international and black presses portrayed the riots as resistance by black people against the indiscriminate police harassment and the imposed poverty and confinement to substandard neighborhoods.

Earlier in the spring, King persuaded the SCLC to sponsor a Poor People's Campaign, and antipoverty activist Marian Wright proposed that the effort include a poor people's march on Washington, D.C. In the months after the riots, the organization planned the campaign and march, but critics predicted violence as tens of thousands of the nation's poor, which included African Americans, whites, and Mexican Americans, planned to participate. King called the protest an "almost desperate plea for the nation to respond to nonviolence the summer threat of more violence."

While the SCLC prepared for the march, King went to Memphis to support black sanitation workers on strike. He was assassi-

The Poor People's March, Washington, D.C. (Library of Congress)

nated there, but the Reverend Ralph Abernathy, who became president of the SCLC, and Whitney Young, executive director of the National Urban League, called for the march as dozens of riots occurred after King's death. Young also called for the "titans of business and labor" to support the march and his request for a Domestic Marshall Plan to aid the poor and rebuild the nation's devastated cities. Abernathy and a multiracial committee of 100 urged Congress to quit the war in Vietnam and use the money to end the nation's poverty. Over the next months, tens of thousands organized to march on Washington, D.C., and on city halls across the United States. In June, thousands created Resurrection City on the mall in Washington. After a peaceful march, some of the poor participants began to brawl and the campaign's leaders left. Heavy rains and the assassination of Robert F. Kennedy, who was poised to accept the Democratic nomination for president, further weakened the movement.

The Johnson administration released the Kerner report in early March, one month before King's assassination. The commission's report concluded that the hundreds of riots arose from decades of accumulated anger over years of grievances and black citizens, investigators learned, grew frustrated, then angry, over governments inability or unwillingness to address the problems of decayed schools and urban housing, limited services in hospitals, police and fire protection, garbage collection, and road repair. The damage to stores during the riots arose from consumers angered by the high prices they paid for decayed food, shoddy goods, and poor service.

The Kerner investigations determined that many of the participants in the riots were young men born and raised in the cities. They were the sons and grandsons of migrants. They considered their blighted neighborhoods and under-resourced cities as a result of decades of economic and spatial inequality shaped by their race and class. They watched as the growth in affluent suburbs drained resources from cities that resulted in diminished resources for municipal schools and services. The Eisenhower, Kennedy, and Johnson administrations invested billions of dollars in nations and wars abroad, yet provided little similar commitment to the decayed infrastructure of cities. At the same time federal draft laws required that poor men, including disproportionate numbers of poor black men, go into combat units in Vietnam. City residents grew ever angry about the urban governments' failure to address the dirty streets, inferior schools, and poor services, especially from police. Few of these cities had black, or other nonwhite, representatives on city councils or appointed in municipal positions. By the early 1960s, blacks and other minorities watched city officials ignore their daily needs and they felt excluded from the local and national political processes.

After investigating all of the uprisings, the commission, whose members included New York City mayor John Lindsay and NAACP executive director, Roy Wilkins, concluded that the confluence of poverty, migration, and racial discrimination made America's cities the epicenter for rebellion. The report described the nation as "moving toward two societies, one black, one white, separate and unequal." The commission also sighted poverty as a significant contributor to the riots and that the administration's antipoverty programs did not adequately provide solutions. The report recommended a significant federal effort to produce jobs, job training, and better education and housing. The commission stressed that local and federal agencies needed to enforce civil rights laws. These recommendations were largely those of the Johnson administration, which many critics considered underfunded and poorly executed. Johnson received the report and turned his attention again to the Vietnam War.

CITIES, MIGRANTS, AND MAYORS

The number of urban rebellions as a form of black protest declined in the last decades of the 20th century for several critical reasons. By 1970, many black community activists considered themselves deeply engaged in both antipoverty and antiwar activities. Many activists turned to local politics to effect change in housing, schools, and employment. Some former SNCC and BPP members considered electoral politics the route to change. Antiwar activists, they determined, should get antiwar candidates elected. In many communities, including the District of Columbia, black activism shifted from the streets and storefronts to the voting booth. In less than half a decade, grassroots organizations increasingly leveraged their influence and helped elect black mayors, integrate city councils, and integrate police and fire departments.

Shirley Chisholm, the first black woman elected to the U.S. Congress, was also one of the first to be elected through this process. Elected in 1968 from the Bronx, Democrat Shirley Chisholm became one of the most vocal antiwar critics in the House of Representatives. During her first months in office, she remained optimistic that President Richard M. Nixon would end the war and commit to rebuilding the infrastructure of the nation's cities, schools, and industries. Chisholm quickly discerned that Nixon did not intend to withdraw troops and instead planned to end or diminish important social and economic programs, particularly antipoverty programs, in favor of military spending.

Even as the Vietnam War divided Americans, the belief in American military power held many in its thrall. At the same time, many Americans believed that the social and cultural transformations taking place, the challenges to racial and sexual hierarchies, made the nation vulnerable to attack. Claiming to speak for the silent majority, Nixon argued that grassroots challenges to racial, class, and gender inequalities weakened national security. In this logic, class, racial, gender hierarchy, and war made the nation stronger. Conservatives massaged these fears of mass and unreasonable changes in the social fabric and tied the eroded confidence in traditional religious, military, and political leaders to a politics of coercion, fear, and secrecy. This political and rhetorical mix appeared in various combinations in the 1972 election as Nixon argued for a full use of the state to ensure law and order in Harlem and Saigon.

Paradoxically, while the rhetoric of order persuaded Americans to vote for a president deeply invested in winning in Vietnam and suppressing dissent at home, more African Americans and women ran and won in local, state, and congressional races. Many of the newly elected African Americans had been former community organizers, civil rights activists, and antiwar activists, including in the South. Andrew Young, Yvonne Braithwaite Burke, Cardiss Collins, and Barbara Jordan joined Julian Bond, Shirley Chisholm, Ron Dellums, and Louis Stokes in the House of Representatives. For Chisholm, the 1972 campaign ultimately solidified her stature in the House and the party as she won 87 percent of the vote in her district. Yet, the new coalition of voters that reelected Chisholm and others in local, state, and congressional races could not halt the rise of a New Right. While Nixon resigned nearly two years later, his "southern strategy" united disparate groups that had advocated militarism, anticommunism, and anti-integration in the 1950s into a powerful conservative movement in the 1970s that exploited Americans' fears of communism, immigration, integration, gender equity, and workers' rights.

Many of the newly elected mayors, including Carl Stokes, Whitney Young, Tom Bradley, and Harold Washington, were migrants or the children of migrants. Tom Bradley's family migrated from southeast Texas to Arizona, where he and his mother picked cotton; his father continued to work as a railroad porter. The family moved to Los Angeles in 1924, Bradley's parents divorced, and his mother raised him on her own. By the 1930s, Bradley completed high school and entered the University of California, Los Angeles, on a track scholarship. By 1940, he left college and joined the LA police force, where he served for the next two decades, earned the rank of lieutenant (and a law degree in 1956), and became the highest-ranking black police officer. By 1963, Bradley turned his attention to politics and became the first black city council man. Bradley joined other blacks in California across a wide political spectrum who saw participation in state and national politics promising: Charlotta Bass, editor of the *California Eagle,* had run unsuccessfully as a Progressive candidate in 1950 and in 1952 as the party's vice presidential nominee; Louisiana migrant August Hawkins was elected to Congress as a California representative in 1963; born in Trinidad, Mervyn Dymally served on the California Assembly from 1963 to 1966 and then moved to the state senate in 1967; Texas migrant Willie Brown, who attended college and then Hastings School of Law, was elected to the California Assembly in 1964; and Yvonne

Braithwaite Burke was elected to the California Assembly in 1966 and the U.S. House of Representatives (37th District) in 1973. The son of longshoreman and labor organizer for the Brotherhood of Sleeping Car Porters, Verney Dellums, Oakland native Ronald V. Dellums was elected to the Berkeley City Council in 1967; and then the U.S. House of Representatives in 1970 (7th District). The presence of black migrants in California politics, however, was not unique. Migrants had participated in state politics in the first half of the 20th century, and many continued to do so in the decades after World War II, but the children of migrants were especially visible in the new politics of the civil rights era.

Similar patterns occurred in other states where black southerners had migrated since the late 19th century. Carl B. Stokes first served in the Ohio State House of Representatives before he became the nation's first black mayor of a major city in 1967; his older brother, Louis Stokes, became a U.S. Representative from the state in 1969 (21st District); migrant, Army Air Force veteran, and UAW-CIO labor organizer Coleman Young first served in the Michigan House of Representatives and the State Senate before he was elected as Detroit's first black mayor in 1973; North Carolina migrant Wilson Goode served as mayor of Philadelphia from 1984 to 1992; after serving as Manhattan Borough President in the late 1980s, David Dinkins became mayor of New York City in 1990; and migrant Edward Brooke became a U.S. Senator from Massachusetts (Republican) in 1967.

These wins in large and industrial cities where blacks were also in the minority depended on the connections these candidates forged out of years of local activism in municipal politics, migrant communities, and labor organizations. They also drew on the more recent rhetoric of black power that emphasized pride and community solidarity, especially in cities like Detroit where the black population was large. In contrast, Tom Bradley was elected mayor of Los Angeles in 1973 by a multiracial coalition of whites, African Americans, Latinos, and Asian Americans. He emphasized his commitment to "good government," rhetoric especially powerful in the wake of the national concerns over Watergate.

Regardless of region, many cities had majority black populations, with many living at or below poverty. As more affluent Americans, including 30 percent of black Americans, moved outside urban cores, the concentration of impoverished people living in neighborhoods with the fewest jobs and the worst schools and housing dramatically increased since the 1968 Kerner Report.

Ironically, southern cities showed the greatest integration in schools and housing while northern cities regularly topped the list of having the most segregated neighborhoods. By the 1970s, the dominant term in both academic and popular discussions of the poor was *ghetto*. And the term became imagined as a place where impoverished black people daily lived in dire circumstances. Why they were there and what to do about them became less important to national debates and discussions. Instead, newspapers, popular culture, and everyday discussion consider these spaces as both dangerous and beyond help and repair.

Many African Americans had their own responses to too few jobs, decayed housing, and underfunded schools: they returned to the South.

NOTES

1. Thomas Sugrue, *Sweet Land of Liberty: The Forgotten Struggle for Civil Rights in the North* (New York: Random House, 2008), xv.

2. Quoted in Lizabeth Cohen, *A Consumer's Republic: The Politics of Mass Consumption in Postwar America* (New York: Alfred A. Knopf, 2003), 170.

3. Quoted in *Black/White & Brown: Brown vs. The Board of Education of Topeka, Kansas* (produced by KTWU, Topeka Kansas, 2004).

4. Supreme Court of the United States, *Brown v Board of Education* 347 U.S. 483 (1954), www.nationalcenter.org/brown.html.

5. Jeanne R. Theoharis, " 'I'd Rather Go to School in the South': How Boston's School Desegregation Complicates the Civil Rights Paradigm," in *Freedom North: Black Freedom Struggles Outside the South, 1940–1980*, eds. Theoharis and Komozi Woodard (New York: Palgrave, 2003), 126.

6. George Lipsitz, *A Life in Struggle: Ivory Perry and the Culture of Opposition* (Philadelphia, PA: Temple University Press, 1995, revised edition), 65.

7. James Gregory, *The Southern Diaspora: How the Great Migrations of Black and White Southerners Transformed America* (Chapel Hill: University of North Carolina Press, 2006), 96.

8. Manning Marable, *Race, Reform, and Rebellion: The Second Reconstruction in Black America, 1945–1990* (Jackson: University of Mississippi Press, 1991), 33.

9. Martin Luther King Jr., www.americanrhetoric.com/speeches/mlki haveadream.htm.

10. John Oliver Killens, "Un-Southing the Nation," *New York Amsterdam News*, August 15, 1964, 19.

11. David Segal, *Recruiting for Uncle Sam: Citizenship and Military Manpower Policy* (Lawrence: University Press of Kansas, 1989), 91.

12. Quoted in Christian G. Appy, *Working-Class War: American Soldiers and Vietnam* (Chapel Hill: University of North Carolina Press, 1999), 32–33.

13. Ibid., 32.

14. Malcolm X, *The Autobiography of Malcolm X* (New York: Random House, 1965), 252.

15. M. S. Handler, "Introduction," *The Autobiography of Malcolm X*, xiii.

16. Quoted in Hasan Kwame Jeffries, *Bloody Lowndes: Civil Rights and Black Power in Alabama's Black Belt* (New York: New York University Press, 2009), 1.

17. Yohuru Williams, "From Oakland to Omaha: Historicizing the Panthers," in *Liberated Territory: Untold Local Perspectives on the Black Panther Party*, Williams and Jama Lazerow, eds. (Durham, NC: Duke University Press, 2008), 3.

18. Reverend Martin Luther King Jr., Telegram to President Johnson, July 25, 1967, http://americanradioworks.publicradio.org/features/king/telegram-7–25–67.html.

Epilogue: Overlapping Migrations in the Black Diaspora, 1975–2005

Since 1965, three trends have appeared in blacks' patterns of voluntary migration in, and immigration to, the United States that simultaneously signal important continuities and dramatic ruptures in their century-long movements for freedom and equality. While African Americans have continued to leave the South, especially the Deep South, in appreciable numbers, these departures have been eclipsed by a larger influx of migrants who returned to the region. During and after the Great and Second Migrations, many former migrants and their northern-born children returned to southern homes for extended periods of time; others resettled in the South permanently. Few observers, however, attempted to quantify how many migrants returned to the South in these earlier periods. When this trend of African Americans' reverse migration first appeared in 1965, numerous surveys of the returnees revealed most were born in the South and they resettled near or in their former homes. Other African Americans moving to the South tended to be children or grandchildren of migrants who left the region before 1950. The second change in black population movement appeared in data from 1980, which showed that the majority of black southerners who were born in the South have remained in the South. Only black Mississippians' migration continues to outpace the number that returns to the state. And as blacks migrated back to the South after 1965, the number of immigrants from Africa has surpassed 500,000 and more than double this number of immigrants from the Caribbean and Latin and Central Americas have arrived and settled permanently in the United States.

The reasons for the reversal in the internal population flows are diverse, and African Americans who decided to remain in, or who returned to, the South often responded to the diminished economic, social, and political opportunities in Northeast and Midwest cities. Many of these returnees initially left the South as children or they are children of post-1945 migrants. They have professional degrees and technical skills, and they found better and more career opportunities in the South than were available elsewhere. This group has typically concentrated in cities and states with the most favorable economic, political, and social conditions. For many, going south in search of work has become as much a necessity as it has been a choice.

Even when work opportunities drew blacks back to the South, a sizeable portion of this population returned to the towns and cities of parents and grandparents. Some of the returnees who were born outside the region had spent summers in the South. Working parents who needed childcare once school ended for the summer typically sent their children to visit older relatives. This practice dates to the Great Migration when migrants sent their children south to help grandparents and other relatives with farm work. During the Second Migration, many families sent children down south for the summer because northern black teenagers faced rising levels of violence and a limited availability of jobs. Others sent their children to relatives in the South to experience the rhythms of rural life or the slower pace of southern towns and cities. These visits maintained family ties and social connections between those African Americans who still lived in the South and those who had left. These intimate and familiar connections meant that many regularly compared the social and cultural experiences of the South with those outside the South. More than nostalgia drew African Americans back to the South.

Many returnees who arrived in the North during the Second Migration had more typically lived in segregated neighborhoods and schools outside the South, which meant they considered the struggle for equality to be a national problem. However, different in the North, these African Americans shared the frustrations of segregation with their southern kin. Blacks in Nashville and Philadelphia simultaneously organized boycotts, marches, and sit-ins in the 1950s and 1960s to dismantle Jim Crow. Northern blacks, too, struggled to integrate schools, workplaces, and neighborhoods. African Americans in the North may have had greater access to the ballot, but they also battled for full citizenship and equal access to all areas of American life. The 1964 Civil Rights Act and the 1965 Voting Rights Act provided the foundation for blacks' participation in the social, civic, and economic life in the South, but this legislation impacted blacks' lives everywhere else. Investigations into the reasons behind the hundreds of riots that erupted in the North between 1964 and 1970 revealed that African Americans were frustrated by their limited representation by public officials attuned to their needs. The increase in black representatives in municipal, state, and national offices was as pronounced in the North after 1965 as it was in the South.

Blacks' struggle for equal access to housing and schools had similarly mixed results inside and outside the South. Between 1980 and 2000, some African Americans experienced steady declines in residential segregation, but as a group, they remained more segregated than other social groups in their housing opportunities. Ironically, cities and suburbs in the South and West have had greater declines in residential segregation than in areas of the Northeast and Midwest. Since the 1970s, cities and older suburbs in the regions that attracted many migrants have consistently remained the least integrated in the nation—although Atlanta, Georgia, and Mobile, Alabama, are also in the 10 most segregated cities in the United States. These patterns of residential segregation exacerbated the segregation in public schools outside the South. Whites' departure from cities and the simultaneous overt and subtle exclusion of African Americans from many suburbs have led to segregated schools from Boston to Newport News, Virginia; from Atlanta to Oakland. While many southern school districts resisted desegregation in the two decades after the *Brown* decision, others integrated, out of choice, necessity, or federal pressure.

More than any other reason, the absence of adequate work has influenced African Americans' return to the South. Just as migrants leaving the South before 1970 assessed the availability of work in the region against employment opportunities in other regions, African Americans who left Northeast and Midwest cities considered the work available to them in the South. Between 1950 and 1981, employment increased by only 2.8 percent in New England states and by 1.1 percent in North East Central states. In the mid-Atlantic states, employment opportunities declined by 15.7 percent. By comparison, manufacturing employment grew by 81.6 percent in the South Atlantic states, 97.5 percent in the East South Central region, and 76.2 percent in the West South Central states. Manufacturing and agricultural opportunities in many of the Mississippi Delta states continued to vanish, but seasonal and service work, especially in tourism, began to increase sharply.

Despite the seeming expansion of employment opportunities in the South, the last two decades of the 20th century have not been advantageous to many southerners, regardless of race. Black men's unemployment in the South overall and in cities in particular is double that of white men's. Black male unemployment rates in other regions show similar patterns. As a group, working-class black women in the South earn the least of any other social group and tend to have greater levels of poverty. Black household incomes in the South are half of white household incomes. Since 1980, the majority of black children under the age of six make up 80 percent of the poor in the region. One-third of southerners, the majority of this group African American, live in trailers, often without electricity or indoor plumbing. The high infant mortality and HIV/AIDS rates have been especially virulent in black southern communities, particularly in Washington, D.C.

The anomalies in African American political life have continued as well. The 1965 Voting Rights Act led to the election of blacks in municipal, state, and national offices in every region. By 1971, 711 African Americans held elective office in the 11 states of the former Confederacy. At the start of the 21st century, however, the number of black elected officials outside the South has dramatically declined. One year before an interracial and intergenerational coalition of voters in states outside the South put a black president in office, two-thirds of elected blacks came from southern states. Black voters have faced restrictions to voting despite the 1965 Voting Rights Act. These restrictions became evident in the 2000 and 2004 national elections when black voters in Ohio and Florida encountered impediments to the polls that appeared to be created to prevent their equal access to voting.

While civil rights activists decried these trends, the barriers to equal voting have increased. In 2010, 24 percent of African Americans in Kentucky were disfranchised; in Ohio, intricate state laws continue to limit and suppress blacks' voting rights. In Wisconsin, the Republican Party sent out mailers to black voters, which were then put in a database and these voters were purged from the rolls. Using a practice called caging, Arkansas Republicans have targeted soldiers—who vote for the Democrats in increasing numbers—and removed them from the polls. Other states have sent out misleading and incorrect information about the location of polls; officials intimidate voters at polls, close parking lots near polls, and provide broken or too few computers at polls in minority neighborhoods.

The immigration of blacks from Africa and the Caribbean has resulted from similar and different reasons from black migration. Though African immigrants compose only a fraction of the black population in the United States—about 3 percent—the increase in their numbers has been steady since 1965. Overall, more immigrants from Africa have arrived voluntarily in the last four decades than the involuntary immigration during the nearly two and a half centuries of the slave trade. Many of these recent immigrants have come as their countries struggled against colonial rule. Many more arrived after 1965 when the United States abandoned the national origins quota in its immigration laws. As their newly independent nations experienced greater economic and political upheavals, many Africans chose to go to former colonial powers, especially Great Britain, France, and Portugal. When these nations established strict immigration laws after 1980, emigrants chose the United States as their destination. New immigration laws have sustained this immigration. The 1986 Immigration Reform and Control Act allowed African immigrants living in the United States to seek citizenship; and the 1990 Immigration Act enacted a lottery system that gave priority to people from underrepresented nations.

Most of these immigrants chose the United States for its educational and professional opportunities, but there are discernible demographic characteristics in this population. The majority of the nearly two million immigrants from Africa have come from Cape Verde, Ethiopia, Nigeria, Ghana, and South Africa. They have settled across the United States, though large populations reside in New York, California, and Maryland. As a group these immigrants tend to be well educated: 49 percent have bachelor's degrees, which is more than twice that (23%) of native-born Americans and 98 percent have completed high school. While they tend to emigrate for professional or educational opportunities, as a group they also tend to migrate to other cities in the United States soon after they arrive.

People of African descent from the Caribbean, Central America, and Latin America have continually emigrated to the United

States for several centuries, but their post-1945 moves to the United States have been more rapid and sustained. Even with restrictions imposed on all groups of immigrants between 1924 and 1965, some migrants from the Caribbean continued to arrive, particularly from Puerto Rico. These moves increased especially during World War II and accelerated after 1945. Through agreements established with Caribbean nations, between 1941 and 1950, more than 50,000 migrants arrived to work in war industries. Under this program, a sizeable portion of this population worked in agriculture, especially in sugar and tobacco. These workers tended to come from the English-speaking areas of the Caribbean, but others arrived from some of the Spanish-speaking nations. The 1952 Immigration and Nationality Act, also known as the McCarran-Walter Act, gave preference to white immigrants from European nations and greatly restricted black migration from the Caribbean. As a result, only those migrants with relatives already in the United States could emigrate.

The 1965 Immigration Act significantly impacted the number and demographic patterns of black migration from the Caribbean. The number of migrants increased from 123,000 in the 1950s to 470,000 in the 1960s. Each decade since, the number of migrants has increased by one-third to one-half. Not all migrants from the Caribbean have experienced equal access to immigration and citizenship, however. Haitians, who live in one of the poorest nations in the world, have found it especially difficult to enter the United States and those already in the United States without proper status found it impossible to seek asylum. President Ronald Reagan, for example, established a policy of interdiction, which allowed the U.S. Coast Guard to board ships and interrogate passengers. Immigrants already in the United States faced deportation. Through this policy, tens of thousands of asylum seekers were forcibly returned to Haiti during the Reagan and Bush administrations. Haitians' ability to enter the United States became only marginally better during the Clinton administration. Congress passed the Haitian Refugee Immigration Fairness Act in 1998, which allowed Haitians already in the United States before 1995 to seek asylum.

As they had in the first half of the 20th century, migrants from the Caribbean have continued to settle in every region of the United States, but more significant populations of Afro-Cubans have settled in Miami and other areas of Florida; many Jamaicans and Haitians have settled in Brooklyn and Queens. Women make up a significant portion of this post-1965 migration. The limited economic opportunities for the majority of blacks in the Caribbean have made it necessary for all classes to migrate in search of work. Among those arriving in the United States, far fewer of these migrants have professional or college degrees.

The cultural production from this Black Diaspora represents the South and the Caribbean less as places to escape and now as critical sources for consciousness and knowledge. Novels and plays by Alice Walker, Toni Morrison, Suzan Lori Parks, Earnest Gaines, and Edward P. Jones explore the tension between what is remembered and misremembered about the southern black past. Jones's two collections of short stories, for example, are set in and around Washington, D.C., which serves as a borderland between the South and North. The majority of residents are African American and they do not have equal representation in Congress. Jones's characters nearly suffocate under the weight of segregation's legacies in the nation's capital. Writers from the Caribbean who reside in the United States, which includes Paule Marshall, Edwidge Danticat, Jamaica Kincaid, Caryl Phillips, and Derek Wolcott, continue traditions of a diasporic literature that began in the early 20th century. The dynamic and extensive list of writers from the Caribbean has been at the epicenter of Black Diaspora literary production.

Black music from the North, the Caribbean, and from Africa has regenerated the blues, jazz, Gospel, soul, and hip-hop. Many of the artists making music in the South are migrants from the other regions; others are immigrants from the Caribbean and Africa. Blues musician Keb' Mo, for example, is a migrant from Los Angeles who now lives in Nashville. New Orleans remains the epicenter of diasporic funk and jazz. Here, the Neville Brothers and the Marsalis family simultaneously nurture longstanding musical traditions, yet create new ones drawn from more recent music from Africa and the Caribbean. Reggaton—a mixture of reggae and Latin music—now thrives in Washington, D.C., and Harlem. Hip-hop had its origins in the urban Northeast where black immigrants from the Caribbean and migrants from the South lived side by side in Harlem and the Bronx, but it also draws from black southerners such as Eryka Badu and immigrants from the Caribbean , including Wyclef Jean, Pres Michel, and Rihanna. And this genre continues to draw its sensibilities in cities where blacks from the Diaspora congregate together, including Washington, D.C., Norfolk, Miami, and New Orleans.

The South and its many pasts figure prominently in the plays of August Wilson. Born Frederick August Kittel in 1945, Wilson lived in the Hill District of Pittsburgh with his parents, Frederick

August Kittel, a German immigrant, and Daisy Wilson, a migrant from North Carolina. His mother, who labored as a domestic, later married David Bedford. By the age of 15, Kittel left high school and two years later he joined the army, but he only served one year. Kittel returned to Pittsburgh, changed his name to August Wilson, and founded the Black Horizon Theater in 1968, where he began writing and producing plays. By the early 1980s, Wilson began to work with Lloyd Richards, a highly acclaimed director of the Yale Repertory Theater.

Over the next 20 years, Wilson wrote 10 plays, each set in a different decade, that chronicled African Americans' experiences in the 20th century. The awards for these plays, which include two Pulitzer Prizes, are numerous. Each play explores the transforming historical events in African American migration history, such as slavery and migration, through the daily lives of working-class men and women. Wilson described these characters as "the transformation of impulse and sensibility into codes of conduct and response, into cultural rituals that defined and celebrated ourselves as men and women of high purpose."[1] In every one of Wilson's plays, the past intrudes even when the catastrophic historical events do not take center stage, such as the Great Depression or the 1960s riots. *The Piano Lesson,* which Wilson set in the 1930s, dramatizes Bernice Charles and Boy Willie's dispute over what to do with an upright piano, which was a family heirloom that dated back to the time of slavery. The owner of their relatives traded them for the piano. Their enslaved great-grandfather carved African portraits into the wood as a memorial to his wife and the young son his owner sold. Decades later, Bernice and Boy Willie's father retrieved the piano and he was killed as a result. Now living in the Hill District of Pittsburgh, Bernice keeps the piano as witness to her family's experiences of slavery and the violence of segregation that drove them from the South. The angry, yet purposeful Boy Willie arrives from "Down South" and he demands his sister give him the piano to sell, which would allow him to buy land in Mississippi.

Set in 1936 Pittsburgh, written in the 1980s, and staged in 1990, the play's plot focuses on a brother and sister arguing over whether or not to sell a piano, but *The Piano Lesson* spans nearly 300 years of African American history, from slavery and past the Great Migration. The characters' travels and memories traverse a wide geography, from Africa through the Deep South and into the urban North. This expansiveness of time and place forces the siblings to stop their personal dispute and use their collective culture—the trem-

bling piano plays spirituals and the blues—to summon their ances-
tors and their memories, which they use to battle the ghost of the
slaveholder.

Wilson has been equally expansive in how the history of black
migration and life in the urban North has influenced his writing.
In numerous interviews he has paraphrased writer James Baldwin,
who was also the child of migrants, to describe his artistic agenda
as a "profound articulation of the black tradition, which included
that field of manners and ritual of intercourse that will sustain a
man once he left his father's house."[2] Like Baldwin's fiction and
plays, Wilson's characters live in the North, but their language and
traditions have been formed by events in the South; southern black
vernacular and oral traditions infuse their vocabulary. Critics have
lauded Wilson's plays as brilliant epics that are also poetic and
musical. The tragedies of William Shakespeare and Eugene O'Neill
have influenced these 10 plays, but African American music, especially jazz and the blues, have given the plays their cadence and
sense of celebration, philosophy, and timbre. Audiences describe
Wilson's characters and settings as intimate and familiar. African
Americans, in particular, have seen their history and family in these
10 plays. Wilson's plays do more than ruminate on the meaning of
the South to African Americans who no longer live in this region.
Each play examines the South's contradictions and considers its
legacy in black culture: is the region a source of collective pain or
cultural renewal?

The slow pace of federal and state response to the suffering of
Delta state residents after destruction caused by Hurricanes Katrina
and Rita in late August and early September 2005 has helped fuel
this debate. Although New Orleans has attracted and retained a
visible population of more affluent African Americans, only 40 percent of black workers in New Orleans held full-time jobs and the
city ranked third in the nation for its high rate of poverty generally, and concentrated black poverty in particular. For the past two
decades, the majority of African Americans, Hispanics, and poor
whites in the city have labored in unstable tourist and gambling
sectors that provide hardly a modicum of subsistence and few, if
any, benefits such as health care. Hampered by low wages and
intermittent work, few families could rely on one income; instead,
many adults in New Orleans households typically worked two and
three jobs. While the poverty rates are undeniably high, most of
the people in this area work, making them the underemployed and
working poor.

In the 48 hours before Katrina arrived, tens of thousands of the working poor and those on social assistance waited for their weekly pay or their end-of-the-month checks. Officials advised residents to evacuate, but did not provide adequate assistance, thus many residents had no money and could not afford to leave New Orleans. Many were recently arrived day workers from Mexico and Guatemala and could not navigate language and financial issues beyond their immediate areas of work. Others stayed to care for elderly loved ones, or because all of their wealth was in their homes—some literally using the walls as banks. The demands of too many low-wage jobs, too few jobs, or too few resources, such as savings, compelled many residents in New Orleans to stay in their homes.

Federal Emergency Management Agency (FEMA) officials ignored the agency's data that had predicted hundreds of thousands of poor in New Orleans would not be able to evacuate. Nonetheless, its director, Michael Brown, declared in the days before the storm that those who stayed behind "deserved what they got." Privately, he told President George W. Bush that the storm would be catastrophic and local facilities were ill-equipped to handle the needs of the city's residents.[3] After Hurricane Katrina made landfall as a Category 4 storm on August 29, 2005, the waters of Lake Pontchartrain breached the levees and rapidly flooded the Ninth Ward in New Orleans, an area with a high concentration of poor African Americans. State and local officials pleaded for assistance, but it took days for federal officials to respond. More than 80,000 residents in the city had no clean water or food. Mothers and fathers of all races made the choice to take formula, water, food, and diapers from locked stores to feed and care for their children and elderly relatives. The media described blacks as "looting" food, and whites as "finding" food. Without acknowledging their own inaction, federal officials expanded the media's representations of black mothers wading chest deep through water and carrying diapers and formula as looters.[4]

As U.S. and international audiences expressed shock at the Bush administration's slow and limited response to the needs of the city's trapped residents, the U.S. Census Bureau released its yearly data on poverty, which had risen for the fourth straight year in the region. New Orleans is not an anomaly. Sociologists Thomas J. Durant and Dawood Sultan have described New Orleans before Katrina as a social and economic disaster. Though a poor city in a poor state in a poor region, Louisianans' poverty, however, cannot top the poverty of Mississippians: This state has the lowest per capita income in the United States. It also has one of the lowest ranked educational systems with one of the highest dropout rates. And it has the highest child poverty rate and the highest infant mortality rate in the nation. Alabama ranks third from the bottom, making these three states the epicenter of the nation's poor. Close to 50 percent of black children in each of these states live below the poverty line. Only 11 percent of white children are similarly situated. Latino Americans have rates equal to that of African Americans. Census data revealed, too, that the poor are overwhelmingly concentrated in the lowest lying areas and in some of the worst housing stock.

Throughout the 20th century, the entire South has experienced repeated and devastating storms that make the catastrophic events of Hurricane Katrina part of a larger pattern of human-made disasters that have irrevocably impacted black southerners' lives. Zora Neale Hurston's 1937 novel, *Their Eyes Were Watching God,* vividly describes black migrations in the context of "natural disasters."

So the beginning of this was a woman and she had come back from burying the dead.

Not the dead of sick and ailing with friends at the pillow and the feet. She had come back from the sodden and the bloated; the sudden dead, their eyes flung wide open in judgment.[5]

These first sentences in the novel make little sense until chapter 18, which begins with a description of lovers creating a whirlwind through nightly jook dances. The real storm begins when a march of people and animals interrupts Janie and Tea Cake's lovemaking/ dancing to warn them of the imminent arrival of turbulent winds: "Going to high ground. Saw grass bloom. Hurricane coming." Seminole and Bahamian cane workers urge Janie and her new husband, Tea Cake Woods, to join them. The couple ignores the warning, and the besotted lovers believe the sun will come out and they can return to picking beans: "[M]oney's too good on the muck," Tea Cake explains. For men and women who earned wages by the day, leaving the fields would mean a loss of income. Besides, they have no way to leave, no way to find safety on higher ground. Whites claim these areas and the segregated Red Cross denied blacks and Seminoles shelter.

The hurricane arrives with quick ferocity. Janie and Tea Cake awaken as "as the winds came back. Everything in the world had a strong rattle, sharp and short like [a drummer] vibrating the drum head near the edge with his fingers." The hurricane that screams across nearby Lake Okeechobee and the Everglades is a "monster rolling and complaining like a peevish world on a grumble." Janie, Tea Cake, and the others sat "staring at the dark, but their eyes were watching God." As the wind roared, their shanties became unmoored, leaving Janie and Tea Cake neck deep in water and buffeted by the fury of 200-mile-an-hour winds. As the dike holding the lake breaks—"the monstopolous beast had left his bed"—Janie shouts "Us can't fly." Instead, they run from the sudden flood, but they cannot find safety on the bridges since whites now occupied these and the other higher elevations. Even in the midst of a disaster, segregation prevailed. Thousands of African Americans, Native Americans, and Bahamians die in the raging water and wind. Afraid Janie might drown in the swirling lake, Tea Cake battles a rabid dog for a bit of dry ground. The dog bites Tea Cake and after the couple escapes the flood, he goes crazy. Unable to care for him and out of fear for her own life, Janie is forced to shoot him.

Hurston could have described any one of the hundred or so hurricanes that made landfall between 1900 and 1935. She might have told the story of the 1927 flooding of the Mississippi Delta that Bessie Smith recalled in "Backwater Blues:"

> Backwater blues have caused me to pack up my things and go
> 'Cause my house fell down and I can't live there no more
> Hmm, I can't live there no more
>
> Hmm, I can't live there no more
> And there ain't no place for a poor old girl to go

But Hurston's fictionalized account of the Category 5 storm that struck the Everglades in mid-September, 1928 particularly informed her imagination. While it happened, few outside of the Everglades heard about one of the most intense hurricanes of the 20th century. Fewer learned that more than 3,000 of the laboring poor died, three-quarters of them blacks from the Diaspora, perhaps half the population in the area. Thousands more died as the storm crossed into the Atlantic and roared over Puerto Rico.

What happened to black residents in the Everglades *after* the 1928 storm was as worse as the storm itself. Officials forced black men to gather the drowned victims and then bury them. Blacks were placed in mass graves. A year earlier during the Mississippi flood, blacks were similarly forced to dig mass graves. Levees were blown up to protect whites' property from the swollen nearby waterways, but blacks lost their homes, property, and land to the flooding that followed. These barriers to a decent burial and the loss of their meager property, like the segregation policies that denied the poor and blacks to seek higher ground, or receive aid continued through Hurricane Betsy (1965) and Hurricane Camille (1969). Each of these storms exacerbated already terrible conditions wrought by segregation in the Mississippi Delta. Long after each storm, blacks migrated out of the South because they had few other options.

During the dozens of hurricanes, tornados, and floods that literally regraded the southern landscape, swamping sugarcane and cotton fields, upending lumber, poor people, especially poor blacks, in the United States have found few options between staying and going. Whatever decision African Americans made about remaining in, or leaving the South, they had much to lose. Sociologist K. Animashaun Ducre argues that the government's response to residents in New Orleans in 2005, when viewed in the larger context of poor federal and state responses to African Americans after hurricanes and other natural disasters in the South, was unremarkable.[6]

The limited support has continued, remaking New Orleans's population. Since 2005, African Americans' access to federal aid and personal resources in the Mississippi Delta has remained limited.

The Ninth Ward in New Orleans shows the devastating aftermath of Hurricane Katrina in 2006. (Library of Congress)

As hurricanes threatened the area in 2007, FEMA's best advice to New Orleanians was that they must depend on their own resources. Thus, only those with substantial personal assets, such as savings, jobs, and insurance, have been able to remain in, or return to, the city to rebuild homes and businesses. Before the storm, blacks comprised two-thirds of New Orleans' nearly 500,000 residents. In 2010, they are less than half the population that now hovers just above 300,000.

As with other storms where a human-made disaster followed, Hurricane Katrina accelerated black out-migration already in progress because of inadequate employment and strained city services. As federal and state officials agreed to "deconcentrate poverty," in the city, they demolished recoverable public and affordable housing. With far fewer personal resources to rebuild and access to affordable housing, the tens of thousands of poor and working-class blacks who were eventually displaced or dispersed to Texas, Colorado, Utah, and Washington, D.C., have found it virtually impossible to return to their homes. The lower Ninth Ward, where many of these residents lived, remains the last area to be recovered and many of the neighborhoods are still desolate. What impact the Louisiana Diaspora will have on the region and the nation remains to be seen. Any argument about blacks' collective return to the South because of its greater opportunities must consider the recent events in New Orleans. Black residents' inability to leave New Orleans during a devastating storm and their mass departure since reveal how the history of migration out of the South continues to be both a choice and a necessity.

Poet Langston Hughes, who participated in the Great Migration and observed the Second Migration, captured in numerous poems and stories African Americans' seemingly quixotic search for personal and collective freedom. In one of his earliest poems published in *The Crisis,* he described blacks' departing the "laughing South/With blood on its Mouth." This South that brutally excavated "Negro's bones" was also seductive and beautiful. African Americans brought this South "many rare gifts/But she turns her back upon" them. When Hughes published this poem in 1922, nearly a million African Americans had left the South over the previous two decades. These migrants, he observed, traveled to "The cold-faced North."

When Hughes died unexpectedly in 1967, he believed the cold-faced North had not thawed. In every region he witnessed African Americans "Groping, hoping,/Waiting for what?" His answer to this question: *"a world to gain."*[7] What would be the questions and answers for migrants and immigrants of the Black Diaspora, or their children and grandchildren, in the second decade of the 21st century?

NOTES

1. August Wilson, "The Ground on Which I Stand." Keynote to the Theatre Communications Group, June 26, 1996. *American Theatre* 13, no. 7 (September, 1996): 14.

2. August Wilson, "How to Write a Play like August Wilson," *The New York Times,* March 10, 1991.

3. http://thinkprogress.org/katrina-timeline.

4. http://www.media-awareness.ca/english/resources/educational/teachable_moments/katrina_2_photo.cfm.

5. Zora Neale Hurston, *Their Eyes Were Watching God* (Urbana: University of Illinois Press, 1978), 9.

6. K. Animashaun Ducre, "Hurricane Katrina as an Elaboration on an Ongoing Theme: Racialized Spaces in Louisiana," in *Seeking Higher Ground: The Hurricane Katrina Crisis, Race, and Public Policy,* Manning Marable and Kristen Clark, eds. (New York: Palgrave McMillan, 2007), 66.

7. Ibid., 549–50.

Selected Bibliography

The voluminous primary and secondary resources available on African American migration and the Black Diaspora are rich and varied. Many are now readily accessible through digitized material on websites and reprints available in libraries. While the bibliography below does not seek to be exhaustive, it does provide a representation of the influential studies alongside more recent publications and resources. These works direct readers to additional bibliographies, appendices, and other critical documents. This bibliography includes a selection of websites either directly related to black migration, or they contain relevant documents, records, and other material, such as films, literature, and oral histories.

GENERAL HISTORIES AND REFERENCE WORKS

Berlin, Ira. *The Making of African America: The Four Great Migrations.* New York: Viking, 2010.

Kusmer, Kenneth L. *Black Communities and Urban Development in America, 1720–1990.* New York: Garland Publishers, 1991.

Marable, Manning, and Leith Mullings, eds. *Let Nobody Turn Us Around: Voices of Resistance, Reform, and Renewal: An African American Anthology.* Lanham, MD: Rowman & Littlefield, 1999.

Reich, Steven A., ed. *Encyclopedia of the Great Migration, Volume 1–3.* Westport, CT: Greenwood Press, 2006.

Rodriguez, Marc S. *Repositioning North American Migration History: New Directions in Modern Continental Migration, Citizenship, and Community.* Rochester, NY: University of Rochester Press, 2005.

Takaki, Ronald. *Double Victory: A Multicultural History of America in World War II.* Boston, MA: Back Bay Books, 2000.

Trotter, Joe William. *The African American Experience.* Boston, MA: Houghton Mifflin, 2001.

Trotter, Joe William, ed. *The Great Migration in Historical Perspective: New Dimensions of Race, Class, and Gender.* Bloomington: Indiana University Press, 1991.

Winant, Howard. *The World is a Ghetto: Race and Democracy since World War II.* New York: Basic Books, 2001.

LETTERS, INTERVIEWS, AND AUTOBIOGRAPHIES

Angelou, Maya. *I Know Why the Caged Bird Sings.* New York: Random House, 1969; reprint, New York: Ballantine Books, 2009.

Baraka, Amiri. *The Autobiography of Leroi Jones.* New York: Freundlich Books, 1984.

Brooks, Sara. *You May Plow Here: The Narrative of Sara Brooks.* New York: Touchstone Books, 1986.

Denby, Charles. *Indignant Heart: A Black Worker's Journal.* Detroit, MI: Wayne State University Press, 1989.

Hughes, Langston. *The Big Sea, an Autobiography.* New York: Alfred A. Knopf, 1940; reprint, New York: Hill and Wang, 1993.

Hunter, Jane Edna. *A Nickel and a Prayer.* Cleveland, OH: Elli Kani, 1940.

Malcolm X. *The Autobiography of Malcolm X.* New York: Random House, 1965.

Rice, Sara. *He Included Me: The Autobiography of Sarah Rice.* Athens: University of Georgia Press, 1989.

Shaw, Nate. *All God's Dangers: The Life of Nate Shaw.* New York: Alfred A. Knopf, 1974.

Wilson, August. "The Ground on Which I Stand." Keynote to the Theatre Communications Group, June 26, 1996. *American Theatre* 13, no. 7 (September, 1996): 14.

Wright, Richard. *Black Boy.* New York: Harper & Brothers, 1945; reprint, New York: Harper Perennial, 2006.

BIOGRAPHIES, ESSAY COLLECTIONS, AND LITERATURE

Baldwin, James. *Notes of a Native Son.* New York: Beacon Press, 1955; reprint, New York: Beacon Press, 1984.

Cross, Charles R. *Room Full of Mirrors: A Biography of Jimi Hendrix.* New York: Hyperion, 2005.

Danticat, Edwidge. *Breath, Eyes, Memory.* New York: Soho Press, 1994; reprint, New York: Vintage Books, 1998.

Dunbar, Paul Lawrence. *The Sport of the Gods.* New York: Signet Classic, 1999.

Ellison, Ralph. *Invisible Man.* New York: Random House, 1952; reprint, New York: Vintage Books, 1972.

Himes, Chester. *If He Hollers Let Him Go.* New York: Doubleday, 1945; reprint, New York: New American Library, 1971.

Hughes, Langston. *The Collected Poems of Langston Hughes,* Arnold Rampersad, ed. New York: Alfred A. Knopf, 1994.

Hurston, Zora Neale. *Their Eyes Were Watching God.* Urbana: University of Illinois Press, 1978.

Johnson, James Weldon. *The Autobiography of an Ex-Colored Man.* New York: 1912; reprint, New York: Hill and Wang, 1960.

Jones, Edward P. *All Aunt Hagar's Children: Stories.* New York: Amistad, 2006.

Jones, Edward P. *Lost in the City: Stories.* New York: Amistad, 1992.

Kincaid, Jamaica. *Lucy: A Novel.* New York: Farrar Straus and Giroux, 1990.

Larsen, Nella. *Quicksand and Passing.* Deborah McDowell, ed. New Brunswick, NJ: Rutgers University Press, 1986.

Lipsitz, George. *A Life in Struggle: Ivory Perry and the Culture of Opposition.* Philadelphia, PA: Temple University Press, 1995, revised edition.

Locke, Alain, ed. *The New Negro: An Interpretation.* New York: Albert and Charles Boni, 1925; reprint, New York: Atheneum, 1980.

Marshall, Paule. *Brown Girl, Brownstones.* New York: 1959; reprint, Old Westbury, NY: Feminist Press, 1981.

Morrison, Toni. *The Bluest Eye.* New York: Holt, Rinehart and Winston, 1970.

Morrison, Toni. *Jazz.* New York: Plume, 1992.

Morrison, Toni. *Paradise.* New York: Alfred A. Knopf, 1998.

Morrison, Toni. *Song of Solomon.* New York: Alfred A. Knopf, 1977; reprint, New York: Plume, 1987.

Petry, Anne. *The Street.* New York: 1946; reprint, New York: Liveright, 1975.

Wilson, August. *Fences.* New York: New American Library, 1985.

Wilson, August. *The Piano Lesson.* New York: Plume, 1990.

Wright, Richard. *Native Son.* New York: Harper & Brothers, 1940; reprint, New York: Harper Perennial, 1993.

GENERAL HISTORIES

Adams, Luther. *Way Up North in Louisville: African American Migration in the Urban South.* Chapel Hill: University of North Carolina Press, 2010.

Ayers, Edward. *The Promise of the New South: Life after Reconstruction.* New York: Oxford University Press, 1992.

Biondi, Martha. *To Stand and Fight: The Struggle for Civil Rights in Postwar New York City.* Cambridge, MA: Harvard University Press, 2003.

Blackwelder, Julia Kirk. *Styling Jim Crow: African American Beauty Training during Segregation.* College Station: Texas A&M University Press, 2003.

Boehm, Lisa Krissoff. *Making a Way Out of No Way: African American Women and the Second Great Migration.* Jackson: University Press of Mississippi, 2009.

Bontemps, Arna, and Jack Conroy. *They Seek a City.* Garden City, NY: Doubleday, 1945.

Borchert, James. *Alley Life in Washington, 1850–1970.* Urbana: University of Illinois Press, 1980.

Broussard, Albert S. *Black San Francisco: The Struggle for Racial Equality in the West, 1900–1954.* Lawrence: University Press of Kansas, 1993.

Brown, Leslie. *Upbuilding Black Durham: Gender, Class, and Black Community Development in the Jim Crow South.* Chapel Hill: University of North Carolina Press, 2008.

Cecelski, David S., and Timothy B. Tyson, eds. *Democracy Betrayed: The Wilmington Race Riot of 1898 and Its Legacy.* Chapel Hill: University of North Carolina Press, 1998.

Clark-Lewis, Elizabeth. *Living in, Living Out: African American Domestics and the Great Migration.* New York: Kodansha International, 1996.

Cohen, Lizabeth. *A Consumer's Republic: The Politics of Mass Consumption in Postwar America.* New York: Alfred A. Knopf, 2003.

Cohen, William. *At Freedom's Edge: Black Mobility and the Southern White Quest for Racial Control, 1861–1915.* Baton Rouge: Louisiana State University Press, 1991.

Countryman, Matthew, J. *Up South: Civil Rights and Black Power in Philadelphia.* Philadelphia: University of Pennsylvania Press, 2006.

Curry, Dwane Y., Eric D. Duke, and Marshanda A. Smith, eds. *Extending the Diaspora: New Histories of Black People.* Urbana: University of Illinois Press, 2009.

Dailey, Jane. *Before Jim Crow: The Politics of Race in Postemancipation Virginia.* Chapel Hill: University of North Carolina Press, 2000.

Davis, DeWitt. *Reverse Black Migration.* Columbus: Dept. of Geography, Ohio State University, 1976.

Devlin, George Alfred. *South Carolina and Black Migration, 1865–1940: In Search of the Promised Land.* New York: Garland Publishing, 1989.

Dickerson, Dennis C. *Out of the Crucible: Black Steelworkers in Western Pennsylvania, 1875–1980.* Albany: State University of New York Press, 1986.

Dodson, Howard, and Sylviane Diouf, eds. *In Motion: The African-American Migration Experience.* Washington, D.C.: National Geographic Society, 2004.

Donald, Henderson Hamilton. *The Negro Migration of 1916–1918.* Washington, D.C.: Association for the Study of Negro Life and History, 1921.

Drake, St. Clair, and Horace Cayton. *Black Metropolis*. New York: Harcourt, Brace and Company, 1945; reprint: Chicago, IL: University of Chicago Press, 1993.

Dray, Philip. *At the Hands of Persons Unknown: The Lynching of Black America*. New York: Modern Library, 2003.

Du Bois, W.E.B. *Darkwater: Voices from Within the Veil*. New York: Harcourt, Brace and Howe, 1920; reprint: New York: Washington Square Press, 2004.

Elam, Harry J., Jr. *The Past as Present in the Drama of August Wilson*. Ann Arbor: University of Michigan Press, 2006.

Epstein, Abraham. *The Negro Migrant in Pittsburgh*. Pittsburgh, PA: University of Pittsburgh, 1918; reprint: New York: Arno Press, 1969.

Everett, Anna. *Returning the Gaze: A Genealogy of Black Film Criticism, 1909–1949*. Durham, NC: Duke University Press, 2001.

Fligstein, Neil. *Going North: Migration of Blacks and Whites from the South, 1900–1950*. New York: Academic Press, 1981.

Foner, Eric. *Reconstruction: America's Unfinished Revolution, 1863–1877*. New York: Harper & Row Publishers, 1988.

Foner, Nancy. *Islands in the City: West Indian Migration to New York*. Berkeley: University of California Press, 2001.

Fossett, Mark Alan, Omer R. Galle, and Jeffrey Allan. *Racial Occupational Inequality, 1940–1980: The Impact of the Changing Regional Distribution of the Black Population on Inequality at the National Level*. Austin: Texas Population Research Center, University of Texas at Austin, 1986.

Fox, Ted. *Showtime at the Apollo*. New York: Quartet Books, 1985.

France, Edward E. *Some Aspects of the Migration of the Negro to the San Francisco Bay Area since 1940*. San Francisco: R and E Research Associates, 1974.

Frey, William H. *Black In-migration, White Flight, and the Changing Economic Base of the Central City*. Madison: University of Wisconsin Press, 1979.

Frey, William H. *The New Great Migration: Black America's Return to the South, 1965–2000*. Washington, D.C.: Brookings Institution Center on Urban and Metropolitan Policy, 2001. http://www.brookings.edu/urban/pubs/20040524%5FFrey.pdf.

Gilmore, Glenda. *Gender and Jim Crow: Women and the Politics of White Supremacy in North Carolina, 1896–1920*. Chapel Hill: University of North Carolina Press, 1996.

Goings, Kenneth W., and Raymond A. Mohl, eds. *The New African American Urban History*. Thousand Oaks, CA: Sage Publishers, 1996.

Goldberg, David, and Trevor Griffey, eds. *Black Power at Work: Community Control, Affirmative Action, and the Construction Industry*. Ithaca, NY: ILR Press, 2010.

Gotham, Kevin Fox. *Race, Real Estate, and Uneven Development: The Kansas City Experience, 1900–2000*. Albany: State University of New York Press, 2002.

Gottlieb, Peter. *Making Their Own Way: Southern Blacks' Migration to Pittsburgh, 1916–1930.* Urbana: University of Illinois Press, 1987.

Gottlieb, Peter. *The Origins of Black Migration.* Urbana: University of Illinois Press, 1987.

Green, Laurie B. *Battling the Plantation Mentality: Memphis and the Black Freedom Struggle.* Chapel Hill: University of North Carolina Press, 2007.

Gregg, Robert. *Sparks from the Anvil of Oppression: Philadelphia's African Methodists and Southern Migrants, 1890–1940.* Philadelphia, PA: Temple University Press, 1993.

Gregory, James N. *The Southern Diaspora: How the Great Migrations of Black and White Southerners Transformed America.* Chapel Hill, NC: The University of North Carolina, 2006.

Griffin, Farah Jasmine. *"Who Set You Flowin'?": The African-American Migration Narrative.* New York: Oxford University Press, 1995.

Grossman, James R. *Land of Hope: Chicago, Black Southerners, and the Great Migration.* Chicago, IL: University of Chicago Press, 1989.

Grossman, James R., and Martin Paul Schipper. *Black Workers in the Era of the Great Migration, 1916–1929.* Frederick, MD: University Publications of America, 1985.

Guralnick, Peter. *Dream Boogie: The Triumph of Sam Cooke.* New York: Little, Brown and Company, 2005.

Hahamovitch, Cindy. *The Fruits of their Labor: Atlantic Coast Farmworkers and the Making of Migrant Poverty, 1870–1945.* Chapel Hill: University of North Carolina Press, 1997.

Hahn, Steven. *A Nation under Our Feet: Black Political Struggles in the Rural South from Slavery to the Great Migration.* Cambridge, MA: Harvard University Press, 2003.

Hahn, Steven. *The Political Worlds of Slavery and Freedom.* Cambridge, MA: Harvard University Press, 2009.

Harris, Abram Lincoln. *Negro Migration to the North.* New York: New York Times Company, 1924.

Haynes, George Edmund, and Sterling Allen Brown. *Negro Newcomers in Detroit and Washington.* Washington, D.C.: Federal Writers Project, 1937; reprint: New York: Arno Press, 1969.

Henri, Florette. *Black Migration: Movement North, 1900–1920.* Garden City, NY: Anchor Press, 1975.

Herman, Max Arthur. *Fighting in the Streets: Ethnic Succession and Urban Unrest in Twentieth-Century America.* New York: Peter Lang, 2005.

Hine, Darlene Clark, and Jacqueline McLeod. *Crossing Boundaries: Comparative History of Black People in Diaspora.* Bloomington: Indiana University Press, 1999.

Hinshaw, John H. *Steel and Steelworkers: Race and Class Struggle in Twentieth-Century Pittsburgh.* New York: State University Press, 2002.

Hinshaw, John H., and Paul Le Blanc. *U.S. Labor in the Twentieth Century: Studies in Working-class Struggles and Insurgency.* Amherst, NY: Humanity Books, 2000.

Hirsch, Arnold. *Making the Second Ghetto: Race and Housing in Chicago, 1940–1960.* Second edition. Chicago, IL: University of Chicago Press, 1998.

Hunter, Tara. *'To Joy My Freedom: Southern Black Women's Lives and Labors after the Civil War.* Cambridge, MA: Harvard University Press, 1998.

Jacobson, Matthew Frye. *Barbarian Virtues: The United States Encounters Foreign Peoples at Home and Abroad, 1876–1917.* New York: Hill and Wang, 2000.

James, Winston. *Holding Aloft the Banner of Ethiopia: Caribbean Radicalism in Early Twentieth-Century America.* New York: Verso Press, 1998.

Johnson, Charles S. *Shadow of the Plantation: Peonage in the South.* Urbana: University of Illinois Press, 1972.

Johnson, Daniel Milo. *Black Return Migration to a Southern Metropolitan Community, Birmingham, Alabama.* Columbia, MO: The Author, 1973.

Johnson, Daniel M., and Rex R. Campbell. *Black Migration in America: A Social Demographic History.* Durham, NC: Duke University Press, 1981.

Jones, William P. *The Tribe of Black Ulysses: African American Lumber Workers in the Jim Crow South.* Urbana: University of Illinois Press, 2005.

Jung, Moon-Ho. *Coolies and Cane: Race, Labor, and Sugar in the Age of Emancipation.* Baltimore, MD: Johns Hopkins University Press, 2006.

Katznelson, Ira. *Black Men, White Cities: Race, Politics, and Migration in the United States, 1900–30 and Britain, 1948–68.* London: Published for the Institute of Race Relations by Oxford University Press, 1973.

Kelley, Blair L. M. *Right to Ride: Streetcar Boycotts and African American Citizenship in the Era of Plessy v. Ferguson.* Chapel Hill: University of North Carolina Press, 2010.

Kiser, Clyde Vernon. *Sea Island to City: A Study of St. Helena Islanders in Harlem and Other Urban Centers.* New York: Columbia University Press, 1932.

Kusmer, Kenneth. *A Ghetto Takes Shape: Black Cleveland, 1870–1930.* Urbana: University of Illinois Press, 1982.

Lemann, Nicholas. *The Promised Land: The Great Black Migration and How it Changed America.* New York: Alfred A. Knopf, 1991.

Lemke-Santangelo. *Abiding Courage: African American Migrant Women and the East Bay Community.* Chapel Hill: University of North Carolina Press, 1996.

Lewis, David Levering. *When Harlem Was in Vogue.* New York: Vintage Books, 1982.

Lewis, Edward Erwin. *The Mobility of the Negro: A Study in the American Labor Supply.* New York: Columbia University Press, 1931.

Manning, Patrick. *The African Diaspora: A History through Culture.* New York: Columbia University Press, 2010.

Marable, Manning. *Race, Reform, and Rebellion: The Second Reconstruction in Black America, 1945–1990.* Jackson: University Press of Mississippi, 1991.

Marks, Carole. *Farewell—We're Good and Gone: The Great Black Migration.* Bloomington: Indiana University Press, 1989.

Massey, Douglas S., and Andrew B. Gross. *Black Migration, Segregation, and the Spatial Concentration of Poverty.* Chicago, IL: Population Research Center, NORC and University of Chicago Press, 1993.

Massood, Paula J. *Black City Cinema: African American Urban Experiences in Film.* Philadelphia, PA: Temple University Press, 2003.

McKiven, Henry M. *Iron and Steel: Class, Race, and Community in Birmingham, Alabama.* Chapel Hill: University of North Carolina Press, 1995.

Moore, Shirley Anne Wilson. *To Place Our Deeds: The African American Community in Richmond, California, 1910–1963.* Berkeley: University of California Press, 2000.

Mumford, Kevin. *The History of Race, Rights, and Riots in America.* New York: New York University Press, 2007.

Odum, Howard W. *Race and Rumors of Race: The American South in the Early Forties.* Chapel Hill, NC: University of North Carolina Press, 1943; reprint: Baltimore, MD: Johns Hopkins University Press, 1997.

Okpewho, Isidore, Carole Boyce Davies, and Ali Al'Amin Mazrui. *The African Diaspora: African Origins and New World Identities.* Bloomington: Indiana University Press, 1999.

Okpewho, Isidore, and Nikru Nzegwu, eds. *The New African Diaspora.* Bloomington: Indiana University Press, 2009.

Osofosky, Gilbert. *Harlem: The Making of a Ghetto, 1890–1930.* New York: Harper Torchbooks, 1963.

Painter, Nell Irvin. *Exodusters: Black Migration to Kansas after Reconstruction.* New York: Alfred A. Knopf, 1977.

Phillips, Kimberley L. *AlabamaNorth: African-American Migrants, Community, and Working Class Activism in Cleveland, 1915–1945.* Urbana: University of Illinois Press, 1999.

Phillips, Kimberley L. *War! What Is It Good For? Black Freedom Struggles and the U.S. Military from World War II to Iraq (2012).* Chapel Hill: University of North Carolina Press, 2011.

Pleck, Elizabeth Hafkin. *Black Migration and Poverty, Boston, 1865–1900.* New York: Academic Press, 1979.

Rachleff, Peter. *Black Labor in Richmond, 1865–1890.* Urbana: University of Illinois Press, 1989.

Ransbey, Barbara. *Ella Baker and the Black Freedom Movement.* Chapel Hill: University of North Carolina Press, 2005.

Rooks, Noliwe. *Ladies' Page: African American Women's Magazines and the Culture that Made Them.* New Brunswick, NJ: Rutgers University Press, 2004.

Rudwick, Elliott M. *Race Riot at East St. Louis, July 2, 1917.* New York: Atheneum, 1964.

Scott, Emmett J. *Negro Migration during the War.* New York: Oxford University Press, 1920; reprint, New York: Arno Press, 1969.

Self, Robert O. *American Babylon: Race and the Struggle for Postwar Oakland.* Princeton, NJ: Princeton University Press, 2003.

Sernett, Milton C. *Bound for the Promised Land: African American Religion and the Great Migration.* Durham, NC: Duke University Press, 1997.

Shaw-Taylor, Yoku, and Steven A. Tuch, eds. *The Other African Americans: Contemporary African and Caribbean Immigrants in the United States.* Lanham, MD: Rowman & Littlefield Publishers, 2007.

Shenk, Gerald E. *"Work or Fight!": Race, Gender, and the Draft in World War One.* New York: Palgrave, 2005.

Sides, Josh. *L.A. City Limits: African American Los Angeles from the Great Depression to the Present.* Berkeley: University of California Press, 2003.

Sitkoff, Harvard. *A New Deal for Blacks: The Emergence of Civil Rights as a National Issue, the Depression Decade.* New York: Oxford University Press, 1978.

Smethurst, James Edward. *The Black Arts Movement: Literary Nationalism in the 1960s and 1970s.* Chapel Hill: University of North Carolina Press, 2005.

Smith, Suzanne E. *Dancing in the Street: Motown and the Cultural Politics of Detroit.* Cambridge, MA: Harvard University Press, 1999.

Spear, Allan. *Black Chicago: The Making of a Negro Ghetto, 1890–1920.* Chicago, IL: University of Chicago Press, 1967.

Stack, Carole. *Call to Home: African-Americans Reclaim the Rural South.* New York: Basic Books, 1996.

Steward, Jacqueline Najuma. *Migrating to the Movies: Cinema and Black Urban Modernity.* Berkeley: University of California Press, 2005.

Strickland, Arvarh E., and Robert E. Weems, Jr., eds. *The African American Experience: An Historiographical and Bibliographical Guide.* Westport, CT: Greenwood Press, 2001.

Sugrue, Thomas J. *The Origins of the Urban Crisis: Race and Inequality in Postwar Detroit.* Princeton, NJ: Princeton University Press, 1996.

Sugrue, Thomas J. *Sweet Land of Liberty: The Forgotten Struggle for Civil Rights in the North.* New York: Random House, 2008.

Sullivan, Patricia. *Days of Hope: Race and Democracy in the New Deal Era.* Chapel Hill: University of North Carolina Press, 1996.

Sullivan, Patricia. *Lift Every Voice: The NAACP and the Making of the Civil Rights Movement.* New York: The New Press, 2009.

Taylor, Quintard. *The Forging of a Black Community: Seattle's Central District from 1870 through the Civil Rights Era.* Seattle: University of Washington Press, 1994.

Taylor, Quintard, and Shirley Ann Wilson Moore. *African American Women Confront the West: 1600–2000.* Norman: University of Oklahoma Press, 2003.

Theoharis, Jeanne F., and Komozi Woodard. *Freedom North: Black Freedom Struggles Outside the South, 1940–1980.* New York: Palgrave, 2003.

Thomas, Richard Walter. *Life for Us Is What We Make It: Building Black Community in Detroit, 1915–1945.* Bloomington: Indiana University Press, 1992.

Tolnay, Stewart Emory. *The Bottom Rung: African American Family Life on Southern Farms.* Urbana: University of Illinois Press, 1999.

Trotter, Joe William. *African Americans in Pennsylvania: Shifting Historical Perspectives.* University Park: Pennsylvania State University Press, 1997.

Trotter, Joe William. *Black Milwaukee: The Making of an Industrial Proletariat, 1915–1945.* Urbana: University of Illinois Press, 1985.

Turner, Elizabeth Hutton, ed. *Jacob Lawrence: The Migration Series.* Washington, D.C.: The Rappahannock Press, 1993.

Watkins-Owens, Irma. *Blood Relations: Caribbean Immigrants and the Harlem Community, 1900–1930.* Bloomington: Indiana University Press, 1996.

Weisenfeld, Judith. *African American Women and Christian Activism: New York's Black YWCA, 1905–1945.* Cambridge, MA: Harvard University Press, 1997.

White, Shane, and Graham White. *Stylin': African American Expressive Culture from its Beginnings to the Zoot Suit.* Ithaca, NY: Cornell University Press, 1998.

Wiese, Andrew. *Places of their Own: African American Suburbanization in the Twentieth Century.* Chicago, IL: University of Chicago Press, 2004.

Wilkerson, Isabel. *The Warmth of Other Suns: The Epic Story of America's Great Migration.* New York: Random House, 2010.

Woodard, Komzi, and Jeanne F. Theoharis. *Groundwork: Local Black Freedom Movements in America.* New York: New York University Press, 2005.

Woodson, Carter Godwin. *A Century of Negro Migration.* Washington, D.C.: Association for the Study of Negro Life and History, 1918; reprint, Mineola, NY: Dover Publications, 2002.

Woofter, Thomas Jackson. *Negro Migration: Changes in Rural Organization and Population of the Cotton Belt.* New York: W. D. Gray, 1920; reprint, New York: Negro Universities Press, 1969.

Wright, Richard. *Black Boy.* New York: Harper & Brothers, 1945; reprint, New York: Harper Perennial Modern Classics, 2006.

Wright, Richard. *12 Million Black Voices.* New York: Viking Press, 1941; reprint, New York: Arno Press, 1969.

ARTICLES

Biegert, M. Langley. "Legacy of Resistance: Uncovering the History of Collective Action by Black Agricultural Workers in Central East Arkansas from the 1860s to the 1930s." *Journal of Social History* 32, no. 1 (Fall 1998): 73–98.

Butler, Kim D. "Defining Diaspora, Refining Discourse." *Diaspora* 10, no. 2 (Fall 2001): 189–219.

Byfield, Judith. "Introduction: Rethinking the African Diaspora." *African Studies Review* 43, no. 1 (April 2000): 1–9.

Collins, William J. "When the Tide Turned: Immigration and the Delay of the Great Black Migration." *Journal of Economic History* 57, no. 3 (September 1997): 607–32.

De A. Reid, Ira. "Methodological Notes for Studying the Southern City." *Social Forces* 19, no. 2 (December 1940): 228–35.

De A. Reid, Ira. "Special Problems of Negro Migration During the War." *The Milbank Memorial Fund Quarterly* 25 (July 1947): 287–88.

Hamilton, Kenneth M. "The Origin and Early Developments of Langston, Oklahoma." *The Journal of Negro History* 62, no. 3 (July 1977): 270–82.

Hawkins, Homer C. "Trends in Black Migration from 1863 to 1960." *Phylon* 34, no. 2 (Winter 1973): 140–52.

Heathcott, Joseph. "Black Archipelago: Politics and Civic Life in the Jim Crow City." *Journal of Social History* 38, no. 3 (Spring 2005): 705–36.

Hill, James L. "Migration of Blacks to Iowa 1820–1860." *Journal of Negro History* 66, no. 4 (Winter 1981–1982): 289–303.

Hughes, Langston. "My Early Days in Harlem." *Freedomways* (Summer 1963): 312–14.

Lewis, Earl. "To Turn as on a Pivot: Writing African Americans into a History of Overlapping Diasporas." *American Historical Quarterly* 100 (June 1995): 765–87.

Lichtenstein, Alex. "Proletarians or Peasants? Sharecroppers and the Politics of Protest in the Rural South, 1880–1940." *Plantation Society in the Americas* 5 (Fall 1998): 297–331.

Long, Herman H. "Racial Desegregation in Railroad and Bus Transportation." *Journal of Negro Education* 23, no. 3 (Summer 1954): 214–21.

Mack, Kenneth W. "Law, Society, Identity, and the Making of the Jim Crow South: Travel and Segregation on Tennessee Railroads, 1875–1905." *Law & Social Inquiry* 24, no. 2 (Spring 1999): 377–409.

Milloy, Courtland. "Black Highways: Thirty Years Ago in the South, We Didn't Dare Stop." *The Washington Post* (June 11, 1987), B1, B4.

Patterson, Tiffany Ruby, and Robin D.G. Kelley. "Unfinished Migrations: Reflections on the African Diaspora and the Making of the Modern World." *African Studies Review* 43, no. 1 (April 2000): 11–45.

Powell, Richard J. "Jacob Lawrence: Keep on Movin.'" *American Art* 15, no. 1 (Spring 2001): 90–93.

Rousey, Dennis C. "Yellow Fever and Black Policeman in Memphis: A Post-Reconstruction Anomaly." *Journal of Southern History* 51, no. 3 (August 1985): 357–74.

Scott, Emmett J. "Letters of Negro Migrants of 1916–1918." *The Journal of Negro History* 4, no. 3 (July 1919): 290–340.

Scott, Emmett J. "More Letters of Negro Migrants of 1916–1918." *Journal of Negro History* 4, no. 4 (October 1919): 412–65.

Seiler, Cotton. "'So We As a Race Might Have Something Authentic to Travel By': African American Automobility and Cold-War Liberalism." *American Quarterly* (2006).

Sewell, Stacy Kinlock. "The 'Not-Buying Power' of the Black Community, Urban Boycotts and Equal Opportunity, 1960–1964." *Journal of African American History* 89, no. 2 (Spring 2004): 135–51.

Wilson, August. "How to Write a Play like August Wilson." *The New York Times*, March 10, 1991.

AUDIO, ORAL HISTORIES, AND DOCUMENTARY FILMS

American Public Media, American Radio Works. "Remembering Jim Crow." www.americanradioworks.publicradio.org/features/remembering/

American Social History Project. City College of New York, Center for Media and Learning. "Up South: African-American Migration in the Era of the Great War." www.ashp.cuny.edu/ashp-documentaries/up-south/

Eyes on the Prize, Series II (1990, Public Broadcasting Service).

Fordham University. "Bronx African American History Project." www.fordham.edu/academics/programs_at_fordham_/bronx_african_americ/index.asp/

Goin' to Chicago (1996, California Newsreel).

Jazz: The Story of American Music (2000, Public Broadcasting Service).

July '64 (2006, California Newsreel).

Little Senegal (2001, Tadrart Films).

National Park Service. "In Those Days: African American Life near the Savannah River." www.nps.gov/seac/ITD/longversion/itd-lg1.htm/

Struggles in Steel (1994, California Newsreel).

WEBSITES

General History

The Black Past. "African American History in the American West." www.blackpast.org/?q=aaw/african-american-history-american-west

Civil Rights Digital Library. "Documenting America's Struggle for Racial Equality." www.crdl.usg.edu/?Welcome/

Serving History. "African American History." www.servinghistory.com/topics/african_american_history/

Documents and Databases

Chicago. "Chicago Race Riot of 1919." www.chicago.urban-history.org/evt/evt01/evt0100.shtml/

Gilda Lehrman Center for the Study of Slavery, Resistance, & Abolition. White, Walter. "The Causes of the Chicago Race Riot." www.yale.edu/glc/archive/1126.htm/

History Matters, City University of New York. "7 Letters to the Chicago Defender." www.historymatters.gmu.edu/d/5332/

Library of Congress. "The African American Mosaic." www.loc.gov/exhibits/african/afam001.html

New York Times. "Immigration Explorer." www.nytimes.com/interactive/2009/03/10/us/20090310-immigration-explorer.html/

Seattle Civil Rights and Labor History Project. "African Americans and Seattle's Civil Rights History, Oral Histories." www.depts.washington.edu/civilr/African%20Americans.htm/

Seattle Civil Rights and Labor History Project. "Seattle Black Panther Party History and Memory Project." www.depts.washington.edu/civilr/BPP.htm/

University of North Carolina. "Documenting the American South." www.docsouth.unc.edu/neh/

Online Exhibits and Educational Sites

Chicago. "Encyclopedia of Chicago." www.encyclopedia.chicagohistory.org/pages/545.html/

Nebraska Studies. www.nebraskastudies.org/0700/frameset_reset.html? http://www.nebraskastudies.org/0700/stories/0701_0131.html/

New York Public Library, Schomburg Center for Research in Black Culture. "In Motion: The African American Migration Experience." www.inmotionaame.org/home.cfm/

Phillips Collection. "Jacob Lawrence: The Migration Series." www.phillipscollection.org/migration_series/index.cfm

Index

About the Author

KIMBERLEY L. PHILLIPS is professor of History and Dean of the School of Humanities and Social Sciences, Brooklyn College-CUNY. She was recently the Frances L. and Edwin L. Cummings Associate Professor of History and American Studies at the College of William and Mary. Her scholarship includes *AlabamaNorth: African-American Migrants, Community, and Working-Class Activism in Cleveland, 1915–1945* (1999) and *War! What Is It Good For?: Black Freedom Struggles and the U.S. Military from World War II to Iraq* (2012).

Recent Titles in
The Greenwood Press Daily Life in the United States Series

Immigrant America, 1870–1920
June Granatir Alexander

Along the Mississippi
George S. Pabis

Immigrant America, 1820–1870
James M. Bergquist

Daily Life in the Progressive Era
Steven L. Piott